) 2026 (
HOROSCOPES

Week-by-week
predictions for
every zodiac sign

PATSY BENNETT

THE MOON'S PHASES FOR THE YEAR

On the following pages are the moon's phases for 2026 for both the southern and northern hemispheres.

JANUARY

S	M	T	W	T	F	S
				1	2	3
4	5	6	7	8	9	10
11	12	13	14	15	16	17
18	19	20	21	22	23	24
25	26	27	28	29	30	31

FEBRUARY

S	M	T	W	T	F	S
1	2	3	4	5	6	7
8	9	10	11	12	13	14
15	16	17	18	19	20	21
22	23	24	25	26	27	28

MARCH

S	M	T	W	T	F	S
1	2	3	4	5	6	7
8	9	10	11	12	13	14
15	16	17	18	19	20	21
22	23	24	25	26	27	28
29	30	31				

APRIL

S	M	T	W	T	F	S
			1	2	3	4
5	6	7	8	9	10	11
12	13	14	15	16	17	18
19	20	21	22	23	24	25
26	27	28	29	30		

MAY

S	M	T	W	T	F	S
					1	2
3	4	5	6	7	8	9
10	11	12	13	14	15	16
17	18	19	20	21	22	23
24	25	26	27	28	29	30
31						

JUNE

S	M	T	W	T	F	S
	1	2	3	4	5	6
7	8	9	10	11	12	13
14	15	16	17	18	19	20
21	22	23	24	25	26	27
28	29	30				

2026 SOUTHERN HEMISPHERE MOON PHASES

JULY

S	M	T	W	T	F	S
			1	2	3	4
5	6	7	8	9	10	11
12	13	14	15	16	17	18
19	20	21	22	23	24	25
26	27	28	29	30	31	

AUGUST

S	M	T	W	T	F	S
						1
2	3	4	5	6	7	8
9	10	11	12	13	14	15
16	17	18	19	20	21	22
23	24	25	26	27	28	29
30	31					

SEPTEMBER

S	M	T	W	T	F	S
		1	2	3	4	5
6	7	8	9	10	11	12
13	14	15	16	17	18	19
20	21	22	23	24	25	26
27	28	29	30			

OCTOBER

S	M	T	W	T	F	S
				1	2	3
4	5	6	7	8	9	10
11	12	13	14	15	16	17
18	19	20	21	22	23	24
25	26	27	28	29	30	31

NOVEMBER

S	M	T	W	T	F	S
1	2	3	4	5	6	7
8	9	10	11	12	13	14
15	16	17	18	19	20	21
22	23	24	25	26	27	28
29	30					

DECEMBER

S	M	T	W	T	F	S
		1	2	3	4	5
6	7	8	9	10	11	12
13	14	15	16	17	18	19
20	21	22	23	24	25	26
27	28	29	30	31		

○ New moon ● Full moon

2026 NORTHERN HEMISPHERE MOON PHASES

JANUARY

S	M	T	W	T	F	S
				1	2	3
4	5	6	7	8	9	10
11	12	13	14	15	16	17
18	19	20	21	22	23	24
25	26	27	28	29	30	31

FEBRUARY

S	M	T	W	T	F	S
1	2	3	4	5	6	7
8	9	10	11	12	13	14
15	16	17	18	19	20	21
22	23	24	25	26	27	28

MARCH

S	M	T	W	T	F	S
1	2	3	4	5	6	7
8	9	10	11	12	13	14
15	16	17	18	19	20	21
22	23	24	25	26	27	28
29	30	31				

APRIL

S	M	T	W	T	F	S
			1	2	3	4
5	6	7	8	9	10	11
12	13	14	15	16	17	18
19	20	21	22	23	24	25
26	27	28	29	30		

MAY

S	M	T	W	T	F	S
					1	2
3	4	5	6	7	8	9
10	11	12	13	14	15	16
17	18	19	20	21	22	23
24	25	26	27	28	29	30
31						

JUNE

S	M	T	W	T	F	S
	1	2	3	4	5	6
7	8	9	10	11	12	13
14	15	16	17	18	19	20
21	22	23	24	25	26	27
28	29	30				

2026 NORTHERN HEMISPHERE MOON PHASES

JULY

S	M	T	W	T	F	S
			1	2	3	4
5	6	7	8	9	10	11
12	13	14	15	16	17	18
19	20	21	22	23	24	25
26	27	28	29	30	31	

AUGUST

S	M	T	W	T	F	S
						1
2	3	4	5	6	7	8
9	10	11	12	13	14	15
16	17	18	19	20	21	22
23	24	25	26	27	28	29
30	31					

SEPTEMBER

S	M	T	W	T	F	S
		1	2	3	4	5
6	7	8	9	10	11	12
13	14	15	16	17	18	19
20	21	22	23	24	25	26
27	28	29	30			

OCTOBER

S	M	T	W	T	F	S
				1	2	3
4	5	6	7	8	9	10
11	12	13	14	15	16	17
18	19	20	21	22	23	24
25	26	27	28	29	30	31

NOVEMBER

S	M	T	W	T	F	S
1	2	3	4	5	6	7
8	9	10	11	12	13	14
15	16	17	18	19	20	21
22	23	24	25	26	27	28
29	30					

DECEMBER

S	M	T	W	T	F	S
		1	2	3	4	5
6	7	8	9	10	11	12
13	14	15	16	17	18	19
20	21	22	23	24	25	26
27	28	29	30	31		

○ New moon ● Full moon

Patsy Bennett is a rare combination of astrologer and psychic medium. Her horoscopes are published in newspapers and magazines in Australia and internationally and she has appeared on several live daytime TV and radio shows, including the *Today Extra* show and ABC Radio. Her books *Astrology: Secrets of the Moon* and *Sun Sign Secrets*, her oracle card deck *Zodiac Moon Reading Cards* and the annual *Astrology Planner/Astrology Diary* are published by Rockpool Publishing.

Patsy provides astrology and psychic intuitive consultations and facilitates astrology and psychic development workshops. She also runs astrocast.com.au and patsybennett.com.

f patsybennettpsychicastrology | ⓘ patsybennettastrology

FURTHER INFORMATION

For an in-depth personal astrology chart reading contact Patsy Bennett at patsybennettastrology@gmail.com.

Astronomical data can be obtained from the following:

- *The New American Ephemeris for the 21st Century, 2000–2100*, Rique Pottenger, Starcrafts Publishing, USA, 2006 (reprinted 2012).

A Rockpool book
PO Box 252
Summer Hill
NSW 2130
Australia

rockpoolpublishing.com
Follow us! f ⓘ rockpoolpublishing
Tag your images with #rockpoolpublishing

ISBN: 9781923208025

Published in 2025 by Rockpool Publishing
Copyright text © Patsy Bennett 2025
Copyright design © Rockpool Publishing 2025

All rights reserved. No part of this publication may be reproduced, stored in a retrieval system, or transmitted in any form or by any means, electronic, mechanical, photocopying, recording or otherwise, without the prior written permission of the publisher.

Design and typesetting by Sara Lindberg, Rockpool Publishing
Edited by Lisa Macken

Printed and bound in China
10 9 8 7 6 5 4 3 2 1

All dates in this book are set to Greenwich Mean Time (GMT). Astrological interpretations take into account all aspects and the sign the sun and planets are in on each day and are not taken out of context.

CONTENTS

THE MOON'S PHASES FOR THE YEAR • ii

INTRODUCTION • 2

MERCURY AND VENUS RETROGRADE PERIODS IN 2026 • 2

ARIES • 3

TAURUS • 29

GEMINI • 55

CANCER • 81

LEO • 107

VIRGO • 133

LIBRA • 159

SCORPIO • 185

SAGITTARIUS • 211

CAPRICORN • 237

AQUARIUS • 263

PISCES • 289

INTRODUCTION

There is so much to be excited about in 2026, especially the opportunity to innovate, imagine and incorporate new activities into your life. This will be an excellent year for bringing your true strengths into play and making them count. The transformations you make in your life could take you into fresh territory and bring exciting developments.

Consider how you'd like to see your life progress in 2026. It may sound like a pipe dream, but with the necessary focus on practicalities and in tandem with inspiration and motivation you could truly make your dreams come true.

This horoscope book is a guide for you, with weekly horoscopes highlighting your options and the areas of your life that will thrive or gain focus. There is also a round-up of the predominant themes for each month, divided into the following important areas of your life: health, finances, home, love life and work. As you gain an appreciation of the areas of your life that will thrive, and how, you'll gain advance information about where best to focus your attention.

The weeks in this horoscope book run from Thursdays to Wednesdays simply because of the way the year falls, beginning as it does on a Thursday on 1 January. By following the sun, moon and stars you'll discover a fresh rhythm in life that encourages you to make the most of your full potential, enables you to work proactively with your positive traits and sidelines your negative characteristics.

Be sure to approach the retrograde phases with patience and the will to learn, and as a result you'll find life much easier and find the time to enjoy a calmer pace during the retrograde phases: especially the Mercury retrogrades.

Above all, be confident that being guided doesn't mean you must act or live your life in a particular way. This horoscope book is intended as a means to bring your best traits forward so you can live your life to the fullest. I hope you have a spectacular year.

To find out more about the daily astrological aspects I use to make weekly predictions, you'll find the *2026 Astrology Planner* (*2026 Astrology Diary* in the southern hemisphere) invaluable.

MERCURY AND VENUS RETROGRADE PHASES IN 2026

Mercury retrograde phases

Venus retrograde phase

26 February to 20 March

3 October to 14 November

29 June to 23 July

24 October to 13 November

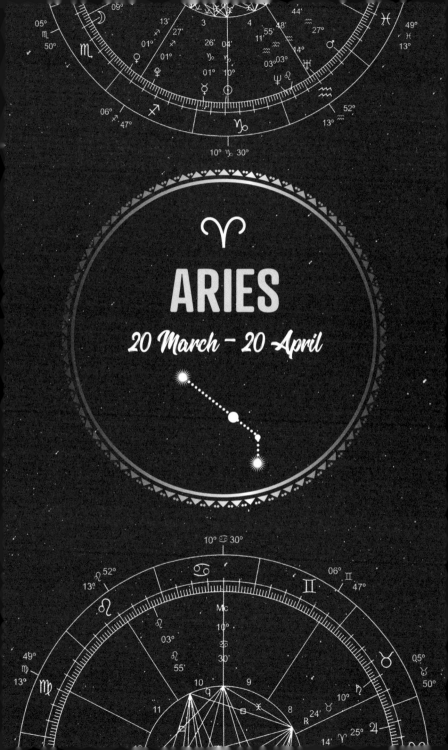

January

WEEK 1: 1–7 JANUARY

A new chapter is about to begin domestically, with family or a property, if it hasn't already. You will gain the chance to turn things around at home, which may impact your work and status or vice versa. Some Aries will enjoy a trip or news from afar, and may also need to adjust to a change of routine due to work or health. Key financial news early in the week will provide clarity.

WEEK 2: 8–14 JANUARY

You may be super busy with your favourite interests and pastimes. You'll enjoy a revitalising development at work or in your personal life early in the week. Take the initiative with your projects but be very wary to avoid crossed lines and misunderstandings, especially on Sunday and early in the week. It's a good week to look after your health.

WEEK 3: 15–21 JANUARY

The more you trust your own abilities the better the outcome, so take the initiative and be positive. You'll enjoy socialising and may even be surprised with the lovely people you meet. Sunday's new moon points to new horizons. Fresh territory may come about through study, travel or simply the chance to broaden your scope and deepen spiritual understanding. Just keep an eye on communications on Friday to avoid mix-ups.

WEEK 4: 22–28 JANUARY

Key news from a group, friend or organisation will broaden your mind. A connection with your past or health could be important in this context, so be sure to think outside the square about your options. Your sign's ruler Mars meets Pluto in your social and status zones. You could progress in relation to a group or organisation. Be calm and focused: this could be an empowering week.

HEALTH

This will be a valuable month to consider whether the people around you are a good example of healthy living. If not it's time to look for a well-being posse who will help you be your healthiest self. Keep an eye on your health, especially mid-month, as overwork and too much play could tire you. The entry of Mars in Aquarius on the 23rd will help you to feel more energised, so don't give up if fatigue strikes mid-month.

FINANCES

You'll gain the opportunity to truly boost your finances and circumstances, so be prepared to go the extra hard yards to improve your situation. The new moon on the 18th may already bring a synchronicity that confirms you're on the right track. Just be sure to avoid gambling, both with money and your job, especially around the 16th. It's far better to research carefully and wait for the inevitable positive outcome to arise as a result.

HOME

You'll appreciate the chance to turn a corner with your domestic circumstances in January, with the first week being particularly productive in this regard. Developments in connection with a group, friend or organisation will have an effect on your home life or a property, so be sure when making decisions regarding others that you consider your home life too and make it a priority.

LOVE LIFE

You have the opportunity to alter your status this month, and that includes whether you're single or married. If you're married and your love life has been lacklustre it's time to take the bull by the horns and bring more zest into your life. If you're single and looking for someone fun or a commitment, keep an eye out mid-month as you're likely to meet someone sensual even if it's under surprising conditions.

WORK

This month is ideal for moving forward, especially with your career and direction, and for many this will come about through the people you know so socialising and networking will certainly bring excellent results. Be prepared to reach out to new groups, friends and organisations to improve your working situation as your efforts will be rewarded, especially in the third week of the month. The new moon on the 18th could even spark a fresh work move.

February

WEEK 1: 29 JANUARY–4 FEBRUARY

Monday's Leo full moon and the conjunction of Mercury and Venus point to a passionate and changeable week. Expect important meetings, and you'll enjoy socialising and networking. There will also be key developments with family, creative projects and in your love life: it is the run-up to St Valentine's after all! A key matter of principle or a favourite project will require discussion.

WEEK 2: 5–11 FEBRUARY

Links with your past due to a reunion or return to an old haunt may include surprising developments. Be sure to plan travel well to avoid delays as much as possible. A group, organisation or social setting could bring something new and exciting into your life. Thursday and Monday may feature some tough communications, so be prepared to see things from the perspective of others.

WEEK 3: 12–18 FEBRUARY

Get set to turn a corner. This will involve fresh ideas, a new work ethic and, for some, restored health and vitality. A fresh opportunity in one or all of these areas could be ideal, but you will need to be ready to move forward with some of your preconceived ideas. Above all avoid impulsive decisions, as these may seem adventurous but could cause mistakes. Be spontaneous instead!

WEEK 4: 19–25 FEBRUARY / WEEK 5: 26 FEBRUARY–4 MARCH

WEEK 4: beautiful aspects bring an ideal time to progress at work. Some Aries will be ready to make an important commitment, both at work and at home. This is also a particularly romantic or sociable time. A health matter may deserve attention. **WEEK 5:** try to get key paperwork and decisions clear before 26 February to avoid having to redo them at a later date. The lunar eclipse on 3 March will bring resolution to important developments.

HEALTH

The conjunction between Saturn and Neptune could unearth latent health issues. For some this conjunction will counsel against overdoing things in January. You may simply feel the need to slow things down. It's far better to manage your health early in the month than to have to dig deep and discover you've exhausted yourself by the end of the month and must then use remedial action to boost your health.

FINANCES

You may be surprised by some developments both at the start and end of the month, and if these are not to your liking you'll gain the opportunity as a result to reconfigure important financial measures. To mitigate fallout, find ways during the month to manage finances with an even, long-term perspective and always maintain a slush fund for a rainy day.

HOME

The wonderful aspect between Venus and Jupiter towards the end of the month will bring a sense of progress, nurturance or simply contentment at home, with family or someone special. If you've been considering making changes at home, this will therefore be a good month to gear up to do exactly that. If you have been fatigued, this will also be a good time to feather your nest so it becomes a true relaxing haven.

LOVE LIFE

The Leo full moon on 1 March brings the chance to reassess both your personal life and domestic obligations. You may also be drawn to make changes at home in line with your new sense of priorities and duties towards someone special. For some mid-April–born Aries a reconfiguration of your closest friendships and circles is likely in February, so be prepared to seek friendships and circles who support you as opposed to the opposite.

WORK

In February you will be drawn to interact with a new and perhaps different group of people. For some Aries this will mean the prospect of fresh work parameters or even a change in the organisations you work with or for. A fresh opportunity in early February could come out of the blue and it may also mean a change in finances for a short while, so be prepared to negotiate clear terms for the best results.

ARIES • FEBRUARY

March

WEEK 1: 5–11 MARCH

As Venus enters your sign you'll notice your attention go to the areas in your life that bring you a sense of pleasure. For some this will translate as more attention to money and the way you earn it, and for others there will be more focus on your love life and romance. It's certainly a positive week to get work and domestic projects underway, so take the initiative.

WEEK 2: 12–18 MARCH

You'll receive news from the past or regarding a project at work. It's a good week to get on top of a health and work routine and for a reunion. Keep communications super clear for the best results. You can improve both your finances and self-esteem this week, and developments at home will deserve extra focus towards the middle of next week.

WEEK 3: 19–25 MARCH

Venus still in your sign continues to bring your focus to love and money. This week's new moon in Pisces will be ideal for devising a fresh daily, work or health routine, one that more fully supports your aims and goals. You may even hear unexpected news that alters your usual schedule. You will enjoy getting together with someone whose company you like.

WEEK 4: 26 MARCH–1 APRIL

In the lead-up to the full moon in your opposite sign of Libra next week you'll already notice your focus going more towards finding peace, harmony and balance in your life. You may receive important news at work. If health has been an issue or an area you'd like to improve, this week's stars could be beneficial for improving well-being.

HEALTH

You will be drawn early in March to invest in your appearance and find well-being practices that support a healthy body and mind. The idea that your health is reflected in your face is something you'll embrace, and this will encourage you to look for modalities that promote serenity. You are likely to be drawn towards a particular health practitioner or benevolent influence mid-month and towards the new moon on the 19th and coming up to the 26th.

FINANCES

You are on a generally upwards spiral in relation to your finances, so it is as well to always keep an eye on where you wish your investments and finances to be in the bigger picture and long term as well, as your current decisions will of course determine the future. Key news either to do with work or health will also encourage you to consider your finances in a new light.

HOME

The positive sun–Jupiter aspect early in March points to the opportunity to improve your home life. You may be drawn to return to an old haunt or will be receiving visitors, such as family. This will also be a good time to consider refreshing your home décor or making other important domestic changes, as they are likely to succeed. However, you will need to be careful with communications mid-month to avoid arguments.

LOVE LIFE

Venus enters your sign in the first week of March and this will encourage you to look increasingly at how to bring more love into your life. You'll certainly experience an uptick in romantic interest at the start of March, which will at the very least boost your self-esteem. You may also be drawn to improve your appearance and health. You're likely to feel more romantic than usual, and for this reason singles will be more attracted to others.

WORK

The conjunction between Saturn, Neptune and Venus in Aries early in March will encourage you to take action to bring more activities into your daily work life that you actually enjoy. For this reason you are likely to be drawn to either look for a promotion or for avenues of work that provide a sense of purpose, especially around the new moon on the 19th. Be sure to be practical but don't lose sight of your ideals.

April

WEEK 1: 2–8 APRIL

Thursday's full moon will be in Libra and will encourage you to formulate a fresh daily health or work routine, and if you were born in March to find more balance in your relationships. Be sure to gain clarification concerning unclear issues, especially this weekend, which will also be a good time to avoid arguments or a Mexican stand-off at home.

WEEK 2: 9–15 APRIL

Mars, your sign's ruler, enters your sign now, where it will be until mid-May. Mars will provide an energy boost that you'll appreciate. However, it may contribute to you appearing to others to be feistier, even if you feel you are simply being bold, so be aware you may be perceived as bossy now. Nevertheless, Sunday and Monday are perfect for indulging in the comforts of life. Romance could thrive.

WEEK 3: 16–22 APRIL

This will be an invigorating week in your personal life and at work as the new moon will be in Aries on Friday. Be sure to take the initiative. You may be aware already that your various projects and work could point you in a different direction, which will prompt you to put in extra effort. Key news or a get-together during the week will motivate you to succeed.

WEEK 4: 23–29 APRIL

You may be pleasantly surprised by developments on Thursday and Friday, and a surprise is likely to boost your ego or finances. Just be careful with communications at the weekend and avoid a battle of wills. Next week you may experience an improvement either financially or in your personal life. This is a good week to improve your appearance, as long as you are clear about the look you're going for.

HEALTH

This month it is important to take advantage of astrological influences that can help you find more peace and calm, as this will benefit your health. April-born Aries are in an especially strong position to gain an increasing sense of balance in your health and outlook, so take the initiative! Circumstances towards the 17th will give you the heads-up about your health or that of someone close.

FINANCES

You may be drawn to spend a little more time and effort on your home or a property and with your family in April, which will provide a sense of well-being and enable your relationships at home and with family to thrive, especially mid-month. Just avoid overspending if you're considering making investments at home as you may be liable to do so, especially towards the 12th and 13th.

HOME

You will appreciate the opportunity to indulge a little in creature comforts, especially mid-month. A visit or development in your home could be ideal and you'll enjoy the opportunity to provide a nurturing and comfortable home not only for yourself, but also for those you love. In mid-April you may be drawn to look after your own health and well-being a little more than usual, so providing a nurturing ambience at home will appeal.

LOVE LIFE

The full moon in your opposite sign of Libra on the 2nd and the new moon in your sign on the 17th indicate an important turning point in a close relationship. You may also experience a considerable development at home or with family, and this will impact your approach to someone special. It will be a good month to seek a balanced and calm outlook. Romance could thrive on the weekends of the 11th, 12th and 24th.

WORK

If you were born in April you are likely to experience a fresh daily or work routine in April, beginning already at the start of the month. It will be in your interest then to weigh the relative importance of a study schedule that enables you to enjoy your downtime as well. The new moon in your sign on the 17th could help reinvigorate your work and career, so be sure to take the initiative with meetings then.

May

WEEK 1: 30 APRIL–6 MAY

A fresh approach to a relationship may appeal. Negotiations will be necessary, and to be on top of developments research will be beneficial. The aspect between Mercury and Chiron at the full moon on 1/2 May, depending on where you are, counsels care with communications, travel and health. You may enjoy a reunion this weekend. A financial or ego boost will improve your mood.

WEEK 2: 7–13 MAY

You'll appreciate the chance to discuss financial and personal arrangements in a constructive way and to make agreements with the people or organisations that can help you progress. This is a good week to make domestic changes. You may enjoy a reunion and creating a steady schedule that supports your health and well-being. Your efforts are likely to be worthwhile.

WEEK 3: 14–20 MAY

This weekend's new moon supermoon signals a fresh chapter financially. Developments could boost your circumstances but you must be clear about terms if you're in debt and should now catch up with your past investments. You may enjoy an impromptu trip or get-together or will receive unexpected news early next week. If undecided, be sure to stick with your big-picture goals.

WEEK 4: 21–27 MAY / WEEK 5: 28 MAY–3 JUNE

WEEK 4: you'll enjoy an impromptu get-together or an unusual event towards the weekend. Should a difference of opinion arise over the next two weeks, avoid allowing it to lead to conflict. **WEEK 5:** you may be drawn to make a surprising investment as the full moon in Sagittarius on 31 May will offer the chance for an adventure, but you must base your decisions on realities rather than expectations.

HEALTH

The start of the month will be ideal to set in place a fresh health schedule. You may be drawn to a trusted health routine that you have already used in the past. Be practical about your daily life and what your body needs to function at its best capacity. The conjunction of Mars and Chiron in your sign on the 16th may predispose you to minor bumps and scrapes, so avoid rushing then.

FINANCES

You'll enjoy a financial boost early in the month. For some Aries, though, the positive Venus–Saturn aspect on 1 May will offer the chance to reconfigure your finances so they suit you better, so do take the initiative. The new moon supermoon on the 16th/17th will help you organise your finances in a new light, especially if you have amassed debt. The full moon on the 31st will help you see shared finances in a new light.

HOME

Jupiter in your home sector makes a fortunate aspect both with the sun and Mercury early in May, bringing the likelihood that you'll appreciate positive developments in this area. For example, you may enjoy receiving a visitor or paying someone else a visit yourself. If you've considered investing in your home your efforts are likely to be successful, especially around the 10th to the 12th.

LOVE LIFE

May will be bookended by two full moons, both of which will spotlight your love life and the areas you share in your life. The full moon on 1 May will spotlight an important and for some intense issue in your love life that will benefit from clarity. Be careful with communications at this time, as misunderstandings may be prevalent. The full moon on the 31st will provide insight into the best way forward regarding shared plans.

WORK

You may be drawn to see your work and earnings in an idealistic light this month, and for that reason it will be important to spend a little time looking with fresh eyes at which areas you love in your work and which you no longer do. You'll gain the opportunity moving forward to decide whether the financial benefits of aspects of your work have more allure than the unenjoyable aspects of your work.

ARIES · MAY

June

WEEK 1: 4–10 JUNE

Agreements and changes at home, with family or someone special, will require delicate handling. An expert could help with a financial or personal matter, but you must be prepared to do your own research as well. If you're making a commitment, be this at work, financially or to a health schedule, be sure you have researched the variables as impulsiveness could be a true pitfall now.

WEEK 2: 11–17 JUNE

This is a good time to keep an eye on your health and fitness or those of someone close, as your efforts will succeed. Consider enlisting the help of an expert if it's needed. Monday's new moon supermoon could revitalise your communications; you may consider a fresh communications device, for example. Be patient with domestic or family circumstances, particularly where you need the co-operation of others to reach your goals.

WEEK 3: 18–24 JUNE

You'll enjoy investing more time in yourself with a treat such as a night out. Romance is on the cards; singles should mingle towards Thursday and Friday! Your artistic side will look for expression. Avoid arguments, as these could escalate. Careful negotiations and talks could produce a fresh agreement with someone in charge or an expert. This is a good week for a medical appointment.

WEEK 4: 25 JUNE–1 JULY

You'll appreciate the sense that your projects are falling into place, and a happy coincidence or chance to move forward this weekend could not only surprise but also delight, especially in connection with your creative projects, family and/or home life. This week's full moon will effectively earth your projects, giving you a little more sense of stability. Aim to turn a corner as new ventures, travel and study appeal.

HEALTH

Towards the new moon supermoon mid-month will be an excellent time to look at ways to strengthen your well-being: mentally, spiritually, emotionally and physically. You may need to work hard to understand a family member or someone close at this time. As a particularly proactive person, you can tend to rush into projects and agreements before having adequately thought them out. Be sure to maintain a close eye on your energy levels as you may be inclined to overwork in June.

FINANCES

You may experience an unexpected financial boost towards mid-June, which will certainly raise morale and especially if you've been careful financially recently. The full moon on the 29th/30th will offer opportunities to improve your finances by way of making changes within your status, career or general direction. For the best results, avoid get rich quick schemes and making arrangements you have not adequately researched.

HOME

The conjunction of Venus and Jupiter on the 9th will put the focus on your domestic life, property or family. You may be drawn to bring more peace and comfort into your home, or even to make considerable changes such as a move or welcoming family members. The lead-up to the new moon on the 15th may spotlight various aspects of a relationship that bring out your or someone else's vulnerabilities. Luckily you gain the chance to improve communications.

LOVE LIFE

It's likely mid-month that your sensitivities or those of your partner's are heightened, so be sure to look at what you're learning through this – for example, your or your partner's triggers – and how you could improve your relationship. If things are truly tough this would be a good month to enlist the help of an expert or adviser for the best results. Communications skills can always be improved, and doing so can help you improve your love life.

WORK

Developments could take you to another level at work, but you must be prepared to discuss your options. A situation may become intense towards the 18th and at this time discussions could turn out to be productive, so take the initiative. The full moon on the 29th/30th will encourage you to turn a corner with your career and projects. If you're making long-term decisions, ensure you have all the information and details before committing to ventures.

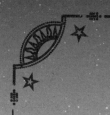
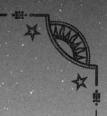

July

WEEK 1: 2–8 JULY

As your sign's ruler, Mars, aligns with changeable Uranus you may feel the winds of change and at least a sense of restlessness this week. This is a good time to initiate change even if it's challenging, especially in the areas of finances, collaborations and work. Developments are likely to take a momentum of their own so be prepared to slow things down if necessary.

WEEK 2: 9–15 JULY

A reunion or return to an old haunt is likely to be both therapeutic and nostalgic. You may hear from an old friend or work-related colleague and will need to decide whether this is kismet or whether it's a distraction from your best-laid plans. You are likely to make progress with domestic matters now but must avoid rushed financial decisions.

WEEK 3: 16–22 JULY

There are many therapeutic aspects to the week; you may even find yourself in a brand-new work or financial situation. Some Aries may be considering where a fresh approach to your daily life, personal circumstance and status will take you. Be sure to look at details carefully as this can be a groundbreaking time for you.

WEEK 4: 23–29 JULY

Saturn will turn retrograde in your sign this week, and you may discover you need to focus a little more on your personal interactions. Be prepared to choose your words carefully, both at work and at home. This aside, this is likely to be an upbeat and creative week when you will enjoy a reunion and your creative abilities really come to the fore both at work and at home.

HEALTH

You'll find out in the first week of the month whether you have taken on too much, either at work or in your daily chores or even family commitments. If so, take a breath and configure a fresh plan. You'll gain the opportunity to improve your health and well-being, especially in the days preceding the new moon mid-month and towards the 26th, so be sure to take the initiative then.

FINANCES

The conjunction of Mars and Uranus at the start of the month may bring financial surprises your way. You'll have to think quickly to avoid missing out on a good opportunity. However, you will need to be careful at this time financially, as mistakes can be made. Be sure to enlist the help of one if not two experts to help you navigate important financial decisions. Avoid gambling and snap decisions, especially towards the 13th and 26th.

HOME

Hopes and plans to make changes at home could be therapeutic, but if you encounter a hiccup or the need to alter your plans early in July then rest assured you will gain a grace period to do exactly that. The conjunction between Mercury retrograde with the sun just before the new moon supermoon mid-month will enable you to cover old ground and repair any aspects of your home life you need to. Just avoid impulsive decisions at this time.

LOVE LIFE

You may be drawn to the past with regard to your love life, and while there are romantic aspects to a nostalgic outlook you risk seeing only the good from the past as opposed to the reality of the present and may be disappointed for this reason. Nevertheless, July, especially mid-month, is particularly healing regarding your love life, and should you rekindle a romantic liaison just keep an eye on practicalities to avoid disappointment.

WORK

Developments are going to be rapid this month, especially in your communications and day-to-day interactions, so be sure to be on top form with your interactions, especially at the start of the month and towards the end of July. Because Mercury is retrograde you will need to focus twice as hard as usual on facts and figures to avoid mistakes. When you do you could make long-term progress in your usual daily routine and at work.

ARIES · JULY

August

WEEK 1: 30 JULY–5 AUGUST

You'll enjoy a creative, fun activity or family project. If you're single, prepare for your status to change if you wish to welcome a partner in your life. Take positive steps towards meeting someone new and you'll gain ground. Organise dates. However, you must avoid power struggles this week as these may become long-standing. There is still tension in the air from the recent full moon.

WEEK 2: 6–12 AUGUST

The total solar eclipse on the 12th/13th will usher in a fresh cycle in your personal life. Singles may meet someone alluring, so be sure to organise a date. A fresh creative or family venture will appeal. Developments are all about romance and exciting activities that can, paradoxically, bring more stability to life. You may be drawn to make a commitment to a new venture or person.

WEEK 3: 13–19 AUGUST

News and developments will bring a change in your usual routine, and for some important news connected with family or a creative project. Be careful towards Monday with communications, especially at work, as it will be important to establish details. You may be forgetful early in the week too, so be extra attentive for the best results. You may receive an unexpected boost or financial improvement.

WEEK 4: 20–26 AUGUST / WEEK 5: 27 AUGUST–2 SEPTEMBER

WEEK 4: this will be a good week to get your ducks in a row with regard to personal and work projects. You'll enjoy a lovely reunion this weekend. **WEEK 5:** key news will be therapeutic for some, and for others the opportunity to indulge a little more in creating good health. The partial lunar eclipse will spotlight the unpredictable nature of some of your arrangements. Be prepared to create your own path to happiness irrespective of the erratic natures of others.

18 ✦ *2026* HOROSCOPES

HEALTH

August is an excellent month to improve your health and vitality, although you must be careful to avoid making snap decisions regarding health routines you have not adequately researched as you may be mistaken in the choices you make. The partial lunar eclipse on the 28th will help you formulate a fresh health and well-being program. You may find around this time that you meet therapeutic or health-conscious people who encourage you towards this goal.

FINANCES

You may experience unusual financial developments in August and these are likely to improve your circumstances, especially if you've been careful with your financial planning in the past. News towards mid-August could even bring a fortunate or surprise financial development your way. Just be sure at this time and also towards the 28th to avoid gambling, as this is likely to backfire or will complicate your financial circumstances.

HOME

If you have been planning major changes at home, domestically or with family this month will enable you to take big steps forward. The solar eclipse on the 12th combined with the transit of the sun, Mercury and Jupiter through your domestic zone will provide perfect opportunities to transform this important part of your life. However, if you're making serious financial commitments you must be careful with details, especially around the 10th, 17th and 28th.

LOVE LIFE

The total solar eclipse on the 12th/13th will bring your focus on people close to you, including those in your love life and family. In the lead-up it is in your interest to look at creative and fun ways to bring more romance into your life, especially if you're single, as this solar eclipse could considerably alter your status. Towards the 21st you may be drawn to make a commitment to someone.

WORK

You can make wonderful headway at work and with organising your daily life so it suits you better, so be sure to take the initiative. The opposition between Venus and Neptune on the 10th may even bring an ideal scenario. However, if you are making serious financial commitments ensure you adequately research circumstances. Significant developments at work are likely mid-month and towards the partial lunar eclipse on the 28th. Just be sure to double-check details to avoid mistakes.

ARIES · AUGUST

September

WEEK 1: 3–9 SEPTEMBER

As you allow the dust to settle after the eclipse season it is an excellent week to get things shipshape at work and health-wise, but you must also avoid pushing yourself and others too hard or you could make mistakes or exhaust yourself. Be practical and reasonable. Make the most of a positive opportunity to enjoy yourself towards the end of the weekend or even on Monday.

WEEK 2: 10–16 SEPTEMBER

Friday's new moon could kick-start a fresh cycle at work and in your daily routine. You may achieve a goal. You'll also be drawn to boost your health and well-being at this time. Romance or a creative project should flourish, although someone close may be feeling a little sensitive or even vulnerable. If it's you, ensure you take time out to destress.

WEEK 3: 17–23 SEPTEMBER

An important decision or discussion may have a surprising outcome in that it will bring the opportunity to create more stability and security. It will demonstrate exactly where you feel you're best motivated to make changes in some of your projects or activities. However, for some this week's developments may bring the need to be patient with a work or health matter.

WEEK 4: 24–30 SEPTEMBER

This weekend's Aries full moon signals a fresh chapter in a personal or work arrangement, so be positive about making agreements. For many the full moon signals a new work arrangement and daily routine. Developments may be unexpected or even disruptive. Luckily this weekend there will be an opportunity to improve your health. You'll also gain the chance to experience something ideal but must avoid rushing and making rash decisions.

HEALTH

September is an excellent month to boost your health and well-being as the new moon on the 11th and the full moon in your own sign of Aries on the 26th/27th put you in a strong position to do so. If you need additional information about a health issue, mid-month and around the 17th will be ideal times to find out more. This is also an excellent month to improve your appearance and spiritual and emotional health.

FINANCES

You can make a great deal of financial progress in September and may even experience unexpected financial improvement, especially towards the 12th and 14th. Just be careful towards the 15th with joint financial arrangements as you may be prone to arguing or even come into conflict over money at that time. Work discussions could also revolve around financial arrangements towards the 17th. Be sure not to underestimate your value.

HOME

Mars in your domestic sector will motivate you to progress aspects of your home life you would like to change. This is a good month for improving your domestic circumstances and relationships at home. You will appreciate the opportunity to connect with like-minded people but must avoid feeling that things should be a certain way, in narrow terms, especially towards the end of September, as this may needlessly rock the boat. Nevertheless, you will need to reach certain agreements.

LOVE LIFE

There is a transformative aspect in a key relationship in September and you'll discover more about someone close towards the 10th. You may even discover something significant about your own emotional make-up at this time. If you or someone close feels super sensitive or vulnerable you may be wise to avoid making snap decisions at this time and towards the end of the month and to wait until some of the intensity wanes.

WORK

You'll discover how you truly feel about your work circumstances, which may initially come through uncertainty or even confusion. You will, however, gain the opportunity to revitalise key aspects of your daily working life towards the new moon on the 11th and towards the 17th, and the full moon on the 26th/27th, and this will enable you to better pursue your goals. Just be sure to gather all the facts and information you need to make decisions.

ARIES · SEPTEMBER

October

WEEK 1: 1–7 OCTOBER

A new agreement may be forged at work or regarding past decisions. However, communications are likely to be intense, so be patient and keep your goals in mind to avoid distractions. You may need to be spontaneous or encouraged to reveal matters you wish to avoid or keep secret, so be diplomatic where possible. It's a good weekend to get on top of creative projects and for romance.

WEEK 2: 8–14 OCTOBER

A fresh approach to someone close could ring in changes at work and a new, more practical attitude to someone at home could bring more stability into your life, but you must be prepared to negotiate in both cases. This weekend's new moon energy will encourage you to consider fresh ways to relate with those you have an unavoidable connection with, including colleagues and family.

WEEK 3: 15–21 OCTOBER

This is a good time for making agreements. You may find that you feel particularly creative and outgoing. A lovely event should boost your feel-good factor, as an upbeat character brings humour into your life. Just be careful towards mid-week next week to keep an eye on good communications skills to avoid misunderstandings and arguments.

WEEK 4: 22–28 OCTOBER / WEEK 5: 29 OCTOBER–4 NOVEMBER

WEEK 4: Mercury turns retrograde on the 24th, so try to get key matters such as agreements on the table beforehand to avoid frustration further down the line. The Taurus full moon on the 26th may illuminate a surprise or something unexpected that merits clarification. **WEEK 5:** be careful with communications towards the 30th due to potentially crossed lines. You'll appreciate a change of pace towards 4 November.

HEALTH

The beginning of the month is ideal for looking into a steady routine that can bring a strong foundation for good health into your daily life. Consider joining a club or enlisting the help of a fitness expert if you need the motivation to maintain a regular fitness schedule. You may even consider seeing some fitness schedules as a part of your usual domestic/everyday chores such as gardening and cleaning.

FINANCES

This is a lovely month to look at your income and expenditure in a fresh way as you will gain the opportunity to move some of your projects and investments forward into different territory. If you are unable to gain new perspective consider enlisting the help or guidance of an expert. You'll be drawn to invest in your home or family, which will provide more stability in the long term.

HOME

A change of pace will be revitalising for your home life. If you work from home, consider rearranging your home office so you can separate your work from the rest of your life. You may experience rapid changes with a domestic circumstance, so the more adaptable within reason you are the better for you. Aim to put in place fail-safe mechanisms that bring more security and stability, especially towards the 16th, as your efforts are likely to succeed.

LOVE LIFE

There is a tinderbox feel to certain communications early in the month and towards the new moon on the 10th/11th, so be careful to avoid arguments and unnecessary conflict. Aim to organise events carefully to avoid disappointment during the first weekend of October. Towards the 7th you may enjoy a spontaneously fun event, and singles may even meet someone attractive at this time. To avoid delays with shared plans, aim to have arrangements sorted before the 24th.

WORK

A fresh arrangement at work early on in the month may appeal, especially if you were born after mid-April. It's certainly a good time for all Aries to discuss work matters, but you must be prepared to reveal vulnerabilities because in this way you will grow throughout October. Be prepared to negotiate and discuss your ideas in practical terms to avoid tension and even misunderstandings, especially towards the 9th and 20th.

ARIES • OCTOBER

November

WEEK 1: 5–11 NOVEMBER

This will be a perfect week to gain deeper understanding of a circumstance, of someone else or yourself. You may experience the strength of your intuition and will be guided by this to make changes in your life. A collaboration, contract or agreement could flourish this week as you may receive information that could improve your daily life, health or work.

WEEK 2: 12–18 NOVEMBER

Life can move forward at a fast pace now. If you're looking for love and romance be sure to make dates from the 12th to the 16th as you're likely to meet someone special. Just avoid rushing things. There may even be a predestined feeling to the meeting. If you're more focused on work and/or health, significant meetings could progress your position so be positive and proactive.

WEEK 3: 19–25 NOVEMBER

There are therapeutic aspects to the end of your week. However, it is important that you do not enter into or recommence arguments with someone you must share duties, finances or responsibilities with. Romance could thrive towards the end of the weekend, and the full moon on Tuesday promises to help you turn a corner either financially or within your personal life.

WEEK 4: 26 NOVEMBER–2 DECEMBER

You are likely to see a marked improvement in your work, career or status this week and may even be surprised by developments. However, you may benefit from a healthy break to avoid fatigue. This weekend is an excellent time to look after yourself and those you care about, and a health or beauty appointment will appeal. Avoid misunderstandings, though.

HEALTH

You'll enjoy the opportunity to bring more beauty and self-care into your daily life already early in the month. You'll find mid-November is particularly constructive regarding your health and well-being as you will gain the opportunity to indulge in healing activities at that time that may prove particularly effective, so be sure to take the initiative to improve your health. The entry of Mars in your health sector on the 25th will provide increased energy moving into December.

FINANCES

You are still in the midst of a transformative phase financially, and if you look back towards July you will see that many of your efforts relate to developments dating from that time. The full moon supermoon on the 24th/25th could indicate a turning point. You may experience unusual or unprecedented circumstances. Be sure to maintain a view of your goals, even if you are prone to doubting their feasibility at times.

HOME

There is a great deal of focus during November on your relationships, work and happiness. For this reason it would be relatively easy for you to ignore the importance of your home life. However, there are super-therapeutic aspects concerning not only your health and well-being but also some relationships that will benefit from the nurturance of a relaxed domestic setting. As a result, investing a little time on your décor and comfort level will be beneficial.

LOVE LIFE

You'll gain the motivation to factor someone special into your life on a more daily basis, especially if you have been neglecting them of late. Romance could thrive on the 10th, 12th, 16th and 23rd. If you're single be sure to organise dates between the 12th and 16th and on the 23rd, as you may meet someone you feel fated to be with. However, you must maintain a sense of discernment and avoid rushing in.

WORK

You may receive good news towards the 10th and once again towards the end of the month that encourages you to take strides ahead in your work arrangements. Key meetings between the 12th and 16th could put you on track to a fresh development, especially if you were born before mid-April. If you are a creative Aries, November is also a good month to be outgoing with your endeavours as you can make great inroads in your projects mid-month.

ARIES • NOVEMBER

December

WEEK 1: 3–9 DECEMBER

Venus will ramp up your lust for life; you'll certainly enjoy seasonal festivities. The Sagittarius new moon on the 9th kick-starts a fresh phase where you will be drawn to reconnect with favourite activities and people and travel is also likely to appeal to you. You may find fresh ways to share duties or even space at home and finances. Be sure to plan ahead to avoid delays next Wednesday.

WEEK 2: 10–16 DECEMBER

Developments regarding work or someone you collaborate with may bring about a little soul searching. A strong connection with your past or to do with health could produce excellent results, so be sure to initiate conversations and research your position. A friend or collaborator may prove to be particularly helpful either at work or with personal issues. You will enjoy romance this weekend and a reunion early next week.

WEEK 3: 17–23 DECEMBER

As you sail towards next week's solstice you have the wonderful opportunity to experience a therapeutic and uplifting development. You may be lucky to embark on a trip, and at the least a positive change in your usual schedule will prove uplifting. However, you must avoid succumbing to seasonal pressure and checking all itineraries to avoid unnecessary delays and misunderstandings.

WEEK 4: 24–31 DECEMBER

It's all systems go, especially with collaborations and domestic matters that require updating or transformation. For some a change of scenery may produce a flurry of activity. Centre stage will be good communications and the need to sort out logistics. A change of location could cause tension, but if you maintain focus on your goals you're likely to overcome obstacles. You'll enjoy feeling things are on track by New Year's Eve.

HEALTH

You'll appreciate creating your own happiness as you gain the incentive to plan lovely get-togethers via travel and your favourite activities and interests. You're likely also to feel more passionate about life and for this reason will feel motivated to enjoy your month. A fun or upbeat weekend of the 12th may include a boost in your health. You will appreciate the opportunity to engage in a truly therapeutic activity towards mid-December, which you will enjoy.

FINANCES

There is no doubt that this month financial change is afoot for you. Whether this is a positive outcome or the opposite depends to a great degree on the level of attention to details you have paid to your finances in recent months and years. However, for many a work development could truly boost your financial outlook, so be sure to work towards your goals earlier in the month as you may already see positive developments by the 18th.

HOME

You'll experience a pleasant change of environment in December that for many will be connected with Christmas, as travel takes shape or visitors arrive at this time of year. However, some developments will feel even more therapeutic in connection with some of the changes you make at home. You are likely to see the domestic aspects of your life as healing. The full moon supermoon on Christmas Eve will spotlight your relationships. Avoid taking other people's actions personally.

LOVE LIFE

Venus in passionate Scorpio from the 4th onwards will provide you with a truly passionate need to connect with your partner. Singles may enjoy the festive season more than usual, with fun being a priority. The 12th and 14th may be particularly conducive to romance. Keep an eye on communications during the last week in December, as miscommunications and misunderstandings may be prevalent and could interfere with an otherwise enjoyable time.

WORK

You are in line to experience a positive change in your usual working day or experience at work. For some Aries this will simply mean that you are embarking on a holiday; however, for many it is possible that you make a breakthrough at work and especially towards the 18th. To ensure your safe passage into improved circumstances at work avoid battles of will and be meticulous, especially towards the 23rd, to avoid mistakes.

January

WEEK 1: 1–7 JANUARY

A trip, transportation or key news will put the spotlight on the necessity to be a little careful about travel and communications. You may be ready for a long trip or are returning from one. You'll appreciate the chance to find a more secure way forward, especially regarding financial, legal, study, travel or personal matters. Be prepared to collaborate and find out more about your options.

WEEK 2: 8–14 JANUARY

You'll enjoy pursuing a favourite activity or interest this weekend. A trip or reunion will appeal. You may meet someone attractive and will enjoy music, the arts and a fun atmosphere. Romance could flourish. However, misunderstandings are possible both at work and at play, so keep an eye on mix-ups. You'll gain an increasing sense of direction early in the week.

WEEK 3: 15–21 JANUARY

You'll appreciate the opportunity to socialise this weekend; the festivities will see you in your element. The new moon on Sunday may kick-start a fresh agreement or arrangement at work or in your personal life, and take you in a fresh direction. If you feel this week that some events are challenging or surprising then make time for research, especially if you're making big changes.

WEEK 4: 22–28 JANUARY

Key developments in your career, direction or status could signal a fresh course of action. A contract or agreement may be on the table. Check details to ensure a collaboration is fair and, if so, it could be ideal. Avoid tempers and think clearly. Be prepared to step into fresh territory within your usual daily routine as this will prove to be constructive for you.

HEALTH

Be prepared to look after your health, especially mid-month, as you will otherwise risk over-tiring yourself in January and will need either to take extra holidays or take one at least, if you didn't already. The last week of the month is likely to be fairly intense, so be sure to find an outlet for a build-up of pressure or of activity so you are able to pace yourself.

FINANCES

You'll gain the opportunity to improve your financial circumstances as you will receive key news either to do with work or with your status in general. Be constructive with your various projects, and if you have been considering stepping into fresh territory in the way you organise your financial and work schedules you will gain the opportunity to do so, but you must ensure you have all the information before making rash decisions.

HOME

There will be considerable focus on where you are going to be setting your compass for the year and it will be important not to underestimate the relevance and value of a settled home life. You will encounter exciting opportunities to broaden your horizons, both through your work and your personal life. It would be easy to take certain people or circumstances at home for granted so you must remember that in many respects your home life anchors you.

LOVE LIFE

There is focus in January on your status and direction in life and there will be exciting opportunities to step into fresh territory. Whether you are single or married, attached or not looking for a partner you will gain the opportunity now to consider or at least imagine new arrangements. While you are feeling inspired, be sure to maintain a strong understanding of who is and who is not important in your life.

WORK

You have a wonderful opportunity in January to boost your work and personal circumstances, and your status could thrive as a result. Be sure to take the initiative with your various projects and ventures, as you're likely to see positive results by the 18th if not before. Be prepared to look outside the box at your options and to collaborate. Just avoid mid-month looking only at the negatives, as this could be a pitfall.

TAURUS · JANUARY

February

WEEK 1: 29 JANUARY–4 FEBRUARY

Sunday/Monday's full moon will shine a light on domestic, family and property developments; you may already anticipate changes in these areas. News or a get-together this Thursday may be intense, with travel or work obligations bringing you in touch with like-minded people. Your personal life is due change, so be prepared to be flexible and if possible avoid prioritising work over home.

WEEK 2: 5–11 FEBRUARY

You may need to reassess a situation or change your perspective. Avoid attempting a broad sweep; be selective. You may be surprised by developments. Pluto in Aquarius could create intensity in your life so be sure to take things one step at a time. News to do with work, travel, overseas, your status, ventures or general direction is on the way.

WEEK 3: 12–18 FEBRUARY

You'll enjoy doing something new involving a group, organisation or friend. You'll find out more about how to work with someone whose ideas differ from yours. Try to avoid seeing only the black and white in a circumstance, as there may be many advantages to being flexible now. Do your research if venturing into new territory and then you could excel.

WEEK 4: 19–25 FEBRUARY / WEEK 5: 26 FEBRUARY–4 MARCH

WEEK 4: there are many ideal aspects this weekend. You'll enjoy get-togethers. This is also a good time for making a commitment to a person or plan and for creating a solid base for yourself. For many this will revolve around work and a firm health plan, and for some a commitment to a friend or organisation. **WEEK 5:** the lunar eclipse on 3 March will bring a sense of stability or at least resolution within your personal life, enabling you to anchor some of your projects.

HEALTH

An inquiring mind will serve you well in early February, as in this way you can get on top of niggling health issues. Avoid overwork as this could precipitate a cycle that will be difficult to exit later in the month. The third week of the month will be conducive to making a commitment to better health and well-being. At this time you may also discover new health practices that are motivational and improve morale.

FINANCES

There will be considerable developments going on behind the scenes in your life, changes that will become clearer as the month goes by. Many of these will involve your work and daily schedule and this will invariably alter your financial approach, as you either change up a gear at work or decide you're ready for a slower pace. As your health will also factor into considerations, it's important to consider how to maintain the status quo in your finances.

HOME

February will be a good month to focus on your domestic priorities such as your family, home or a property, as the full moon on 1 February indicates fresh opportunities that will affect this key part of your life. For many Taureans this may be due to changes at work or your personal status, such as from single to married and vice versa. The eclipse season also indicates developments with your family and love life, so aim to keep your home a haven.

LOVE LIFE

Your love life and social life can flourish in the third and final weeks of February, and especially on the weekend of the 21st. You may even find that some get-togethers have a therapeutic quality. If you're planning a lovely event, that weekend will be conducive to romance. Singles may even meet someone particularly alluring at this time, so keep an eye out! If you find your love life becomes a little all-absorbing you'll relish the resolution that the lunar eclipse on 3 March provides.

WORK

Your approach to matters will determine the outcome of your month, especially early on in February. You may need to adapt to changing goal posts, and for some Taureans there may even be reason to alter your daily work schedule or big-picture career goals. Be prepared to look at the bright side of circumstances as otherwise you may turn out to be your own worst enemy, especially towards the 5th, 8th and 27th.

March

WEEK 1: 5–11 MARCH

This is a good week to move ahead with domestic-, family- or property-related matters as you are generally communicating well. A lucky event or coincidence could boost your mood. Some Taureans will appreciate a visit or enjoy a short trip. Romance could blossom, so be sure to take the initiative! You'll enjoy socialising and getting back in touch with someone you love.

WEEK 2: 12–18 MARCH

This will be a lovely week for get-togethers, both socially and at work. You are likely to meet someone who has already played an influential role in your life or who is about to. You may also be drawn to travel and to a reunion or visit an old haunt. Just be careful towards mid-week next week, when some developments will require more attention than usual.

WEEK 3: 19–25 MARCH

You'll enjoy socialising and taking the time to enjoy time spent with your favourite people. Thursday's new moon will encourage you to turn a corner with a particular group or organisation. You may receive an attractive job offer. If your current circumstance has become restrictive, you'll feel motivated to change this. Be sure to follow your ideals but also be practical.

WEEK 4: 26 MARCH–1 APRIL

Be open to new developments at work and a change in your schedule. Thursday and Friday are good days to focus on a beauty or health appointment. You may enjoy an impromptu get-together with a group, organisation or friend at the weekend. Romance and the arts could thrive mid-week next week, so be sure to organise a date then!

HEALTH

You'll enjoy socialising in early March, which will boost your mood. You may enjoy a trip or visit that provides a sense of expansion but also of belonging. Mid-month you may be particularly busy, so be sure to organise relaxation time. This will also be a positive month to set in motion a more active fitness schedule, especially after the 19th, so be sure to find a group or organisation you wish to work with.

FINANCES

The conjunction between the sun, Saturn and Neptune in your work sector points to developments at work that could truly take you into fresh territory. This makes March an excellent month to put your negotiation skills to good use, so therefore you have the potential to improve your finances via a better work arrangement. You may even be surprised by opportunities to do so, especially towards the end of the month.

HOME

For some Taureans early March will revolve around the opportunity to bring a sense of expansion in your home life, including the relationships you enjoy at home or associate with your home such as your family ties. For others a trip or visit will take you into different territory but will nevertheless provide a sense of belonging. Changes at work or health-wise will require you to remember to feather your nest.

LOVE LIFE

The second week of the month running through to mid-March will be a particularly positive time for socialising, so if you are single you may meet someone either from your past or with whom you feel already familiar even though you have just met, especially between the 13th and 18th. Couples will enjoy spending time with like-minded people and also might consider joining groups or organisations where you both feel a sense of growth.

WORK

You'll gain the opportunity, especially mid-month, to progress within your work and/or career trajectory. You may even be in a position to commit to a role that suits you and is more upbeat or outgoing than your current position. At the start of the month be sure to look out for opportunities and get your ducks in a row so you're ready to make the most of this proactive time.

TAURUS • MARCH

April

WEEK 1: 2–8 APRIL

Thursday's full moon will spotlight your personal life including family, love life and, for some, home life. You may need to priorities those you love over work or an organisation, so be prepared to look at where your true loyalties lie. It's a sociable and potentially busy time, so be sure to pace yourself. Avoid a battle of wills if possible this weekend and early next week.

WEEK 2: 9–15 APRIL

The arrival of Mars in your 12th house of work and health will prompt you to devote more energy to these important areas of your life. You may even receive ideal news in one or both of these areas towards the weekend and or on Monday. Take the initiative with work and romantic gestures as you are sure to enjoy and appreciate a get-together with someone special.

WEEK 3: 16–22 APRIL

If you like a challenge you will succeed with your endeavours now, but if you tend to shy away from obstacles this week may feel like a tough time. Keep lines of communication open or you risk limiting your options moving forward. You will be drawn to begin a fresh chapter either at work or regarding your health routine.

WEEK 4: 23–29 APRIL

Friday's developments may be a surprise. For some this will simply be unexpected news, and for others an impromptu get-together that may be financial or romantic in nature. You may benefit from an expert's help financially, especially if you discover an anomaly towards the 24th, and the entry of Uranus in Gemini suggests this would be a good time to consider ways to stabilise your budget for the foreseeable future.

HEALTH

The full moon on 2 April will be in Libra, and this will be a particularly powerful full moon for you and an opportunity to put in place a balanced health schedule. You may also be drawn to alter your appearance. The new moon on the 17th will shine a light on the state of your health or that of someone close. This is a good time to focus on your well-being.

FINANCES

The conjunction of Venus and Uranus on the 24th and the entry of Uranus in your financial zone suggest you may be surprised by financial developments towards the end of the month. If you have been meaning to find ways to stabilise your budget and keep income and expenditure on an even keel, April will be a good month to do this so you are in a strong position moving forward over the next few years.

HOME

There will be so much focus this month on your work and well-being, so it will be very important to create a stable and healthy home life for yourself as you may otherwise feel under more pressure than necessary, especially towards the new moon mid-month. Be sure early in April already to build creature comforts for yourself and create a balanced situation for the best results.

LOVE LIFE

The Libran full moon on the 2nd will spotlight key relationships for you. For some these will be at work, while for others these relationships will involve family and friendships. It may be a fairly intense full moon, but if you focus on good communication skills and camaraderie you could build some truly strong, secure foundations for yourself and those you love.

WORK

The month begins with promising developments at work and, in the bigger picture, in your career, and you will gain the opportunity to build solid foundations for yourself moving forward this month as long as you avoid an ego battle either with colleagues or a boss or clients early in the month, especially around the 5th. Mars in your 12th house of work until mid-May will provide you with a boost in energy and motivation, so be sure to take the initiative.

TAURUS • APRIL

May

WEEK 1: 30 APRIL–6 MAY

Your expertise will be in demand early in May. The Scorpio full moon on 1 May could shine a light on someone's intense beliefs. If you agree with them all well and good, but if their beliefs are conflicting aim to maintain a tactful approach to avoid intense interactions – at least up until 6 May, when communications may be difficult. You may need to reconsider some of your plans.

WEEK 2: 7–13 MAY

A trip or get-together will be uplifting. Creative Taureans will find this a particularly productive week and you could accomplish a great deal, not only at home but also at work. A change of routine may produce good results, especially financially, and could also boost your ego. It's a good week to be outgoing with communications, both verbally and via the internet, paperwork and so on.

WEEK 3: 14–20 MAY

This weekend's new moon supermoon will be in Taurus and signifies the start of a fresh phase in your life, especially if it's your birthday. Prepare to welcome a more stable phase, even if a surprise arises. It's a good time to focus on your health and/or that of someone close. If you need advice be sure to ask for it, because it will be available for you now.

WEEK 4: 21–27 MAY / WEEK 5: 28 MAY–3 JUNE

WEEK 4: you'll enjoy sharing time with like-minded people. You may hear unexpectedly from someone or receive surprise news. A refreshingly different approach to the areas you share in life such as finances, space at home and the office will thoroughly benefit you now. **WEEK 5:** a discussion may bring issues to a head, in which case it's best to overcome differences of opinion before they escalate, especially from the 26th to the 29th.

HEALTH

The conjunction of Mars and Chiron on the 16th will be particularly motivational for you to find ways to boost your health and well-being or to help someone close do the same. If you work in the health industry you may be particularly busy at this time. It is a good time to look for therapeutic ways to also boost your self-esteem and confidence.

FINANCES

Keep an eye on finances this month, especially towards the end of the month when Venus makes a tough aspect with Neptune and Mars with Pluto. Ensure you have the right information if you're making key decisions both financially and at work and regarding your big-picture goals, as you may otherwise be inclined to make uninformed choices either due to feeling pressured or misinformation. Research the facts for the best effect if you're making key choices.

HOME

The second week of May is going to be particularly productive for you at home, especially if you were born in April, although all Taureans will find this a productive time whether you focus your creativity and productivity at home or at work. If you are lucky enough to enjoy some travel in May it is likely to bring you in touch with new ideas that you can then incorporate into your home or domestic relationship dynamics.

LOVE LIFE

Your love life may prove intense around the full moon in your opposite sign Scorpio on 1 May, especially if you are an April-born Taurean. Aim to find clever ways to communicate clearly as otherwise intense emotions may take you down a complex or even conflicting path. Focus on common ground for the best effect, as opposed to your differences, if talks take an awkward turn.

WORK

For many Taureans the full moon on 1/2 May will spotlight a change in a work schedule, and at least the desire to alter your usual working parameters. This may be experienced as an intense or conflicting time, so be sure to keep your emotions out of important decisions but make sure those decisions are based on your values and principles. You may also be in a position to reconsider some of your past decisions.

TAURUS · MAY

June

WEEK 1: 4–10 JUNE

You can make a great deal of progress with work- and health-related matters but must avoid impulsiveness and stubbornness. Be flexible to maximise your options. A domestic, property- or family-related event may be significant, especially if you were born before mid-May. If you were born later in May a conversation or trip could bring you in touch with people who will stimulate change in your personal life.

WEEK 2: 11–17 JUNE

This weekend it's in your interest to keep communications and financial transactions on an even keel as you'll enjoy events, but you may also experience mistakes or misunderstandings. Monday's new moon supermoon will provide insight into your circumstances from a practical, financial point of view. Your values will come into sharp focus, enabling you to make clear decisions. A repaid debt or reunion could be a catalyst to positive action.

WEEK 3: 18–24 JUNE

A change of pace or perspective will include the chance to bring more contentment into your home or to visit an area of beauty. Travel, a fun activity and romance will all appeal, so be sure to organise a treat. An important conversation or news will enable you to move ahead with key matters such as work and finances even if there is still hard work to be done.

WEEK 4: 25 JUNE–1 JULY

Commitments will be made, and for some these may involve long-term arrangements. A work decision or personal commitment will offer a sense of security, but if you feel that current circumstances are more limiting than you'd prefer this will be your motivation to make changes that align more with a sense of adventure and to embrace your favourite interests in your life and work ethics.

HEALTH

With Mars in your sign until the 28th you are likely to feel more active and vibrant this month. Be sure to plan your activities to maximise this potentially revitalising time. However, you may be prone to overestimating your physical stamina, especially during the first and second week of June and particularly towards the 13th, so be sure to pace yourself. It's a good month to invest in your well-being to help boost energy levels.

FINANCES

The new moon on the 15th will kick-start a new financial phase for you, so the lead-up to mid-June will be an ideal time to reconfigure your budget and investments if it's necessary. You may be surprised by some lucky developments that put you in a better position in June, however, but if you experience the opposite this will be the ideal month to seek expert advice or help as it will be available to you.

HOME

Developments will put the focus on your home, family and personal life. It will be an excellent time to consider how you derive a sense of nurturance from your home and interpersonal dynamics and to invest in this important part of your life. However, some Taureans may come to the realisation that your home no longer supports your requirements and you must make a tough call. A trip or visit mid-month may provide perspective in this respect.

LOVE LIFE

Mid-month you'll appreciate the opportunity to spend time with someone special in a domestic setting or simply relax in an environment that is conducive to romance. However, someone is likely to feel a little vulnerable or under the weather, so sensitivity to their feelings on your part will be needed. If it is you who is feeling under the weather you may need to ask for a little more support from your partner or someone close.

WORK

The new moon supermoon on the 15th kick-starts a fresh financial chapter in your life, and this may well be due to changes within your working circumstance. Be open to new opportunities that could broaden your horizon but avoid making changes for the sake of them. The Capricorn full moon on the 29th/30th will encourage you to make a commitment to work or a project that could provide stability. However, you must ensure you are not limiting your options too much.

July

WEEK 1: 2–8 JULY

There will be unexpected or even unprecedented developments this week, so be sure to keep your feet on the ground and be practical about changes that stem from past actions, ideas and decisions that need acting upon now. You may be called on to help someone in need, and if you need support or advice it will be available. A financial or work development may be a surprise.

WEEK 2: 9–15 JULY

There are therapeutic aspects to the week and this is a good time to build bridges with anyone you have argued with, such as family or even an ex. Any kind of reunion with an ex must, however, be carefully analysed, and unless you can guarantee positive outcomes there is the likelihood that unanticipated variables outweigh the positives. There will be unexpected news either from work or the past.

WEEK 3: 16–22 JULY

The Uranus–Pluto trine can put you onto a fresh path in your life, and this may be ideal. It is important that you double-check all paperwork and communications as you may be inclined to look at developments through rose-tinted glasses. Once you have determined that all is kosher, be prepared to step into something new.

WEEK 4: 23–29 JULY

You have a wonderful opportunity to move either your work or domestic life forward so take the initiative. You may receive specific news connected with someone close, either at home or in your personal life. This will be a good time to review your daily work and health routines to ensure they support you as best they possibly can.

HEALTH

The start of the month will be a good time to decide to carry on the way you wish to for the rest of the month as key health matters – your own or those of someone close – need attention. You may simply need to manage strong emotions or must contend with pressure that dictates your feelings for now. Take this as an opportunity to develop strength of mind and resilience.

FINANCES

Developments stemming from past actions that affect your current career or financial situation will arise early in July. For some these will be positive developments, although many Taureans will nevertheless need to adapt to fresh circumstances. As developments in July are likely to be fairly swift despite the Mercury retrograde, it is in your interest to double-check all financial transactions as you and others may be liable to make mistakes.

HOME

If you have been waiting for news connected with your home or family it is likely to arrive this month. For many the news is likely to be positive, but for some there may be a little upheaval that needs to be negotiated before the healing can begin. Be prepared to deal with the unexpected, and in this way you will be a few steps ahead. A reunion or return to an old haunt will be significant.

LOVE LIFE

You could alter your status – for example from single to married – this month and developments are likely to be rapid. Be prepared to alter your usual routine or way of meeting people if you are single, as you may be surprised by who you meet. The Uranus–Pluto trine could affect your love life as you step from single to married or from married to single once again.

WORK

Developments early in July, mid-month and towards the 27th may be surprising. You could make changes very rapidly now, so be sure to be on the ball and make the most of opportunities that arise. Some may unfortunately appear to be obstacles, and if so maintain a positive outlook as opportunities to improve circumstances will arise. The Uranus–Pluto trine on the 18th could take you to another level, so be prepared to make changes.

TAURUS · JULY

August

WEEK 1: 30 JULY–5 AUGUST

This week's developments are likely to validate some of your recent actions and decisions, especially at home or with family. It's certainly a good time to make solid plans that are both realistic and practical, because in this way you will see positive results for all your hard work. Many Taureans will gain the opportunity to turn hard work into pleasant gain.

WEEK 2: 6–12 AUGUST

The total solar eclipse on the 12th/13th will encourage you to make changes to a domestic or personal arrangement, with the aim of securing a sense of security with someone close. A trip and arrangements you make now may create excitement, even if at first they represent a degree of upheaval. They are likely to bring long-term happiness but could involve disruption in the short term.

WEEK 3: 13–19 AUGUST

Much of your focus will be on a change of circumstance concerning your personal life, home or family. You may feel a little sensitive this week, so it's an excellent time to take things step by step. Avoid feeling things are outside your control by gently managing your response to circumstances over which you do have control. Be careful with significant financial and work transactions to avoid making mistakes.

WEEK 4: 20–26 AUGUST / WEEK 5: 27 AUGUST–2 SEPTEMBER

WEEK 4: you may be in a position to make a commitment to a work or health project, and this could be beneficial as long as you do not limit your future options too far. There is a therapeutic aspect to a reunion towards the weekend.
WEEK 5: the partial lunar eclipse on the 28th will bring a personal chapter into focus where circumstances may be unexpected. However, you could make great progress with a personal or work project.

HEALTH

August and right up until early March 2027 will be an excellent time to re-evaluate your current health schedule and put something new in place, so be sure to look at your various options. August will be an excellent time to consider ways to improve your appearance and peace of mind. Both these are connected, and the more you look for balance and harmony in your daily routine the more this will radiate from your face.

FINANCES

Mars in your money zone continues to bring opportunities to improve your financial circumstances but equally the likelihood that you overspend, so it will be important at least until the 12th to keep an eye on maintaining balance in your accounts. Tough astrological aspects on the 10th and 17th could predispose you to making mistakes, so if you're undertaking important transactions at this time be careful to check the facts.

HOME

As an earth sign, planning and organisation are two of your strong points. However, this month you may be prone to make snap decisions at home or with family, but as long as you maintain a sense of perspective you can move forward into pleasant territory. Just avoid impulsiveness as this will backfire. News towards the 17th could turbocharge your plans, but again you will need to take good, solid information as opposed to supposition into account.

LOVE LIFE

An eclipse season is being entered, with the first eclipse being on the 12th/13th depending on where you are. The second eclipse on the 28th could bring romance to a high point for you. Both these eclipses signal an intense month for you in your love life. If you love intensity you will love August, but if it does not appeal this is a good time already early in August to establish a contingency plan to funnel intense emotions into productive activities.

WORK

You will gain the opportunity to align your work activities with a deeper sense of purpose. This may come about as you realise you are on an unfulfilling career path or, alternatively, you realise you are doing exactly what you love. While both these eventualities would seem opposite, what they have in common is that you gain the opportunity now to become truly single-minded about your work.

TAURUS · AUGUST

September

WEEK 1: 3–9 SEPTEMBER

Your hard work will pay off, so if you're uncertain of your path right now ensure you research your circumstances and then pay close attention to details and show your willingness to make things work. You will appreciate the opportunity to get together with a favourite person towards Sunday or Monday and engage in favourite activities, so be sure to take the initiative.

WEEK 2: 10–16 SEPTEMBER

Get set for a fresh chapter in a creative venture. If you're particularly musical, inventive, romantic or simply love luxury in life you'll enjoy incorporating more of these qualities in your life. However, you must avoid mix-ups and misunderstandings this week, especially at work and on Friday and at the weekend. This aside, you could make a great deal of progress both at work and with your ventures.

WEEK 3: 17–23 SEPTEMBER

If you're looking for a commitment from someone or you'd like to make a particular decision, this is the week to do it. Financial matters deserve your full focus, and a little attention either to your health or that of someone close will put you in a strong position. You will find a friend, group or organisation particularly helpful, so do reach out.

WEEK 4: 24–30 SEPTEMBER

You'll progress with a venture; news will enable you to move forward with more clarity. A fresh approach to a friend or organisation will provide the chance to deepen some friendships and to leave others you have outgrown. Avoid taking other people's circumstances personally unless you're directly involved. Be prepared to put your home life first if you experience a clash of duties towards Sunday. Avoid rushing.

HEALTH

Developments towards the 10th, 17th and 26th could spotlight a key health or beauty appointment. This is certainly a good month to look at your health from a big-picture point of view and gain insight into your best way forward. You may be drawn particularly to improve your appearance towards the 26th, but if you are undertaking serious measures be sure to adequately research what you are looking for to avoid misunderstandings.

FINANCES

Positive aspects this month can improve your finances considerably, largely through choices and opportunities you gain to improve your work situation. Be prepared to consider your finances in the long term rather than making short-term arrangements that could leave you vulnerable to market forces. Be prepared to put your spending at home first so that you always know you have your bases covered, as this will avoid needless angst.

HOME

This is a constructive month for putting effort into your home life, as your efforts are likely to succeed. The more practical and realistic yet also big-hearted you are the better will be the outcome. By the same token it will be important not to push your own agenda or pressure yourself or others in the hope of a certain outcome, as you may miss important factors that could actually take you to a better place.

LOVE LIFE

If you are looking for a particular commitment from someone close, September is the month when discussions could take you closer to that outcome. However, you may in the process discover either your own or someone else's vulnerabilities and will need to work constructively with these in mind to create a sense of commitment. Singles may be particularly drawn to new groups and organisations where you can meet like-minded people and this is certainly possible, especially towards the 26th.

WORK

Be super clear about what you would like in your working life and career in general, because you will gain the opportunity to turbocharge your plans and projects in September. The new moon on the 11th will be a particularly beneficial time to float fresh ideas and plans, especially if you are a creative Taurean. You will increasingly gain motivation to succeed and perhaps even in unexpected ways, especially towards the end of the month.

TAURUS • SEPTEMBER

October

WEEK 1: 1—7 OCTOBER

Your sign's ruler Venus turns retrograde this week, and you'll gain the opportunity to re-evaluate important aspects of your life such as your primary relationships and work. A change of routine or unexpected development needn't set the cat among the pigeons. Rely on your good sense of timing and you could make developments a success, especially at work and home. Just avoid arguments, especially on Friday.

WEEK 2: 8—14 OCTOBER

This is an excellent week to organise your schedule for the months to come so you gain more peace and balance in your daily life. You'll appreciate the chance to touch base with someone special on Friday or at the weekend but must avoid tense or complex topics, especially at work. Be prepared to negotiate with someone important this weekend as otherwise disagreements could flare up.

WEEK 3: 15—21 OCTOBER

You're likely to enjoy the company of upbeat people or the chance to indulge in a favourite activity. You'll enjoy socialising towards the weekend. You may experience a boost in your working week and may even be happy to see a project take off. However, mid-week next week it'll be in your interest to be careful with communications, most notably at work and concerning health and well-being. Be tactful.

WEEK 4: 22—28 OCTOBER / WEEK 5: 29 OCTOBER—4 NOVEMBER

WEEK 4: a new chapter may involve a surprise or fresh circumstance. For many this will involve work or health, and for some there will be a fresh agreement with someone special particularly if it's your birthday at the full moon. **WEEK 5:** be prepared to discuss your options with those they concern such as work and personal collaborators and things will look up towards 4 November.

HEALTH

Early in the month you will already gain insight into important health matters, either yours own or those of someone close. If you have become lazy about maintaining good health you'll gain the opportunity in October to review your health schedule and get it back in tip-top order, especially around the new moon on the 10th/11th and towards the 16th. A friend or organisation may prove helpful in this respect.

FINANCES

The stars align mid-month to create positive opportunities at work and, at the very least, produce an improvement in your usual daily schedule. Whether you gain a promotion at work or simply take a holiday your finances will be affected by developments in October, so be ready to manage them accordingly. Developments towards the end of the month may predispose you to make important investments for long-term financial security.

HOME

The beginning of the month sees excellent astrological influences for your home, domestic and property circumstances, so be sure to be proactive in these areas then. However, you may need to make a tough call between your home and other considerations. For some these will revolve around work, and for others health considerations and your status. Avoid intense interactions, especially on the 2nd, 10th, 20th and 30th, as these could derail the best-laid plans.

LOVE LIFE

Your sign's ruler Venus turns retrograde on the 3rd, which can mean important discussions with someone special are on the way. For some Taureans a partner will have important news or will simply need to discuss their feelings more than usual, so October is an excellent month to spend that little bit extra time discussing shared concerns and especially around the 9th, 10th, 20th and 26th to ensure talks run smoothly.

WORK

Venus retrograde through your work zone brings a retrospective aspect to the month. If you think sometimes that you're going backwards, avoid feeling stuck and look at current circumstances as opportunities to quietly re-evaluate where you are and place more attention on your health and happiness. You will still be able to make progress at work and may even be surprised by some developments early in October and towards the 10th, 15th and 26th.

TAURUS · OCTOBER

November

WEEK 1: 5–11 NOVEMBER

Monday's new moon signals a passionate phase romantically that will motivate you to be more adventurous and outspoken with that someone special, especially if you were born before the 9th. If you were born later, be prepared to turn a corner at work. Ensure you take the initiative as you could see your profile and status blossom. You'll enjoy a fun event towards Tuesday.

WEEK 2: 12–18 NOVEMBER

There will be a predestined feeling to the week for you, especially in relation to your personal life and specifically your family and love life. For some developments will move very quickly, so be sure to be on your toes and evaluate circumstances in your own time. There are therapeutic and healing aspects to developments. Creative projects including the arts and performance are likely to be busy.

WEEK 3: 19–25 NOVEMBER

This will be a good week to build bridges with those you have argued with. However, tempers are likely to be frayed so avoid igniting further arguments. You'll enjoy a reunion, and some Taureans may be drawn to romance. The full moon supermoon mid-week will spotlight the erratic nature of a particular relationship; however, you may also be pleasantly surprised towards Wednesday by a business or personal partner.

WEEK 4: 26 NOVEMBER–2 DECEMBER

This is an excellent week to take the initiative at work, as your efforts are likely to succeed. Avoid taking things personally if an event or circumstance falls short of expectations. This weekend a health or beauty appointment may appeal. It's a good week to improve both your appearance and health, so take the initiative. You'll appreciate all things artistic, creative and beautiful this weekend.

HEALTH

Stress is a strong indicator in ill-health, and as November goes by it is in your interest to find ways to manage either your stress or that of someone close who can be a little explosive now and then. You'll gain the expert advice of someone who can support your aims to improve stress levels, so be sure to reach out. You may even experience a breakthrough towards the full moon supermoon on the 24th/25th and on the 28th.

FINANCES

The full moon on the 24th/25th will bring a fresh cycle for you in a key work or personal relationship, and for many this will involve finances. You may even be surprised by developments associated with a business or personal partner or family. You'll gain the opportunity to improve your own circumstances over time, so be sure to take the initiative and negotiate the outcome of important changes in your career or status.

HOME

Developments mid-month could signal considerable changes in your home life, especially if you have been planning changes with family. A therapeutic or health-related circumstance will make your options so much clearer moving forward. If you have been planning to add to your family it's possible a window will open for you mid-month. You will also appreciate the opportunity to invest time and energy in your family or home later in the month.

LOVE LIFE

You'll appreciate the opportunity to flirt with your partner, and if you're single to enjoy the arts, romance, dance and music. However, be careful as sparks could fly if you don't find the middle ground between tact and honesty with a partner. Singles: be sure to mingle from the 12th to the 16th as you may meet someone who seems familiar but whom you have never met before. Romance can thrive towards the 23rd, so consider organising a social event.

WORK

You may be pleasantly surprised towards the end of the month by developments that could elevate your position at work. Be sure to be diligent with your various projects throughout the month even if you sometimes feel that you are not appreciated as much as you could perhaps be. A positive link with an organisation around the full moon on the 24th/25th and developments towards the 28th could illuminate fresh options for you.

TAURUS • NOVEMBER

December

WEEK 1: 3–9 DECEMBER

Venus brings a passionate phase for you, especially in your partner. If you're single this will be an excellent weekend to socialise, as romance could thrive. Just be careful with misunderstandings, both in your personal life and at work, as these could trip you up. Wednesday's new moon could kick-start a fresh business or personal arrangement but some communications will be intense, so be sure to avoid arguments.

WEEK 2: 10–16 DECEMBER

A close friend, group or organisation will promote a little food for thought this weekend; you may simply enjoy socialising. It's likely to be a productive week work-wise, and a serious decision will require insight or research. You will appreciate being able to alter your usual daily health or work routine early in the week to accommodate someone special.

WEEK 3: 17–23 DECEMBER

Developments will gather momentum, so be sure you're happy with the direction they are taking earlier in the week rather than once events have gained speed. You'll enjoy wonderful get-togethers from Friday and into this weekend that prove uplifting. You may need to tread carefully with someone special, but when you do you will appreciate the outcome. Double-check details next week, especially with an organisation, to avoid mix-ups.

WEEK 4: 24–31 DECEMBER

The Christmas Eve full moon supermoon will kick-start a fresh chapter in your personal life that could have wide-ranging consequences. A financial or personal matter may hold the key to future developments so ensure you approach both finances and your personal life with an open mind and avoid arguments, as these may become long-standing. A change of pace or of place or key news will signify the option for something new.

HEALTH

You will appreciate the opportunity to devote time to your health and well-being in December, and the weekend of the 12th could be particularly re-energising or beneficial health-wise. You may also be drawn to indulge in a beauty treat or fresh look for the festive season. A therapeutic phase towards the 18th will certainly raise morale and you may also enjoy a variety of company that boosts your emotional well-being.

FINANCES

If you have allowed your finances to take their own course the new moon on the 9th will encourage you to rein in spending, which unfortunately may prove to be difficult at this time of year. It will be in your interest to set in place a budget that factors in the importance of a short break around the holiday period and the necessity to look after yourself and those you love.

HOME

A fair degree of tension in the air at the start of December points to the need to find ways to defuse this before it gains magnitude. If you have important matters to discuss, the weekends of the 12th and 19th may be conducive to finding common ground as therapeutic stars could help you improve domestic and family relationships. However, you must at that time avoid entering a battle of egos. Ensure you double-check facts to avoid misunderstandings.

LOVE LIFE

The start of December is a mixed bag as you may experience therapeutic developments in your love life but, on the other hand, there is an equal likelihood of tension and perhaps even disappointment. The key to ensuring therapeutic developments lies in good communication skills. If you are single be sure that any prospective companion is on the same page as you romance-wise. You will appreciate towards the 18th deepening your relationships, and a sociable phase will be uplifting.

WORK

Communications at work are best treated carefully as a hastily spoken word can easily be misconstrued and either you or someone else could take offence. This may be particularly likely on the 5th, 9th and 21st. However, the weeks beginning the 14th and the 21st could bring the opportunity to improve work relationships, so be sure to take the initiative. Developments around the full moon supermoon on the 24th will spotlight your true feelings about work and may precipitate an important decision.

TAURUS · DECEMBER

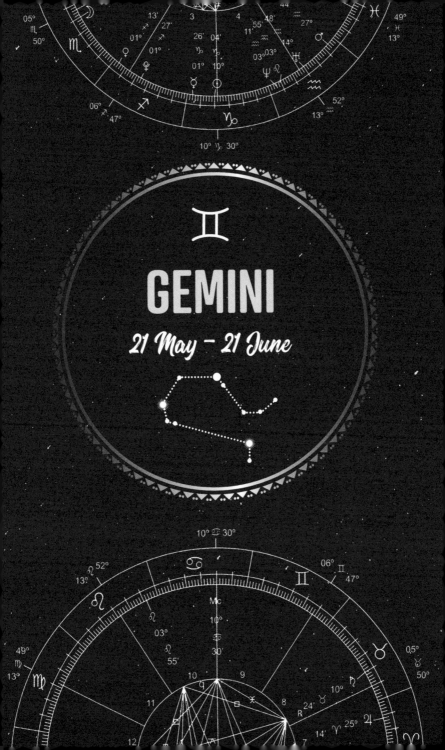

WEEK 1: 1–7 JANUARY

You'll appreciate organising a trip or get-together but must be clear about the details. You may be drawn to update a vehicle or communications device. For some a fresh phase will begin financially, and this may be connected with your career or shared finances such as taxes or legal matters. Tuesday is a good day for romance and collaborations.

WEEK 2: 8–14 JANUARY

You'll enjoy a lovely get-together and romance could flourish, so get set to mingle if you're single. Couples should plan a romantic night out or in this weekend or early in the week. If you're working this weekend, avoid intense conversations as they could escalate. It's a good week to focus on improving your finances, especially those you share with someone.

WEEK 3: 15–21 JANUARY

You'll enjoy socialising or returning to an old haunt. You may enjoy a reunion and the chance to reconnect with a familiar activity. Just avoid complex communications on Friday for the best results. Be prepared to share your space, duties or finances in a new way. A change of routine this weekend could be ideal even if it involves being spontaneous or doing something different.

WEEK 4: 22–28 JANUARY

An exciting adventure may be ideal, yet it could involve a degree of upheaval before you can enjoy it. Luckily, a collaborator such as a partner or group will prove their weight in gold. A fun or exciting activity will delight. Someone who has strong opinions will not be afraid to voice them. Be prepared to be practical. Romance could soar, so if you're single keep an eye out!

HEALTH

Your connection with a group, friend or organisation will encourage you to boost your self-confidence and ability to be hands on and practical about your health. If you've had circumstances that have felt very up and down in connection with health you may be drawn to try something new this January via an organisation that has experience in explorative methods to gain deeper understanding of your health.

FINANCES

The first two weeks of the year will be ideal for improving your finances, especially those you share with someone close such as household expenses and also those you share with a common purse via your taxes. You may even turn a corner towards the new moon on the 18th as you'll gain the chance to boost your work or finances then.

HOME

Your connection with a house or property will come under the microscope as you gain the opportunity to decide exactly who and what is important. Avoid allowing sentimentality and practicalities to determine your decisions in connection with your family and home. Consider, instead, whether aspects of your home life still create a sense of stability but are also inspiring. A trip or adventure will also add perspective to whether you have outgrown a chapter regarding your home life.

LOVE LIFE

The second week of the month will be ideal for love, so be sure to organise some treats and especially around the 8th to the 11th. Be prepared to look at organising your personal life so it suits you better, as the new moon on the 18th will help you bring more fun and zest into your life. You may even decide to share your space or finances in a new way as a sign of commitment or a fresh arrangement.

WORK

This is an excellent month to think outside the square about your work situation. You are in line for a change in your usual routine, which will fuel different opportunities. The new moon on the 18th may even help you enter fresh territory, to study a new area or connect with interesting and upbeat people. Take opportunities towards the end of the month seriously, but avoid making rash decisions.

February

WEEK 1: 29 JANUARY–4 FEBRUARY

An exciting if restless chapter is about to begin and breaking new ground will appeal. You may be drawn to travel or to simply upgrade your communications or a vehicle to satisfy your need for change. A fresh arrangement and understanding with someone special is possible, so be proactive and especially regarding travel and finances. You also will appreciate the opportunity to broaden your perspective and options.

WEEK 2: 5–11 FEBRUARY

You may be surprised by news from the past or an impromptu get-together. A change of schedule will need careful adjustment. Be clear about your priorities and with communications, especially from Thursday through to Monday, and everything else will fall in place. Aim to improve your understanding of someone or something. You may experience intense emotions or a change of pace or of place that requires focus.

WEEK 3: 12–18 FEBRUARY

A change in your status, career or groups you associate with may involve a surprise or simply the chance to do something different. A brand-new chapter comes with the solar eclipse, and the more you can look outside the square at the many benefits in your circumstances the better it will be for you. Not everyone will agree with you, so ensure you get your facts right and avoid conflict.

WEEK 4: 19–25 FEBRUARY / WEEK 5: 26 FEBRUARY–4 MARCH

WEEK 4: the Saturn–Neptune conjunction could stimulate a fresh approach to the people around you and your environment as a delicate blend between your idealism and ability to be practical emerges. In other words, a fantastical plan could work. **WEEK 5:** be ready to research options and make agreements with friends, groups and organisations. You may find resolution around the lunar eclipse on 3 March in connection with your home, work, a property or family.

HEALTH

As you have such an active mind and can be physically restless, sport and physical movement are important to maintain the health both of your mind and body. If you have unfortunately lapsed into a routine where your health takes second priority, this month will be excellent for connecting with groups and organisations that can help you create a stronger well-being plan. Try to organise activities before the 26th as they will be more likely to deliver for you.

FINANCES

This is an important month financially as you will need to consider how best to manage some of your investments, especially in light of a change in your career, direction or status. Towards the end of February you're likely to see a financial improvement. If you have already been angling for a financial commitment from a friend or organisation it is likely to arise at that time, but you must be proactive earlier in the month to see this happen.

HOME

February is a time to weigh up between your idealistic views of your home life and what on a basic level you require from your home. The two are likely to be in stark contrast. Be prepared to somehow navigate between them, but if you're under pressure financially be sure to make decisions based on facts and not expectations. The solar eclipse this month and lunar eclipse next month will open a door for you. Be prepared to step through.

LOVE LIFE

Romance can thrive towards the end of the month, especially during the weekend of the 21st. Be prepared to reach out to your beloved and enjoy special times together; the stars will support your endeavours. Singles may be drawn to make a commitment or find company in new circles and to socialise in new contexts, such as via sports or theatrical groups. There is an adventurous aspect to the month that you'll enjoy.

WORK

Key news and developments early in February may come as a surprise. If you are well on top of your work and schedules it's likely that a change of pace could nevertheless take you into uncharted waters, so be prepared to be proactive but take the time to respond when you're under pressure rather than being impulsive. The solar eclipse on the 17th will spotlight which aspects of your work you love and which not so much. Be prepared to pursue your goals.

GEMINI · FEBRUARY

March

WEEK 1: 5–11 MARCH

You are well known as a good communicator and your negotiation skills will be useful this week. Key financial or personal circumstances are best approached tactfully to avoid a stalemate. You may enjoy a get-together that boosts your financial or personal circumstances this weekend. Be prepared to think laterally regarding your connection with a friend, group or organisation as you could make a valid commitment.

WEEK 2: 12–18 MARCH

You'll enjoy an impromptu event and doing something different mid-week next week. Meanwhile, these will be good days for getting a close relationship back on track. You'll enjoy a reunion or meeting with someone who is both inspiring and can boost your self-esteem. Just avoid sensitive topics and arguments brought about by stress this week, especially towards the 18th.

WEEK 3: 19–25 MARCH

You'll enjoy some lovely get-togethers or events this weekend, so take the initiative. The Pisces new moon is always inspiring and if you are drawn to new ventures and projects this is an ideal time to launch your ideas, especially after Mercury ends its retrograde phase as the sun enters Aries. This is also a good week to overcome past disagreements.

WEEK 4: 26 MARCH–1 APRIL

You may be put on the spot this week so ensure you have the facts at hand, especially with a group or organisation. If you need the help of an adviser or expert be sure to reach out, as help will be available. You may be asked for help yourself. A development at work or from the past may be a surprise but nevertheless could be productive.

HEALTH

The Pisces new moon makes a healthy aspect with Uranus in your 12th house of health, suggesting that quirky or inspired and spiritual modalities will help to improve your health. If you have been under the weather this is an excellent month to look for practitioners, doctors and therapists who can help you. For some Geminis, however, the road to well-being will revolve around altering your daily routine or even lifestyle.

FINANCES

The period between the 5th and the 9th will be productive financially so be sure to take the initiative with arrangements, budgets and investments, as you may be surprised by how swiftly things move ahead. Some Geminis may also be in line to receive a considerable increase either in income or due to an investment. Mid-month will be a good time to look out for someone who can help you financially. However, you must avoid gambling, especially towards the 18th.

HOME

This month a sense of the importance of a well-ordered and tidy house and neighbourhood will put many of your activities into perspective. Much of your attention, nevertheless, will be going to your interactions with groups, organisations and friendship circles and on your career, activities and finances. Being such a busy character, it's important you remember to rest up whenever you can so you truly appreciate the value of your home.

LOVE LIFE

You are essentially a social being: you like the company of other people and feel lonely without it. This week key meetings between the 13th and 18th will bring singles in touch with someone with whom you may have a soul connection, so if you're looking for that special someone then mid-month is the time to be sociable. Couples will also enjoy meeting like-minded people, which will boost your connections.

WORK

You may receive good news regarding work and your status, as your connection with a group or organisation could progress considerably. Be prepared to negotiate as you are in a strong position. You may even discover a perfect scenario or meet an influential character who can boost your work situation. A surprise development towards the 18th may involve a boost to your status and at least your self-esteem. Look at ways of growing within your field.

GEMINI · MARCH

April

WEEK 1: 2–8 APRIL

Thursday's full moon will bring changes at home and, for some, with family. You may be drawn to consider a fresh arrangement in your personal life. If you've been single and would prefer to be a part of a couple, this full moon may spotlight the necessity to take action accordingly. A financial matter will require focus. Avoid arguments at work and find peaceful ways to overcome differences of opinion.

WEEK 2: 9–15 APRIL

You'll notice a change in tempo this week, and if you're working you are likely to be busy. This is a good time to devote effort to your work ventures as your efforts are likely to be successful. Sunday and Monday are particularly advantageous for organising get-togethers, both in your personal life and at work. Some Geminis may even receive a financial boost at the start of next week.

WEEK 3: 16–22 APRIL

You'll appreciate the opportunity this week to connect with someone close, either in person or by phone. As you turn a corner at work and with your long-term projects, conversations or meetings will require detailed consideration. Finances may need focus mid-week next week. Someone may call in a debt or you'll need to evaluate circumstances. Your interactions with a group, friend or organisation will be more significant than usual.

WEEK 4: 23–29 APRIL

The entry of Venus and Uranus in your sign will shake things up a little this week. You may even be surprised by some developments this weekend, and a spontaneous get-together could be enjoyable. Just try to head off intense talks on Sunday/Monday, as they are likely to escalate into conflict or a battle of wills.

HEALTH

The idea early in the month is to find peace of mind within your daily life. Be aware of which aspects of your life create stress. This will be fairly evident, especially around the 5th. Consider how you could minimise stress by altering aspects of your work or daily life and modalities you can adopt to cope better with stress. Mid-April will be an ideal time to consider a fresh look or fitness schedule.

FINANCES

You'll find out now whether some arrangements you already have in place are still working for you. The full moon on the 2nd will spotlight areas where you have overextended yourself financially and you will gain the opportunity as a result to rein in spending if necessary. Be prepared to work constructively with groups and organisations to formulate plans that work for you. You may enjoy a financial boost towards the 13th or will manage to repay a debt.

HOME

This will be an excellent month to evaluate the level of comfort and utility your home life provides you, especially with respect to expenses involved with your home or a property, and finding the sweet spot of being able to enjoy your home life without financial stress. Consider how much your home life supports your mental and physical well-being and focus on creating an environment that also supports your busy schedule.

LOVE LIFE

The full moon in Libra on 2 April will spotlight your personal life from the perspective of your priorities, values and principles. You may need to re-evaluate certain arrangements, especially those concerning finances, so be prepared to discuss any differences in a constructive, balanced way because otherwise you may find conflicts brewing. The 13th will be particularly conducive to romance, so be sure to organise something special then if possible.

WORK

Your work scenario is in the process of long-term change, and while this month will provide to a degree opportunities to gain increasing stability and security in your career you may also experience a little stress early in the month, so be sure to take things in your stride and maintain perspective about your ultimate goals. You may receive good work news around the 13th, so this is a good date to work towards with goals you set yourself.

May

WEEK 1: 30 APRIL—6 MAY

This week's full moon suggests it's time for a fresh approach to your usual daily routine so it provides you with a healthier and more productive schedule. This will be a good week to schedule a health or well-being appointment, as the information you receive is likely to be constructive. Likewise, a sports or fitness schedule begun now is likely to benefit you.

WEEK 2: 7—13 MAY

This is likely to be an upbeat week. You could accomplish a great deal, especially if you are drawn to travel and at work. If you are investing in a new project, just ensure you are not over-spending as Jupiter in your money zone could predispose you towards overindulgence. You'll enjoy a reunion this weekend, and at the least the chance to boost your feel-good factor in life.

WEEK 3: 14—20 MAY

Your relationship with a friend or organisation may improve over the coming days, unless it already has recently. You are likely now to gain direction with work, your daily schedule or health as a more stable phase begins. Be prepared to move into fresh territory workwise. If you are owed money you are likely to receive this, but you may need to chase the debt.

WEEK 4: 21—27 MAY / WEEK 5: 28 MAY—3 JUNE

WEEK 4: the sun, Mercury and Uranus in Gemini point to a busy couple of weeks. You may feel prepared to make a commitment to a fresh plan of action or work scenario. You may make an impromptu change in your usual routine.
WEEK 5: a new understanding in a business or personal partnership can be reached as one door closes and another opens towards the Sagittarian full moon on the 31st.

HEALTH

The start of the month will provide a good indication of your health situation as you gain the chance to put in place a fresh schedule that better suits you. Be sure to take advantage of opportunities to reconfigure your routine, even if they appear to initially present a little disruption. Be practical for the best results. A trip or short holiday will prove revitalising, especially in the second week of the month.

FINANCES

Keep an eye on unnecessary spending early in May, as you may be tempted to splurge or overinvest. If you have overspent in previous days and last month a bill or debt will need to be cleared. You have favourable stars financially towards the 15th, but must be careful mid-month not to overspend. Aim instead to put in place a fresh budget at the new moon mid-month.

HOME

May is an excellent month to decipher where your true loyalties lie in your domestic life and where you find the most sense of stability and growth. If domestic circumstances have been complex, this is an excellent month to consider innovative ways to break into a fresh phase where you find more meaning through your home, family or property. While instigating something new may represent a little upheaval initially, rest assured your efforts will prove therapeutic in the long term.

LOVE LIFE

The month is bookended by two full moons: the first on 1/2 May that will ramp up your lust for life and for that someone special, and the second at the end of the month that will kick-start a fresh chapter for you in your love life, especially if you were born in May. If you were born in June a change of schedule will nevertheless have an impact on primary relationships. Be ready to turn a corner!

WORK

A fresh work schedule will appeal in May, and there's no better time than the full moon on the 1st/2nd to notice due to developments how you could better configure your working life. A change in interests may also dictate a fresh direction for you. Be prepared to follow your true interests, as you have a unique opportunity now to invest in your skill sets and abilities so they feature more heavily in your working day.

GEMINI · MAY

June

WEEK 1: 4–10 JUNE

You'll gain the heads-up about a key arrangement, chat or negotiation that could be altered to make life easier for you. Be careful with discussions as there is the likelihood now that you misinterpret someone's actions or words, especially towards next Wednesday. Some Geminis will be drawn to travel or receive visitors. There will be a larger-than-life aspect to the week.

WEEK 2: 11–17 JUNE

You know you have the gift of the gab; however, this week you must be careful with communications as not everyone is as gifted as you. Monday's Gemini new moon supermoon signifies a fresh chapter. Be true to yourself to make key and valid decisions, especially in your personal life. You're a maverick and only you can know if your ideas will work. The new moon will help you proceed.

WEEK 3: 18–24 JUNE

Developments that span across your career and home life may require additional focus. Changes will merit patience and good communication skills. You'll appreciate the therapeutic effect of a get-together with like-minded people. You'll also enjoy the opportunity to indulge in your favourite activities even if some are particularly intense. It's a good week for a health or beauty treat to raise morale.

WEEK 4: 25 JUNE–1 JULY

As Mars enters your sign you're likely to experience improved energy levels over the coming weeks. First, however, your sign's ruler Mercury turns retrograde early next week, making this weekend a good time to float important ideas and get key paperwork on the table where possible. This will avoid potential delays further down the road. The full moon on the 29th/30th presages a financial or personal arrangement that could provide stability for you.

HEALTH

The opportunity to travel and, for some, to receive visitors, will be a drawcard both early in June and after the new moon supermoon on the 15th, and this will provide a breath of fresh air that can only benefit your health. However, you must avoid getting caught up in unnecessary negotiations or discussions that will simply go round in circles, as these will drain your energy. Flashpoints will be mid-June through to the 22nd.

FINANCES

This first week in June will be an excellent time to look at the kinds of transactions that you are undertaking financially. Could there be a better way of doing things? Developments towards the 9th may spotlight areas of difficulty or even financial debt that are best handled sooner rather than later. You are in line to experience an unexpected or unusual financial improvement such as a pay rise mid-month.

HOME

Where do you feel you belong, and could this simply be due to nostalgia or do you truly feel that your home or a property or certain investment is truly fulfilling? If the answer to that question is 'Yes' you will increasingly wish to invest in your home this month. However, if you know you have outgrown your home or a property you will find another way forward, so keep an open mind.

LOVE LIFE

You are known as the zodiac's social butterfly and a good communicator; however you must be careful with communications in June, especially towards the new moon on the 15th. This new moon will bring a fresh chapter in your love life and it's in your power to make this a favourable chapter, so be sure to organise upbeat and bonding events with your partner. Singles may unexpectedly meet someone compatible, so be sure to attend events.

WORK

Work is one of the most important parts of your daily life and it must bring a degree of fulfilment. If you notice this month, however, that the area or position you work in no longer provides a sense of purpose or accomplishment it could be your cue to begin looking for something more suitable. Twins born after mid-June may already begin something new now. However, you must avoid making changes at work simply due to restlessness.

GEMINI · JUNE

July

WEEK 1: 2–8 JULY

You are ready to step into new territory in a personal context, for many at work. Be prepared for a surprise, especially if you were born around 24 to 26 May. This is likely to be a busy time socially. Be practical with negotiations, especially if your ideas are ahead of their time or out of the ordinary. You may need to be persuasive but avoid being stubborn.

WEEK 2: 9–15 JULY

You will appreciate the opportunity to reconnect with important people in your life both in a business and personal sense. It is a good week for meetings and negotiations; however, you must keep an eye on variables because although there is an overall therapeutic aspect to the week, unexpected news or developments around the 13th could throw a spanner in the works.

WEEK 3: 16–22 JULY

Many of your previous actions come to fruition now. If you have been planning a change of direction either at work or within your favourite activities you will gain insight into the likely outcome. You are likely to experience intense developments either in relationships or via travel and self-development, so it will be important to double-check facts and figures to avoid making mistakes.

WEEK 4: 23–29 JULY

You are in a strong position to make positive changes in your life. It may be a case of overcoming your vulnerabilities and developing a strong sense of resilience and self-confidence to make the most of opportunities. The full moon on the 29th/30th will spotlight your career and general direction in life, so be sure to look at decisions you make from a long-term perspective.

HEALTH

It's all systems go for you in July, as Mars in your sign will improve energy levels. However, with Mercury retrograde until the 23rd you may feel slightly restless or even out of your depth in some matters. Be sure to organise a strong physical and mental training regime that supports your health and happiness. This will be especially important, as you can make seismic changes both in your career and status.

FINANCES

Retrograde Mercury offers you the opportunity to rethink your finances and renegotiate arrangements. A change of plan regarding a domestic or family circumstance will need to be taken into account financially. You will be drawn to invest in the people and activities you love, but you must avoid overspending. As Mercury is in your financial sector it is vital you be careful with financial transactions and avoid gambling. That said, it is possible that you can make true headway financially now.

HOME

Ask yourself where you feel at home. If it's literally in your home then this will be a healing, therapeutic month for you, but if you have a choice between homes or are considering changing your domestic circumstance this question will answer your hesitation. If you no longer feel at home in your current environment it's time for a change. If you have been ignoring this fact, developments mid-month will set you on a fresh track.

LOVE LIFE

Keep an eye on communications early in July and mid-month, as you may be under stress and could misunderstand people and their motives. You or someone close is likely to feel slightly vulnerable around the 2nd and 3rd, mid-month and towards the 29th, so give them or yourself extra leeway. Nostalgic single Geminis may be drawn to the past or even to reconnect with an ex. You will need to decide for yourself whether this is practical and realistic.

WORK

You are in line for considerably fast changes already early in July in your working day or routine. Once again, mid-month will lead to fresh developments; however, some opportunities may come so quickly that you take a leap without having adequately sorted out the arrangements, and this could be a pitfall. Be sure to carefully look into any contracts you sign early in the month and towards the 17th and 29th, as otherwise mistakes can be made.

GEMINI · JULY

August

WEEK 1: 30 JULY–5 AUGUST

You'll begin to see signs of progress with regard to a key agreement with a friend, family or group. Someone may, however, express intense views, which you'll get a chance to discuss. Just avoid if you can fiery exchanges and flighty responses, as these are likely to backfire. This is a good time to make tracks towards fresh understandings and therefore new information will be necessary.

WEEK 2: 6–12 AUGUST

It's all change for you in your personal life as you gain the opportunity to bring more romance into your everyday life. In addition, the solar eclipse on the 12th/13th will offer you the chance to turn an exciting corner that will affect many Twins' home lives or property but will nevertheless create a sense of stability and security in the long term.

WEEK 3: 13–19 AUGUST

You'll enjoy a get-together towards the weekend or will receive key news that puts a great deal into perspective at home, regarding a property and in your general interactions. A key trip may do the same. However, you may feel your values are challenged this week or that you must research your financial or personal circumstances a little more deeply. Romance can thrive, so be sure to organise a date.

WEEK 4: 20–26 AUGUST / WEEK 5: 27 AUGUST–2 SEPTEMBER

WEEK 4: you may be drawn to make a significant commitment to a project or person that could bring you stability, but you must check the facts and figures. **WEEK 5:** there are many therapeutic aspects to this week, despite the fact that events are likely to spotlight unpredictabilities over which you have no control. For this reason it is in your interest to work steadily and methodically towards a required outcome as opposed to simply leaving things to fate.

HEALTH

This will be an excellent month to make a commitment to a particular health outcome or at least to subscribe to a fitness plan, as your will efforts are likely to succeed. As this month also incorporates two eclipses, it is likely that you will be busy and for this reason you will need to be resolute about your commitments to better your health. Developments around the 21st may illustrate the importance of good health and vitality.

FINANCES

The first week of the month will be ideal for sorting out any banking conundrums, although patience will be needed. After the 6th financial transactions may gain a more even keel. You could even be drawn to a particular financial arrangement that may boost your finances, status and self-esteem, but must as with all major financial transactions double-check details, especially towards the 10th and 17th. Mars may predispose you to overspending from the 11th, so be prudent with financial planning.

HOME

A friend or organisation will be helpful at the start of August to help you make solid plans with your home or someone special. Mars in your sign until the 10th suggests that you will tend to leap before you think things through, which is likely to backfire. You may receive key news regarding your home, family or a property towards the 17th that will provide you with a sense of security, especially for May Twins.

LOVE LIFE

The month begins under the lingering aspect between Mars and Venus, which is a tense aspect. While this may be exciting, as it can promote passion, when there is too much tension it can lead to discord. If possible, find ways to inject a little fun into your love life as opposed to getting too tied up in disagreements. Key dates when romance can thrive are the 10th, 17th and 22nd.

WORK

Be prepared to step into fresh territory, because when you do the stars will support your efforts – perhaps even in surprising ways. Avoid being dictated to by your fears but, equally, avoid taking unnecessary risks, especially financially. If you feel drawn to a particular project or job offer, especially around the 10th and 21st, be sure to investigate it as it could be ideal as long as the figures make sense.

GEMINI · AUGUST

September

WEEK 1: 3–9 SEPTEMBER

Building structure in your life brick by brick and being methodical are qualities you will find useful at the moment. If you find being patient is relatively hard, see this as a skill set that is well worth learning. Focus on these abilities this week to navigate around any obstacles. You will appreciate the opportunity to connect with someone upbeat and fun towards Sunday or Monday.

WEEK 2: 10–16 SEPTEMBER

A beauty or health matter will deserve focus towards Friday. You must avoid rushing. For many Twins a new chapter is about to begin regarding your home life or status. You may gain fresh understanding about domestic matters, and some Twins will begin a fresh chapter regarding family. You have a wonderful opportunity to boost your circumstances but you must be careful with facts and figures to avoid making mistakes.

WEEK 3: 17–23 SEPTEMBER

A decision or conversation will ask that you're super focused and take things one step at a time to avoid making mistakes. The chance to indulge in a favourite activity will raise your spirits. If you've been looking for a commitment from someone either in a project or in your personal life, this is a good week to ask. You may experience a positive work development even if a disruption arises.

WEEK 4: 24–30 SEPTEMBER

This weekend's full moon will spotlight arrangements and agreements such as those at work and socially that may be ideal. This is a romantic full moon, so take the initiative. If you discover, however, that some arrangements no longer suit you, you will know certain circumstances are best altered. Luckily you are in a strong position to transform your personal and work circumstances.

HEALTH

You're better known as someone who is sociable and light-hearted but can sometimes tend to flit from one activity to another, never really settling on anything for too long. However, this month, especially at the start and at the end, you may need to exercise other attributes such as diligence and resilience. Being grounded and practical won't necessarily come naturally to you, yet these are wonderful life skills that will bring you peace of mind.

FINANCES

This will be an excellent month to plan finances carefully. If you're tempted to speculate or even to gamble it is likely you will not enjoy the outcome, so it is important as you make financial decisions to base them on facts as opposed to an outcome that is not guaranteed, especially from the 17th to the 22nd and around the 27th. Be sure to obtain expert advice if necessary. When you do you could build significant wealth.

HOME

You will gain a sense of belonging in September and this will come largely due to the appreciation of what you have. It is easy for you to often believe the grass is greener elsewhere, but this month a sense of true gratitude for your home and family will preside, especially towards the 20th to 22nd and around the full moon on the 26th/27th, that could illuminate fresh options for you.

LOVE LIFE

Developments could supercharge your love life as you gain insight into someone close and are able either to deepen your relationship or, contrarily, some may feel that your differences have become too pronounced. The new moon on the 11th may predispose you to being a little self-critical or critical of others, so be sure to maintain perspective at that time. The full moon on the 26th/27th is super romantic, so be sure to organise a date.

WORK

It is possible in September to boost your circumstances through good communication skills, so be sure to take the initiative. However, if you undergo a disappointment you are likely nevertheless to experience a positive development later in the month, so avoid feeling that all is lost. You will be turning a corner, especially if you work in the arts. It's in your interest to be careful with communications, particularly towards the 17th, 20th and 22nd, to avoid mistakes and misunderstandings.

October

WEEK 1: 1–7 OCTOBER

Consider spending a little extra time on interpersonal dynamics, as this will help you move plans ahead both at work and home. Avoid arguments and tempers, especially on Friday. Bring beauty into your life in various ways, such as by visiting beauty spots. You may be ready to make an agreement with a group, friend or organisation, and clarifying the details will put you in a strong position.

WEEK 2: 8–14 OCTOBER

You'll enjoy spending time with someone special – to revel in your spare time or if you're working to truly immerse yourself in that environment – but you must avoid overwhelming yourself or others, especially this Friday and at the weekend. This weekend's Libran new moon will encourage you to look for more peace and harmony, especially in your personal life, at work and in your home life and property.

WEEK 3: 15–21 OCTOBER

Circumstances are likely to work out well. You may find that you're super busy at work or have the opportunity to spend more time on your health and appearance. It's a good week for discussions that lead to new opportunities so take the initiative, both with work and domestic options, as your efforts are likely to succeed. However, you must be careful with negotiations and communications mid-week next week. Avoid slip-ups.

WEEK 4: 22–28 OCTOBER / WEEK 5: 29 OCTOBER–4 NOVEMBER

WEEK 4: news or a change in your schedule may be unexpected or out of the ordinary. The full moon on the 26th/27th will usher in a revitalising chapter, but you must avoid a clash of wills. Seek expert advice health-wise if necessary. **WEEK 5:** you may tend to be impulsive but are better advised to take things carefully, especially at work and home. You'll enjoy a lovely outcome by Wednesday.

HEALTH

You'll appreciate the opportunity to focus a little more on your health and appearance. Consider that a healthy outlook brings a happy and relaxed demeanour, but you must avoid feeling that your health can be improved overnight. Expert advice is available, so be sure to reach out. The days just after the new moon on the 10th/11th and the full moon on the 26th/27th will help your progress. Be careful to avoid minor mishaps on the 21st, 26th and 30th.

FINANCES

Careful negotiations either at work or regarding your home life will be necessary in October, so the better your communication skills and research regarding money the better will be your circumstance. You are in a strong position to gain a positive foothold financially but must avoid being sidetracked by distractions and a battle of wills. Consider your ultimate goals, both at home and work, and as a result you could make a true breakthrough with financial planning.

HOME

There are therapeutic aspects connected with your home, family and property. If someone close needs help health-wise or if it's you, you will find the support you need, especially early in the month. Be careful with communications towards the 9th, 10th, 16th and 30th to avoid unnecessary arguments. You'll enjoy sprucing up your home or welcoming visitors towards 15 October and 4 November. A change of environment will reinvigorate your home life.

LOVE LIFE

If you are looking for a commitment from someone you may find it early in October. However, honest and frank discussions will need to take place in the process, so be prepared to listen carefully and communicate your thoughts and feelings calmly. Otherwise, conflict is likely, especially on the 2nd, although a resolution is possible towards the 4th. Be prepared to see another person's point of view towards the 10th and mid-month, and towards the 30th as well.

WORK

You may be drawn to look at some of your work practices or daily chores in a new light. Some communications are likely to be fairly intense, especially mid-month and towards the 30th. However, with a diligent approach you could make a breakthrough. A little patience may be necessary, especially around the new moon on the 10th/11th when you may be drawn to put in place a fresh work schedule that better suits you and your home life.

November

WEEK 1: 5–11 NOVEMBER

A fresh daily health or work schedule is about to begin that will keep you busy for several months. This is an excellent time to boost your well-being to increase your energy levels so you can take on an extra workload. A family get-together or fun event towards Tuesday may be ideal. For some, though, meetings this week will be oriented towards creativity and romance, which you'll love.

WEEK 2: 12–18 NOVEMBER

Developments at home or with family will have a significant bearing. You may even feel there is a fated or predestined connection that arises regarding a property or your home. There are therapeutic aspects to the week, so be sure to take the initiative with your projects as they could go swimmingly. For some, developments in your career or status will have a direct influence on your home life.

WEEK 3: 19–25 NOVEMBER

This week's full moon supermoon will be in Gemini and signifies a fresh chapter in your personal life and at work. You may, however, need to make a tough call in the process. Avoid difficult communications towards Friday and look for the most therapeutic way forward should developments be disappointing. However, for many the outlook is positive, especially where you are looking for a change in your status and career.

WEEK 4: 26 NOVEMBER–2 DECEMBER

A discussion or transaction could be a catalyst for improved circumstances so be prepared to investigate ways to boost your circumstances, especially at home and work, as your efforts are likely to succeed. However, you may need to undertake some delicate talks in the process, especially towards the 29th. You'll appreciate solid results for your hard work, so be diligent but avoid contentious topics.

HEALTH

The new moon on the 9th ushers in a fresh phase when you'll be drawn to dig deep to establish a sense of peace, calm and harmony. This is a good time to seek spiritual insight or help with cognitive techniques if you feel you could use some emotional, mental or spiritual support. Be sure to be patient with developments in your life so you're not overwhelmed by circumstances that gain momentum of their own, especially mid-month.

FINANCES

Considerable changes can occur this month regarding your status and especially career. If you take the initiative with your various projects and opportunities your finances will change in line with work and career advancement. However, you will need to be careful with communications, especially on the 7th, in the days leading up to the full moon supermoon on the 24th/25th and towards the 29th to avoid making rash decisions that could adversely affect your financial outlook.

HOME

You'll appreciate the opportunity to invest time or energy in your home life, family or property. To make the most of circumstances you may need to review some aspects, either of your investment in your home or property or of your living arrangements. Developments mid-month will be significant and considerably affect your home life, a property or family. Be sure to consider your long-term, big-picture goals as you make changes. You will enjoy a visit or developments towards the 28th.

LOVE LIFE

The full moon on the 24th/25th signifies a fresh chapter in your personal life, and most especially if you were born before 25 May. This may be a truly romantic time and one that could at the least alter your status from single to married or from single to partnered. You are likely to meet someone you feel a strong draw towards but you will nevertheless need to exercise diligence to ensure you are both on the same path.

WORK

The new moon on the 9th and full moon on the 24th/25th both usher in a fresh chapter at work, and the more willing you are to discuss options with those they concern the stronger will be your position to take advantage of new opportunities. For some Twins there will be an important decision to make between your long-term career outlook and domestic investments. Avoid making sudden decisions towards the 19th and you'll see a fresh chapter can truly be transformational.

GEMINI · NOVEMBER

December

WEEK 1: 3–9 DECEMBER

This is a lovely weekend for get-togethers and romance so be sure to organise a treat, but you must avoid ego battles and arguments. Early in the week you may be working hard and will find short breaks very productive to avoid feeling under the pump and navigate potentially unexpected developments. Wednesday's new moon will encourage you to embrace an adventurous, positive approach to work and personal relationships.

WEEK 2: 10–16 DECEMBER

You'll enjoy a sociable week, especially towards Friday and Saturday. A work social event or meeting may be more pleasant than you anticipated. Early next week you'll gain the opportunity to spend a little more time on yourself and those you love. You may even gain the chance to embellish either your home or yourself in preparation for the holiday season or a specific social event.

WEEK 3: 17–23 DECEMBER

You'll enjoy the upbeat atmosphere of seasonal festivities leading into the weekend. Romance can thrive, and family-oriented Twins will enjoy time spent with those you love in a more domestic setting. You may need to choose between domestic duties and work hours, so be sure you choose wisely. Next week a conundrum or mystery may arise, so be sure to get on top of it sooner rather than later.

WEEK 4: 24–31 DECEMBER

The full moon supermoon on Christmas Eve signals a fresh financial agreement for some Twins and the chance to reconsider a personal agreement for others. You may be surprised by some developments this week and a change in your usual routine. Romance could blossom, so singles should mingle and couples could revitalise your love life. Some communications will be difficult but are likely to even out by New Year's Eve.

HEALTH

You'll appreciate spending time with a favourite group or friend who motivates you to invest in your health and well-being. As the festive season approaches tensions can increase so you must be mindful of stress, especially at home, and find ways to de-stress and de-escalate tension. You may be drawn to improve your appearance as you may be sociable from the 11th to the14th and the weekend beginning the 18th. Get-togethers at this time may boost your emotional happiness.

FINANCES

You will gain the impression by the end of this month that you truly are starting a brand-new financial phase. For some this will involve a change in your personal finances and for others a shared situation: for example, with a family member or partner. Be prepared to research your circumstances carefully as you move into this fresh chapter as this will avoid mistakes further down the line due to oversights.

HOME

There is a strong therapeutic influence around your home life in December and you may also find particularly helpful people easier to get hold of than usual. However, some communications will still be tense either with family or housemates, especially around the new moon on the 9th, so a tactful approach may be needed. You'll enjoy investing in your home and family, especially towards the 12th and 14th and the 18th. You may also enjoy a reunion at this time.

LOVE LIFE

The Sagittarian new moon on the 9th enables you to turn a corner in your love life, bringing more adventure and fun into your relationship. However, you may undergo some tense discussions that may be unrelated to your relationship, but unless you're careful could bring tension into your love life. The 12th to the 14th and the weekend beginning the 18th are lovely for singles to meet someone and for couples to deepen your connection, so take the initiative.

WORK

This is a good month to consider fresh ways to relate with colleagues, employers or employees as your efforts are likely to succeed. Just be careful with communications, especially towards the 8th and 9th, to avoid arguments. The developing favourable aspect between Uranus and Pluto will encourage you to look at different fields work-wise, and with adequate research your efforts will be successful. You may gain a work opportunity between the 11th and 14th.

GEMINI · DECEMBER

January

WEEK 1: 1–7 JANUARY

This weekend's Cancer full moon presents a brand-new chapter in your personal life, and at work or regarding your health if you were born after the first week of July. News may even surprise you. This is a good week for negotiations and to devise a shared plan of action, both in your personal life and at work. You may receive good news at work and romance will blossom.

WEEK 2: 8–14 JANUARY

This is a super-intense week for you as you will become acutely aware of your status, be this in your career or general standing in life. Take a moment to reflect before making snap decisions. A key emotional or financial investment will take much of your focus. Romance could go off the dial, but if you're unsure about making a commitment avoid emotional gambling.

WEEK 3: 15–21 JANUARY

Sunday/Monday's new moon will spotlight your agreements and the chance to make fresh ones with a friend, partner or group that could be surprisingly beneficial. You may receive key news from the past that surprises you or motivates you to make changes to how you share your duties or commitments, either at work or home. It's an excellent weekend for socialising and connecting with like-minded people.

WEEK 4: 22–28 JANUARY

News concerning a joint decision or a collaboration will benefit from attention. A powerful business or personal relationship will grab your attention. If you're in two minds about how to proceed you'll gain more insight and calm by considering how current circumstances could take you somewhere new.

HEALTH

January will be a good month to focus on your intuition regarding your health. In other words, you will gain insight into how best to improve your health and well-being by listening to both your body and mind. You will gain the opportunity to deepen your spiritual, mental and emotional understanding of what makes your body work best for you. As you may experience larger-than-life developments in January, be sure to treat yourself well.

FINANCES

Your finances will merit careful focus earlier in the month, as you are likely to enter a fresh phase in which shared responsibilities will require attention towards the end of the month. Shared financial responsibilities include areas such as taxes, debt and household expenses. You will be entering new territory within either your status or career, so be sure to organise a budget earlier in the month if possible.

HOME

Your home is one of the most important areas of your life as it provides you with a sense of nurturing and stability, yet in January your mind will largely be on your career and personal expansion. Be sure to factor the logistics of your home life into any decisions you make regarding your career and status, and whether these will change considerably as a result of the long-term decisions you make.

LOVE LIFE

This will be a good month to focus on improving your love life as the stars will help you. Be prepared to organise romance in the first two weeks of January, and if you're single you're likely to meet someone around the 9th to the 11th, the new moon on the 18th/19th and the 20th to the 30th. You may even meet someone in an unusual circumstance, so be prepared to be spontaneous. Couples will enjoy pepping up your love life and simultaneously deepening your connection.

WORK

During the first half of the month important work or study concerns will be in the spotlight. You may need to make a tough call regarding a collaboration or career step. It's a good time to form associations at work, but you must be careful to avoid rushing and also underestimating your value. You are set to enter fresh territory at work or within your general direction career-wise, so be inspired and ready to embrace new opportunities.

CANCER • JANUARY

February

WEEK 1: 29 JANUARY–4 FEBRUARY

Collaborative arrangements and the way you share finances or even space will change, and your insight and co-operation will help you succeed with joint ventures. Romance is alive and this week's events will bring it centre stage in your life, but you must avoid over-romanticising a relationship, especially if some aspects become intense. The Mercury–Venus conjunction will spotlight a business or personal collaboration and whether it's time to re-evaluate it.

WEEK 2: 5–11 FEBRUARY

A change of perspective will mean that your approach to certain people and friends will change. News this weekend and/or mid-week may be unexpected, and this will kick-start a fresh understanding of someone. Your involvement with a group, friend or organisation may require careful handling. A collaboration or joint initiative may cause intense feelings, so be sure to think before you speak.

WEEK 3: 12–18 FEBRUARY

Maintain an open mind and you could find yourself in a fresh circumstance that will open new doors. You're about to embark on a different understanding of a favourite subject: for some this will involve sport and for others spirituality or studies. Rise to a challenge that will ask you to be super clear about your work, aims or underlying beliefs.

WEEK 4: 19–25 FEBRUARY / WEEK 5: 26 FEBRUARY–4 MARCH

WEEK 4: this is an excellent time to make plans with someone you love such as a partner or family. Romance could blossom, so plan a treat. It's also a good time for talks, especially regarding work and long-term plans. **WEEK 5:** you may experience a change of status that for some will feel like an adventure. If it feels disorienting be sure to carefully research your situation. You will be drawn to travel or a change of pace or environment.

HEALTH

Nurturance both of yourself and of others is of prime importance to you and you have perfect stars in February to truly invest in yourself. You may feel on occasion that you are going backwards with some of your health and well-being plans, but you can make this be to your advantage. For example, if there are health practices you have let fall by the wayside, February is certainly a good month to resurrect them.

FINANCES

February will be a good month to consider how best to organise your finances, especially those you share with others such as a business or personal partner. You may be surprised by news from a group, friend or organisation early in the month, and this will have a bearing on how you share your finances with them. Look at ways to be resourceful and innovative with spending and saving as you enter a fresh cycle.

HOME

You will experience a considerable change of status or of direction now. Be sure to factor the demands of your home life into your choices or you may be tempted to focus more on your career and status to the detriment of your home life. A trip or the arrival of a visitor will remind you of who and what is truly important to you, which will help you make plans for your future that will affect your status for some time to come.

LOVE LIFE

February's stars place the focus on someone special and you may be drawn to turn a corner within this relationship, whether you are single or a committed couple. Someone close to you will enjoy the sense of freedom, and perhaps you will also. It is time to evaluate where you draw the line and find a sense of adventure within your love life. As you alter your approach to someone your relationship dynamics will also alter.

WORK

The solar eclipse on the 17th will open doors for you, especially within your career and general direction. Be prepared to be progressive and innovative and consider your true values and aims, as in this way you will pave the way towards a sense of accomplishment further down the track. Towards the end of the month you may step into an adventurous new role. If it feels overwhelming at first, be sure to research your circumstances.

CANCER • FEBRUARY

March

WEEK 1: 5–11 MARCH

If you're looking for work or wish to alter your personal circumstances, this is the week to do it. A trip, study or the chance for self-development will appeal. You'll enjoy the opportunity to broaden your horizons. It's also a good week for a mini financial review and to discuss serious commitments. It's likely you'll receive news that affects your status or general direction this week. For some this could mean a work improvement.

WEEK 2: 12–18 MARCH

It's an excellent weekend for romance, music and the arts, and you'll enjoy spending time with someone special. A favourite activity such as sports, travel or simply being with someone you love will blossom; however, you'll need to navigate misunderstandings or delays towards mid-week next week. Someone close at work or in your personal life is likely to surprise you.

WEEK 3: 19–25 MARCH

You're ready to turn a corner at work or with your status. You may even be drawn to embrace a completely different direction in life. This will be an exciting time to make new connections at work and/or to seek fresh contracts, as you'll be working well towards goals and with colleagues and associates. Just be sure to be flexible and avoid limiting your options. Be inspired.

WEEK 4: 26 MARCH–1 APRIL

You may be surprised by news. Initially, you may need to exit your comfort zone to get on top of events, but if you are resourceful there is every chance you'll reach a breakthrough with a project or at work. You will appreciate the opportunity to spend quality time with someone you admire or love or at the weekend or on Monday. You may even be surprised by an impromptu get-together.

HEALTH

Jupiter makes strong links with Mercury early in the month, which will encourage you to review and reorganise some of your health practices. This can only benefit you, so rather than feel that you are simply repeating the same cycle you can find ways to overcome habits that no longer support your health. Once Jupiter ends its retrograde phase after the 11th you'll gain strength over the coming weeks and months and begin to feel more motivated and energetic.

FINANCES

As there is so much focus at the moment astrologically on your status and career your finances are likely to alter as well. This is certainly a good month to have a look at your joint responsibilities such as bills and tax obligations, as you could make very positive strides ahead to clear debt and build future wealth. Just avoid making rash decisions towards the 21st, but be prepared to be bold.

HOME

Your home, property and family are important to you, so they can also represent how you see your status. The new moon on the 19th will illuminate how you feel about an important domestic matter and may simply be due to a change of direction. It's in your interest to ensure you maintain a sense of connection with those you love even though you'll be going through a particularly busy phase at work or due to a change of status.

LOVE LIFE

You will enjoy spending time with like-minded people in March, so couples will find that your relationship deepens when you both engage in something you love such as sports or travel. Singles also will be in a position to meet like-minded people, and some of the people you meet may well develop into romantic relationships. You may bump into an ex-flame mid-month and it will be your decision whether or not to rekindle this.

WORK

Be proactive about improving your work circumstances, especially between the 5th and 9th and at the new moon on the 19th, as you are in a strong position to attain a goal. You may be asked to step into a new role or will be drawn to fresh territory if you run your own business, and either scenario will certainly tempt you. Be sure to be positive, as the current stars will support your efforts.

WEEK 1: 2–8 APRIL

The desire to create both excitement but also a degree of stability in your life will come into sharp focus around Thursday's full moon, which will bring key talks, a visit, travel and the chance to find more balance in life. You will need other people's collaboration and therefore may need to make compromises, so you must also sharpen your people skills for the best results.

WEEK 2: 9–15 APRIL

You are likely to gain ground with important projects such as work ventures this week. Meetings towards Monday could go well, although you may also discover where you have underestimated your position. Be sure to be well prepared for next week, as you could make a good impression on people you collaborate with then. Sunday and Monday are also good days for socialising.

WEEK 3: 16–22 APRIL

There are adventurous aspects to the week, and you can certainly move your projects forward. You'll appreciate focusing on a personal or business relationship. Romance comes at the top of your list, and a promising new chapter in a work context could also be ideal. You will gain the opportunity to discuss arrangements and will then be able to put your attention where it is most needed.

WEEK 4: 23–29 APRIL

Thursday will be an excellent day for get-togethers, both at work and socially. You may be drawn to the arts at this time. You could receive unexpected news concerning work or a change of schedule, and this weekend will be excellent for sorting out your priorities. Be sure to plan travel and events well as there may be delays this weekend. Early to mid-next week relationships will again thrive.

HEALTH

As Jupiter gains ground in your sign you will wish to improve your profile and have more of a presence in your everyday life, so this month is a good time to re-evaluate your wardrobe and appearance. Important meetings at work or at play mid-month will merit attention to detail in the way you present. For this reason, improving and maintaining solid fitness schedules and a healthy appearance will appeal now.

FINANCES

Discussions with organisations or groups will produce positive results if you need to reconfigure your finances, so be sure to reach out to organisations or people who you know could help you. You may be surprised by developments that alter either your work or daily routine and so must be sure to put in place a contingency plan should a rainy day arise financially. However, for many Cancerians it's likely a financial boost arises towards the end of the month.

HOME

The full moon on 2 April will fall in your domestic sector, and for some Cancerians will spotlight a difference in values either at home or work. Nevertheless, both scenarios will bring an emotional response that you will chiefly express at home, so you must be careful to avoid making waves purely out of a sense of stress and pressure. Someone you generally rely upon may disappoint you, so you should play to your strengths.

LOVE LIFE

While many of the actions you take are in the name of love and togetherness, this month's developments may bring a slightly more adversarial aspect of yourself or someone close into play so it will be important, especially at the start of the month, to look for ways to collaborate and co-operate for the best effect. The weekend of the 11th is likely to be a sociable time. Singles may meet someone attractive, so be sure to organise events.

WORK

There is a great deal of focus on your career and work in April, so this is an excellent time to make progress. If you are looking for work, circulate your résumé and build connections with prospective employers or colleagues. If you are looking for a promotion, this is a good time to float ideas. You may receive good news mid-month or towards the 28th, and at the very least will find out where you stand if you are in doubt.

CANCER · APRIL

May

WEEK 1: 30 APRIL–6 MAY

This is an excellent weekend to invest a little in yourself. Consider who and what support you and your endeavours, and who and what no longer do. It's a good time to re-evaluate your shared commitments from this point of view and take steps to reconfigure joint duties. A fresh cycle begins in your personal life with the full moon on 1/2 May, so be prepared to welcome the new!

WEEK 2: 7–13 MAY

Jupiter in your sign makes favourable aspects both to the sun and Mercury, creating the opportunity to socialise and spend time indulging in your favourite activities with favourite people. This weekend you may be prepared to make a commitment to a particular path or person, and this promises to be a positive choice. Just avoid burning the candle at both ends.

WEEK 3: 14–20 MAY

You may be surprised by an unexpected development concerning a friend or organisation as the new moon nudges you into fresh territory. You may even experience a bittersweet note to some developments. There is an unanticipated aspect to the week, in that you will find yourself over time in a better circumstance even if some developments right now are not to your liking.

WEEK 4: 21–27 MAY / WEEK 5: 28 MAY–3 JUNE

WEEK 4: you'll enjoy a change of pace or of place this weekend. You may take part in unusual activities and will enjoy the chance to do something different and, equally, will enjoy relaxing. **WEEK 5:** a fresh daily schedule or work timetable towards the end of May will be exciting, but if it's a little confronting or confusing be sure to slow the pace and avoid feeling pressured.

HEALTH

Jupiter in your sign brings joy and abundance and you will enjoy a particularly uplifting and/or sociable time in May. You must, however, avoid overindulgence and overspending while Jupiter is in your sign. You may be inclined to overexert yourself as well and create a little fatigue so be prepared to pace yourself this month, especially during the second week of May and towards the new moon supermoon on the 16th/17th.

FINANCES

May will be an excellent month to look at your shared expenses and investments. Think household expenses and shared duties such as taxes. How could you rethink these areas so they work better for you? Developments in mid-May will put the focus on how best to manage your daily and health expenses. The full moon on the 31st will spotlight a need for adventure and change in your daily life or work. Bear in mind your need to cover expenses.

HOME

Venus in Cancer from the 19th through to mid-June will turn your mind to creature comforts. You're likely to favour a little more luxury and relaxation in a friendly environment, be this your home or through travel. You will also be drawn to reconnect with those you love such as family, especially towards the end of May, and this will motivate you to invest a little more in your home, especially if you are receiving visitors.

LOVE LIFE

The Scorpio full moon on 1/2 May will spotlight your personal life. If you're single you may feel passionately about someone – uncharacteristically so – and will be drawn to pursue a relationship or clarify at least your understanding with someone you feel is close. Couples may feel more passionate about each other, and this is certainly a good month to deepen your ties. Consider a holiday, a change of pace or a fresh way to strengthen your relationship.

WORK

Venus in your 12th house will contribute to the need for a friendly workplace. In mid-May you are likely to determine whether yours is a healthy and supportive environment or vice versa, and as a result you will be able to take necessary action moving forward. A friend or organisation will be helpful in determining the best step forward for you. There is an overriding sense that it is time for you to move into fresh territory.

June

WEEK 1: 4–10 JUNE

This will be a good week to discuss in serious terms your ideas and plans, both at work and with those close to you in your personal life, as you're likely to reach amicable outcomes. A financial or personal commitment will help you turn a corner. For some this will involve the necessity for talks, and for others for making a considerable financial choice as you begin a fresh arrangement.

WEEK 2: 11–17 JUNE

You may be surprised by developments this week such as an unexpected financial or ego boost. Keep communications on an even keel for the best results. As one chapter closes another begins. For you a work, health or daily schedule is soon to change tack, if it hasn't already recently. A change in a business or personal partner's circumstances may be in the works, which could make waves for you.

WEEK 3: 18–24 JUNE

As the sun enters your sign on the 21st it is the solstice, and you are likely to experience increased energy levels over the coming weeks. There will be a focus on your health and well-being and the opportunity to improve both now. Beforehand, though, personal and financial matters will deserve careful focus to avoid making mistakes. You will gain the opportunity to learn how to manage intense emotions.

WEEK 4: 25 JUNE–1 JULY

You'll appreciate the opportunity to get on top of your work commitments, health and well-being this week. If you discover a hole in the bucket financially, it will be your opportunity to stop the leak. A change of environment or simply the chance to do something different will breathe fresh air into relationships. Avoid conflict and work towards common ground and goals, especially at the full moon on the 29th/30th.

HEALTH

Mid-June and the full moon on the 29th/30th will be ideal times to set in motion a fresh health and well-being schedule. Once the sun enters your sign at the solstice on the 21st you will gain the opportunity to focus more on your energy levels. Specifically, if you discover that your reaction to some intense developments this month affects your health adversely it will be your opportunity to find better ways to manage your emotions.

FINANCES

The first week of June will be ideal for discussing important financial matters, both with organisations who can help you and those in your personal life who you must collaborate with on a financial level. The conjunction of Venus and Jupiter on the 9th/10th will bring certain matters into focus. The more information and facts you have at your fingertips the better you will be able to negotiate and decipher your next step forward.

HOME

Your home is very important, as this is an area where you feel most relaxed. However, this month your emotions will be centre stage, and if you find that even despite a relaxing home life you feel either stressed or experience intense emotions, it will be important for you to devote time to your self-development specifically as opposed to expecting your home to be your only haven. Your peace of mind is in reality your safe haven.

LOVE LIFE

There will be intense phases during June, especially around the 9th and 18th, that could spark romance but equally fiery outbursts, so aim to keep things on an even keel. You will become more acutely aware of your true feelings for someone. Be aware, however, that someone may be feeling below par. If it's you then take into account that you're sensitive or vulnerable and avoid making impulsive decisions. Instead, base decisions on clear facts and research.

WORK

Your usual schedule is likely to change now. At the very least it will gain pace, although for some Cancerians there will be reason to consider a fresh job or direction at work. The new moon supermoon on the 15th will kick-start a fresh phase. You may be drawn to new avenues at work but must avoid making changes that you have not researched or you're unsure of. You may receive unexpected offers that could lead to financial gain.

CANCER • JUNE

July

WEEK 1: 2–8 JULY

News at work or a fresh circumstance is on the way. You may even be surprised by developments. Be prepared to look at the big picture if you feel hard done by. If you've been contemplating making changes at work this is a good time to get the ball rolling, especially if you have support. Your link with a friend or organisation will step up to a different level.

WEEK 2: 9–15 JULY

In the lead-up to this week's new moon, which will be in your sign, this is an excellent time to place your attention on what you would like to birth in your life, especially with regard to your personal life. You have the opportunity to enjoy a romantic weekend, so be sure to organise events. Just be wary of misunderstandings or delays towards the 13th.

WEEK 3: 16–22 JULY

The areas you value and wish to celebrate in your life come under full focus this week. It is possible that you'll make enormous headway in your favourite activities and with the people you love; however, there is also an intensity to circumstances that could trip you up unless you are focused, especially regarding joint finances and taxes. Be sure to keep an eagle eye on your finances.

WEEK 4: 23–29 JULY

The sun in Leo will provide a positive outlook for you; however, you must keep an eye on overspending and consider renegotiating some of your arrangements with groups and organisations if you feel they are no longer up to date. There is a synchronicity about events this week that could catapult you to positive circumstances as long as you negotiate arrangements carefully.

HEALTH

You will appreciate the opportunity to try something new in your health schedule. You must be careful, however, early in the month and mid-month to avoid pushing yourself too hard with a fitness plan and/or having a minor accident due to the above or fatigue. The Uranus–Pluto trine mid-month could bring rapid developments health-wise. Be sure to take positive steps at this time to seek the help of experts or join a like-minded fitness group.

FINANCES

If you have overspent in the past you are likely to find out early in the month and will gain the opportunity to set things right throughout July. Be prepared to consult an expert. You may need to liaise with an organisation such as a bank to make the most of a fresh budget. The new moon supermoon on the 14th will be ideal for setting in motion fresh financial plans or to reorganise personal financial agreements.

HOME

The new moon in your sign on the 14th will spotlight some of your commitments, and it's likely that your dreams and plans can take flight. Some of these will affect your home life, so for this reason it is important that you consider this. There is a therapeutic aspect to developments in July. The main stumbling block would be succumbing to pressure or undergoing careless communications and negotiations, so be sure to stay on the ball.

LOVE LIFE

The start of the month is likely to offer opportunities to socialise, especially during the first weekend, so be prepared! Singles could meet someone who is upbeat and potentially also through an unusual circumstance. Be spontaneous, within reason; avoid going too left field, as you may regret your choices. The Uranus–Pluto trine mid-month could catapult your love life into fresh territory, so be sure to enjoy this transformative but also potentially intense time.

WORK

The Mars–Uranus conjunction at the start of the month will bring fresh or unusual circumstances your way. For some this will purely pertain to new links with an organisation. Be prepared to think outside the square, especially if you had already planned to make changes. Developments towards mid-month and the full moon on the 29th/30th could be therapeutic with regard to work, and some developments may even come out of the blue.

CANCER • JULY

August

WEEK 1: 30 JULY–5 AUGUST

The changes you have been engaged in over several weeks and months are likely to show concrete results, especially projects that involve a large financial or personal investment. However, to see the maximum results for all your hard work you must avoid power struggles this week, as the intense influence of the recent full moon is still with us.

WEEK 2: 6–12 AUGUST

The solar eclipse on the 12th/13th will spotlight certain plans: for some these will revolve around key relationships, and for others finances. You'll gain the sense that your plans are viable, even if they have been up in the air recently, but if you experience a setback this week consider your long-term outlook. It's better to have discovered a vulnerability now than further down the line.

WEEK 3: 13–19 AUGUST

A key financial development, transaction or news is best approached carefully to avoid making mistakes. Avoid acting before you totally think things through. When you do you could make considerable progress financially and at home and work this week. You may be surprised by favourable news early next week. Avoid taking developments personally, especially towards Monday, and work towards a favourable outcome.

WEEK 4: 20–26 AUGUST / WEEK 5: 27 AUGUST–2 SEPTEMBER

WEEK 4: this will be an excellent week to make a commitment to a particular person or project, as your plans are likely to succeed as long as you have adequately researched your circumstances. **WEEK 5:** the partial lunar eclipse on the 28th will bring one particular chapter in your life to a close, enabling another, therapeutic circumstance to arise for. For some this will be at home and for others at work.

HEALTH

You have the opportunity at the start of the month to improve your health by taking positive steps and being proactive. Be prepared to find out more about how to live a truly vibrant life. Your efforts will succeed, even if at first it is difficult to exit your usual health schedule. You may even come up with left-field ways to improve your health and vitality towards the solar eclipse on the 12th/13th.

FINANCES

A friend, group or organisation can be helpful with financial planning. Consider engaging the advice of experts as opposed to relying on your hunches now, as risk-taking is unfortunately likely to backfire. Developments before the total solar eclipse on the 12th/13th may be intense and will signal long-term change, so be careful with decisions you make at this time. Key news towards the 17th could signal important developments that boost your circumstances, but you must avoid overspending at this time.

HOME

A tough angle between Mars and Venus early in August suggests a degree of tension or discord either at home or with family. For some there will be an internal struggle between loyalty to work schedules and loyalty to domestic duties, so it will be important to maintain a balanced outlook regarding the importance of your home life. The Venus–Neptune opposition on the 10th/11th and partial lunar eclipse on the 28th could help you make changes at home.

LOVE LIFE

There is a lovely sociable atmosphere at the start of the month that you can take advantage of. You may simply find yourself surrounded by romantic people or events such as family anniversaries or weddings. You have the opportunity to move some of your activities into a more romantic environment, which will promote love: think travel and favourite projects. However, some interactions are likely to be intense, especially around the 12th.

WORK

You have the opportunity in August to gradually build the scenario that you want in your work. It is a case of taking things one step at a time and developing resilience should some developments be slower to eventuate than you would hope. You may experience an unexpected upturn at work in the second week of August. Be prepared to negotiate your terms as you could make promising arrangements, especially towards the 22nd and 28th.

CANCER • AUGUST

September

WEEK 1: 3–9 SEPTEMBER

An eye for detail both at home and work will provide you with an additional skill set this week. However, you must avoid becoming too set on details and in the process miss out on the big picture. You will enjoy a get-together or short trip towards the end of the weekend or early next week, so be prepared to be spontaneous and/or reach out to someone fun.

WEEK 2: 10–16 SEPTEMBER

The opposition between Venus and Chiron may expose vulnerabilities, either in yourself or in someone close. You may simply be re-evaluating some of your loyalties. This aside, you have every option to improve many of your relationships both at work and home. It's time to turn a corner and be innovative and proactive about the life you want, because when you are you are likely to succeed.

WEEK 3: 17–23 SEPTEMBER

A work opportunity may seem to open doors, but it may also limit your free time in the future. Consider your work-life balance. You may need to seek advice from someone at home or work regarding the best way to find the most balance. If making a commitment either way seems challenging, look for a bright solution and be positive.

WEEK 4: 24–30 SEPTEMBER

This weekend's full moon will shine a light on a career decision or change of status, and for some Cancerians this can also mean a change in a family, domestic or property-related matter. It is a good time to re-organise how you see yourself long term, especially if you work from home. If relationships are challenging now avoid impulsiveness and devote more attention to the people who mean the most to you.

HEALTH

Mars in your sign will help you get things done, especially if you base your actions on your intuition, but it's possible you feel the need to rush projects or feel under pressure, so this month may feel frustrating. For this reason it will be important to find ways to manage your daily life and energy levels carefully. With good planning you could make considerable progress in your life in many different fields, not least your health.

FINANCES

Jupiter continues to positively impact your finances. However, on the one hand you are likely to earn more but on the other you are also likely to spend more. The choice in how much you spend is up to you, but if you are prone to gamble this will not work for you this month, especially around the 10th and 27th, when you could make serious losses. Be prudent with important decisions as you could grow financially as a result.

HOME

This will be an excellent month to look at how you could turbocharge your home life so it suits you better and serves exactly the purpose you want. You will gain the collaboration and cooperation of those you love or live with. However, towards the 10th, 18th and 27th especially it is important you avoid a battle of wills. A commitment either to work or a domestic development will need to be adequately discussed to avoid making mistakes.

LOVE LIFE

There is a therapeutic aspect to the month that is likely to improve your relationships, whether you are single or in a partnership. However, around the 10th if you feel particularly vulnerable or sensitive be sure to take time out to re-evaluate how you feel about your current circumstances. This is certainly a good month to try something new in your love life; for example, aiming to meet a different circle, especially if you are single.

WORK

Much of the success in your work scenario will come down to good communication skills. Astrologically, you have excellent stars for making work progress this month. Be sure to be open to collaborate and innovate, and as a result you may surprise yourself with the kind of progress you can make now. Negotiations around the new moon on the 11th and towards the 17th and 26th could set you on a fresh track.

CANCER • SEPTEMBER

October

WEEK 1: 1–7 OCTOBER

News needn't put you in a flurry; your excellent organisational skills will do you proud. Get set to make changes at home, with family or property, as it's time for something new. Be prepared to carefully discuss developments with those they concern, such as family members, partners and business associates. The calmer and more practical you are the better will be the outcome.

WEEK 2: 8–14 OCTOBER

This is a good week to make plans to create more harmony in your interactions, communications and relationships, especially if recent discussions have been difficult. Working Cancerians will be busy, and you may find you must sort out mysteries or conundrums for the people who come your way. A change of routine or impromptu developments will bring variety into your life, even if initially some disagreements need sorting. Avoid gambling.

WEEK 3: 15–21 OCTOBER

You'll embrace change. A trip, get-together or family or financial development may require you to think big or consider the long-term picture. Agreements made now after due research are likely to work out, so be bold! You may receive a financial or work boost. Mid-week next week it will be important to avoid taking someone's circumstances or words personally. Be sure to maintain perspective and be careful with communications.

WEEK 4: 22–28 OCTOBER / WEEK 5: 29 OCTOBER–4 NOVEMBER

WEEK 4: Monday's full moon will foster a fresh agreement with a friend or organisation. You may be surprised by developments. Be practical and look for ways to build understanding with someone special to avoid a battle of wills.
WEEK 5: you can make a breakthrough both in your personal life and financially. The key lies in patience, good communication skills and asking for expert help where and when necessary.

HEALTH

Early in the month you'll feel motivated to revitalise your health schedule. Be sure to listen to impulse! You'll gain the opportunity to vary your activities, which could open doors to different and exciting activities. A boost in self-esteem mid-month will help improve your outlook on life, which will also lift your mood and demeanour and enable you to feel more positive. This could translate also as increased motivation to be healthy, so embrace it!

FINANCES

It's likely that you'll make considerable progress financially already early in the month but this will depend on having the right information, so be sure to carefully investigate investments and financial choices. Obtain the advice of an expert if necessary, as it's far better to gain all the information you need to make clear calls. Avoid gambling, especially towards the 9th, 10th and 30th. You are in line for a financial boost that, for many, will be due to work circumstances mid-month.

HOME

You could make fresh commitments regarding your home life early in October, so be sure to check how you feel about making changes at home, with family or concerning someone special. You could create excellent outcomes, but you must base decisions on facts and not supposition. The full moon on the 26th will spotlight how you feel about someone special and could determine key domestic decisions, especially concerning children and finances.

LOVE LIFE

Your partner or a family member is likely to have significant news early in the month already. The more practical and considerate you can be the better for your relationship. However, someone may have very intense viewpoints, and if these are untenable it may be time to re-evaluate where you stand. It may simply be the case that your values have changed over time or have always been different. Be prepared to re-evaluate circumstances in your own time.

WORK

You may enjoy an improvement in your career or status that will truly boost your self-esteem. You may even receive unexpected news early in the month. Some negotiations may be intense, especially towards the 4th, 9th and 21st, but if you keep an eye on your goals you could make great progress. You may experience an improvement in work conditions or a financial boost towards the 16th. Just be careful with subsequent talks and negotiations.

CANCER • OCTOBER

November

WEEK 1: 5–11 NOVEMBER

Monday's new moon signals a fresh, exciting chapter in your personal life. This could mean more time for romance or for your creativity and love life. For some, though, developments will revolve around family. You may find that some people understand the deeper you, and that you will wish to find out more about someone special too. You may experience an ego or financial boost towards Tuesday.

WEEK 2: 12–18 NOVEMBER

Conversations, trips and get-togethers will be super significant this week, so be sure to pay extra attention to communications and travel. Some meetings may even be therapeutic in nature and could set you on a fresh track, especially regarding your personal life and goals and aspirations. There will be a reunion that is significant to you that puts a great deal of emphasis on family and friendships, which will help you gain perspective.

WEEK 3: 19–25 NOVEMBER

Apart from some stressful days at the end of this week that may put pressure on your communications you have the opportunity now to improve many of your relationships, especially those with a friend, group or organisation. The full moon supermoon in Gemini on Tuesday/Wednesday will help you turn a corner within both personal and work relationships.

WEEK 4: 26 NOVEMBER–2 DECEMBER

You are one of the most intuitive zodiac signs, and this week it's in your interest to trust your gut. You will enjoy a lovely get-together, and if you're looking for romance you'll find it. However, you will need to be discerning. If you find you are disappointed by someone, be prepared to look for constructive ways ahead. You may experience a boost at work on Monday.

HEALTH

There are therapeutic influences this month that can really help you gain a sense of self-esteem and self-confidence, so be sure to take the initiative and seek the expert advice of someone in the health field who has the credentials to help you. If you find your vulnerabilities surface during November, consider looking at psychological techniques that can help you manage sensitivity as your efforts are likely to be successful, especially towards the 19th and 29th.

FINANCES

An investment you made in the past will bring the opportunity to improve your finances, especially towards the new moon on the 9th and also mid-month. As the month goes on you'll have the opportunity to remedy financial circumstances you're unhappy with, so be sure to take the initiative and seek expert help. Advice from a loyal and knowledgeable friend, group or organisation may be particularly helpful in transforming your finances.

HOME

This will be a good month to look at how to improve your personal life, especially your home, as your efforts are likely to succeed. You may even experience an improvement towards the 10th as you gain the opportunity to invest in this important part of your life. You may also appreciate a trip mid-month and towards the 28th that brings you closer to someone you love. You will enjoy sharing time with someone special.

LOVE LIFE

The sexy new moon in Scorpio on the 9th could bring a whole new dimension to your love life. Be prepared to organise something special as you are likely to enjoy spending quality time with someone between the 9th and 16th, when romance can certainly flourish. Towards the end of the month romance can also truly thrive, so be sure to take the initiative and attend or organise events. If vulnerabilities arise look for ways to find emotional stability.

WORK

Activities mid-month will ring in a change of pace at work. For some this will mean a pleasant break from work and for others a super busy time with meetings and get-togethers that need to be attended to. In both scenarios you will feel you make a breakthrough, especially in connection with someone important, and as a result you'll be able to gain more of a sense of identity and independence. You may even experience a particular boost towards the 30th.

December

WEEK 1: 3–9 DECEMBER

Success now will depend on an innovative approach on your behalf, because where previous ventures have failed it's time for something new. Be bold and approach events with a long-term view but be sensitive to the feelings of others, as you otherwise risk a needless battle of wills both at home and work, especially on Friday and mid next week. You may be drawn to a fresh work or health schedule.

WEEK 2: 10–16 DECEMBER

This will be an excellent weekend for the arts, whether you work in the arts sector or simply enjoy music, dance and being creative. Romance could thrive, so be sure to organise a date this weekend. You may receive good news at work or appreciate a change of schedule that takes you to an old haunt. Some Cancerians will enjoy a trip and reunion.

WEEK 3: 17–23 DECEMBER

You'll enjoy a change of pace or of place that will be uplifting on many levels. If you are working this week you are likely to undergo some stressful times but, nevertheless, these are likely to lead to success. However, should a mystery arise at work or staff levels diminish and your workload increases, be sure to pace yourself and avoid taking stress home at the end of the day.

WEEK 4: 24–31 DECEMBER

The Christmas Eve full moon supermoon will be in Cancer, signifying the start of a brand-new cycle in 2027. For some this will involve a fresh chapter at work or in your status, and for a few a fresh situation in your personal life. A change in your usual Christmas schedule will require you and others to adapt to it. You will appreciate regaining your mojo by New Year's Eve.

HEALTH

The new moon on the 9th will kick-start an adventurous phase when being in tiptop condition will appeal. You have excellent stars to enlist the collaboration of someone close to accompany you with health pursuits. Restlessness and/or an argumentative streak early in the month could destroy your peace of mind, so consider activities such as yoga to calm your nerves. Developments around the 18th and 31st could bring ideal opportunities to relax, so be sure to plan breaks or a holiday.

FINANCES

You have the opportunity to make progress financially and the help of an expert may be invaluable. The new moon on the 9th may predispose you to a gambling mindset, but it's far better to make financial plans based on surefire outcomes as opposed to speculation, especially early in the month. Some Cancerians will appreciate a financial boost towards the 18th, but this will depend on previous actions. If you have overspent a fresh budget will be necessary.

HOME

If you feel tension has been brewing already at home it's vital that you de-escalate this, as otherwise you may be predisposed to setting in motion a long-term dispute that you will not appreciate. On the contrary, if you make every effort to infuse your home life with balance and love you will appreciate the outcome. Developments towards the 21st and 29th will especially merit a calm approach to maintain peace, as developments may otherwise try your patience.

LOVE LIFE

The key to a happy love life in December revolves around fair sharing skills. Someone close may have their own idea of what sharing means, so it will be in your interest to find middle ground. You will enjoy socialising during the weekend beginning the 18th and singles may find this a therapeutic time. A change of pace or of place can also revitalise the love lives of couples. Be prepared to be patient around Christmas to avoid unnecessary upheaval.

WORK

You'll gain the opportunity early in December to alter aspects of your working schedule or duties. Some outcomes may even be ideal so be sure to take the initiative, especially towards the 11th and 14th. Some communications may be a little tense, but if you rise to the occasion you could make great progress, especially towards the 18th. Be sure to avoid a battle of wills, and if you feel overwhelmed moving towards Christmas take short breaks whenever possible.

January

WEEK 1: 1–7 JANUARY

The new year full moon will spotlight your past, such as a reunion or return to an old haunt. It's a good week to devise a fresh work or health schedule; look for a supportive schedule or adviser. You'll gain the chance to boost your love life, so if you've been meaning to ask someone out this is the week to do so, especially this weekend and on Tuesday.

WEEK 2: 8–14 JANUARY

Working Leos may enjoy a busy week, and an improvement in your working day will boost your confidence. A change in your usual schedule will mean you must weigh up the relative value of your peace of mind and spare time versus your ability to take on more work. Keep in mind that you must factor in shared circumstances in your new schedule or arrangements. This will also be a romantic week for some mid-August–born Leos.

WEEK 3: 15–21 JANUARY

A change in your usual routine will be constructive. You'll enjoy developments but may also need to adjust to a fresh routine, so be sure to pace yourself. Sunday/Monday's new moon points to doors opening for you: for some this will entail new activities or a fresh work routine and for others a different health schedule. Just be sure to be tactful with communications as you may otherwise land yourself in hot water.

WEEK 4: 22–28 JANUARY

Key developments in your work or health routine will put a fresh schedule in place. A trip or news could be ideal but will also involve a fair degree of adjustment. Some Leos will experience intense or sudden developments. Romance could soar, especially for July-born Leos, so be sure to organise treats, especially around the 22nd. A business or personal partner may have key news and finances will deserve focus towards the end of the month.

HEALTH

Keep your health uppermost in your mind in January, as you may have a tendency to overwork. If you're lucky enough to be on holiday be sure to take a little time to figure out how to gain more work-life balance once your busy schedule resumes, to avoid overwork this year. The new moon on the 18th/19th will be a good time during the following few days to begin a fresh health routine such as a fitness class.

FINANCES

This will be a good month to consider how to improve aspects of your shared finances, such as those you need for business expenses and those you need for domestic overheads. If need be seek out the help of a professional who can help with both. At the end of the month you are likely to experience developments at work or in your personal life that could have a bearing on how you decide to organise your finances moving forward.

HOME

As an essentially outgoing character you do tend to burn the candle at both ends, yet for this precise reason it is important to maintain the status quo in your home life because this is where you can revitalise your energy. As it's quite likely that you will be travelling or welcoming visitors you will appreciate the opportunity to regain your own space at home, as this will allow you to ground yourself in what will be a busy month.

LOVE LIFE

The entry of Venus in your seventh house of partnership will bring more love into your relationships, both at home and at work. This doesn't mean a work romance, simply that your professional relationships can improve now, so be sure to take the initiative and especially after the 17th. At home and romantically you'll enjoy trying new activities to boost the spontaneity in your love life, as this will open doors to a deeper connection.

WORK

It's important to work out what is most important to you in your everyday life: work satisfaction, health and well-being or the chance to spend time with those you love. If work really does grab your focus now you'll gain the chance to improve this important aspect of your life but you must avoid taking on too much, especially mid-month. The new moon on the 18th/19th will open a fresh chapter for you and you may even be surprised by opportunities.

LEO · JANUARY

February

WEEK 1: 29 JANUARY–4 FEBRUARY

You may be ready to turn a corner in your personal life if you were born in July, and if you were born in August in your daily work or health routine. Key talks and developments suggest that you will begin a fresh schedule, one that brings you closer to a sense of purpose both at work and within your favourite activities and interests.

WEEK 2: 5–11 FEBRUARY

A change of circumstance may ask that you better organise or research your situation, especially at work and in your personal life. Good communication skills will boost circumstances, and you must avoid a disagreement as otherwise disgruntlement will arise from a conviction that you are correct. However, there is always room for error, so try to see another person's point of view. Strong emotions will arise and romance could thrive.

WEEK 3: 12–18 FEBRUARY

Get set to share your resources, space or duties in a fresh way. You may be ready to commit to someone in a new way or share your time and energy differently: by delegating chores, for example, or carving out time for romance. For some this week's solar eclipse will signal a fresh opportunity. If you are making long-term decisions ensure you have the facts before committing to plans.

WEEK 4: 19–25 FEBRUARY / WEEK 5: 26 FEBRUARY–4 MARCH

WEEK 4: working Leos are likely to be busy. Be prepared to step into new territory. Someone you work with or the people you meet may be a little distracted or you will need to learn new skill sets and may feel a little overwhelmed, so be sure to take breaks. **WEEK 5:** you'll enjoy a change of environment. Romance could flourish but you must check you're not seeing someone idealistically.

HEALTH

An inquisitive and curious approach to your health and well-being will certainly inform your opportunity to spark on all cylinders in February. You may even be drawn into fresh territory where your health is concerned; for instance, by engaging in activities that take you outside your comfort zone and that you would not normally consider such as complementary medicine, meditation or simply even an unusual fitness class.

FINANCES

This will be an excellent month to get right down to basics and work out who and what mean the most to you. This may seem irrelevant to finances but, in fact, it will help you configure a budget that feels supportive of your efforts rather than the opposite. You will gain the opportunity to improve your finances early in the month but must maintain a realistic approach to your budget.

HOME

The Leo full moon on the 1st/2nd signifies a new chapter in your personal life, especially if you were born in July. For all Leos, however, and depending on where you place your focus – on your love life, work or health – it's likely that you'll welcome a change of environment or of ambience at home and this can feel refreshing, especially if you make this a goal: a revitalising fresh dynamic in your own home.

LOVE LIFE

The Leo full moon on 1/2 February will help you revitalise your personal life, health and/or work. If you were born in August this full moon will help you schedule in more of what you love in your life. If you are in a relationship you'll gain the incentive to be more communicative with your partner and bring zest into your love life. If you are single and were born in July you may even meet someone.

WORK

A change in your usual routine may feel a little intense at first but this month you'll gain the opportunity to settle into a schedule that brings more diversity into your daily life, which you'll enjoy. Leos born in August are likely to experience the most degree of surprise or unsettled developments and a flexible approach from all Leos will help smooth the way, especially around the 5th and 8th.

LEO · FEBRUARY

March

WEEK 1: 5–11 MARCH

You'll enjoy a trip and reunion. You may be drawn to pick up where you left off with a work relationship or romance. Expect changes in a key relationship, some of which may be unexpected, especially if someone tends to keep you guessing. This will be a positive time to consider stepping into new territory either at work or within your status and general direction in the bigger picture.

WEEK 2: 12–18 MARCH

This is a good week to get back to basics, especially concerning areas you share with someone such as with your partner or work mates. You'll appreciate the opportunity to discuss joint finances and may come to a new arrangement concerning duties you share. Singles may meet someone on Friday or Saturday who seems familiar. Someone may even surprise you mid-week. Be prepared to adjust to the demands of a fresh circumstance.

WEEK 3: 19–25 MARCH

You'll appreciate the opportunity to turn a corner with a shared responsibility or arrangement. It's a good week to consider a fresh way to manage your finances, taxes or work duties. Remember to enjoy life, as this is an upbeat week that is ideal for socialising if you like. You may receive an unexpected job offer or change at work around the new moon on the 19th.

WEEK 4: 26 MARCH–1 APRIL

Developments at work will require you to dig deep and come up with answers. Trust that you will be able to do just that and you will succeed. News you receive may be unexpected and you may need to look outside the square at issues. Someone may need your help, and if you need advice it will be available. You'll enjoy a pleasant development late in the weekend or early next week.

HEALTH

Jupiter ends its retrograde phase in your 12th house of health this month, which will encourage you to approach health and well-being from a big-picture viewpoint. If you have been suffering ill health recently you will gradually over the coming weeks and months begin to feel more revitalised. Someone you love or trust is likely to have a positive effect on your health. Just avoid potentially stressful circumstances, especially around the 18th, as these may be super tiring.

FINANCES

You will gain the opportunity to review finances early on in the month and much of your discussion may revolve around past commitments that you are now in a position to alter to suit you better. Be prepared to go over old ground and, if necessary, get in touch with experts, groups or organisations that can help you reconfigure or streamline your finances. Some lucky Leos are in line for a financial boost.

HOME

Developments concerning your career and activities will take much of your focus in March but they will nevertheless have a knock-on effect on your home life. Be sure to maintain the status quo and the balance between work and domestic life, as otherwise you may risk spreading yourself too thin. The end of March is conducive to romance and a chance to enjoy a little comfort and rest, so be sure to organise relaxing domestic events then.

LOVE LIFE

The period between the 5th and the 9th and the end of the month will be particularly favourable for romance and excellent for engaging in activities you love with your partner such as sports, bushwalks, gardening and the arts. You may be drawn to travel or to visit someone. A change of routine will be refreshing. Singles may meet someone you feel a strong link with around the 13th and 18th, so be sure to organise a treat.

WORK

Early March will be excellent for discussing your options as there are good opportunities for negotiations and reaching fresh arrangements that you would be happy with, so do take the initiative if there has been something on your mind for some time that you would like to discuss. Mid-month you are likely to collaborate well with colleagues, so it is a good time to develop positive work relationships. Just be careful with communications around the 18th.

LEO · MARCH

April

WEEK 1: 2–8 APRIL

You'll enjoy a reunion or good news. Be prepared to reconfigure at least some of your shared responsibilities, including work duties and chores around the house. Thursday's full moon will ask that you find a tactful approach to a personal or work matter. You may feel very strongly, and it will be in your interest to express feelings in the best way possible as opposed to creating a difficult situation.

WEEK 2: 9–15 APRIL

You will enjoy a more spontaneous and upbeat feeling to the week. A favourite activity such as sports, travel or spiritual development will be particularly poignant this weekend or on Monday. Some Leos will find this a positive week for work and career advancement, especially on Monday, so be sure to schedule in key meetings with people you'd like to work with or impress.

WEEK 3: 16–22 APRIL

This is a good week for meetings and to organise your activities so you can be more productive and so you can take time out to enjoy life with someone special. Friday's new moon points to a fresh chapter at work or within your status, and it's in your interest to take the initiative and negotiate positive outcomes. Duties and health will dictate your actions.

WEEK 4: 23–29 APRIL

The next few days will be ideal for socialising. You'll enjoy spending time with like-minded people in a group circumstance such as via sports, self-development or another interest you have in common. You may enjoy a spontaneous get-together on Friday. Just be careful at the weekend to avoid delays and misunderstandings. Communications will once again improve at the start of next week.

HEALTH

The first week of April will be particularly good for improving your health and well-being. It will be a beneficial time to consult experts such as doctors, physios or nutritionists to boost your energy levels. A friend or colleague may point you in the right direction towards a group or organisation, so be sure to discuss your options with people around you, especially mid-month and towards the 24th. You'll also be drawn to personal or spiritual development at that time.

FINANCES

The new moon on the 17th is going to kick-start a busy time for you. You will need the resources to pay for your various activities, so the start of the month will be a good time already to budget for the potential for bigger expenditure later in the month. Luckily, work opportunities will arise, and you may be surprised by developments concerning an organisation you are involved with towards the 24th.

HOME

There is a strong focus in April on being busy and spending time with like-minded people. Whether you work or socialise more than usual, your home life is likely to take second place. That said, the need for self-care will also be prevalent this month and there is no better place than your home in which to relax and revitalise, so be sure to spend extra time looking after yourself, especially in the busy second half of April.

LOVE LIFE

The new moon on the 17th will kick-start a fresh phase for you in your status in general. For some Leos this can mean a new status within your love life: for example, from single to married or vice versa. Developments will most certainly be therapeutic in the long term. The third week of April and the 23rd and 24th are particularly romantic, so be sure to organise special events then.

WORK

You may receive good news at work or at least will find ways to get on better with your colleagues early in the month, so be prepared to take the initiative. Be sure to avoid any form of argument or a battle of wills early in April, especially towards the 3rd and 6th, as these are likely to balloon. Towards the 13th, 20th and 24th a particular meeting or news could bring positive developments your way.

LEO · APRIL

May

WEEK 1: 30 APRIL–6 MAY

The full moon will highlight your home life, family and property choices: is it time to refresh some aspects of these areas in your life? You may find a change of status, career or direction will have an impact on your domestic life, so be sure to think outside the box as new options open for you. A desire for change is best addressed, not left to fester.

WEEK 2: 7–13 MAY

This will be an excellent week to take the initiative at work and with your favourite projects, as your endeavours are likely to succeed. Be confident with communications and prepared to lead. You may also be prepared to make a commitment to a particular project or career incentive. You could enjoy a reunion or return to an old haunt.

WEEK 3: 14–20 MAY

This weekend's new moon supermoon will kick-start a fresh chapter in your status, career or general direction, bringing an increasingly stable and secure phase your way over time despite potential surprises or conundrums occurring in the immediate present. Be prepared to contemplate fresh alliances both at work and in your personal life. Your help may be needed, and if you need support it will be available.

WEEK 4: 21–27 MAY / WEEK 5: 28 MAY–3 JUNE

WEEK 4: activities this weekend may take you outside your usual territory or will ask that you be more adaptable. You will be busy or in demand socially. Romance could unexpectedly blossom. **WEEK 5:** look at the bigger picture to ascertain where you could perhaps be more fulfilled. If you find you're often at loggerheads with someone look for ways to defuse tension and avoid an ego battle, especially at work.

HEALTH

Jupiter in your health sector makes fortunate aspects both with the sun and Mercury in the second week of May, making this an excellent time to improve your health. If you have allowed bad habits to enter your health routine this will be a great time to correct any of those negative traits that hold you back. You may also be drawn to reconnect with a favourite pastime that boosts your mood and consequently your health.

FINANCES

May is an excellent month to consider how you spend your money. In other words, are you happy investing your money in yourself or do you find it tends to disappear into bills and expenses before you have even found the time to enjoy some of your wealth? You will gain the opportunity this month to make considerable changes both within your career and domestic and personal lives, so be sure to invest in your immediate present.

HOME

The full moon on the 1st/2nd will be an excellent time to turn a corner domestically as your efforts, especially in the first week of the month, are likely to succeed. Changes may come as a result of developments within your career or general status: think married or single, for example. Try to get the ball rolling with some of your domestic plans before Pluto turns retrograde on the 6th/7th, as this will help you manage your everyday schedule.

LOVE LIFE

The conjunction of Mars and Chiron mid-month will put astrological focus on your status. For some status can signify whether you're single or married, for example, so this conjunction could indicate considerable changes within your marital circumstance from single to married and vice versa. For many Leos there will be therapeutic aspects and developments in your love life in May. You may even be inclined to make a solid commitment to someone special.

WORK

It's time to review a work relationship or how you invest in your daily chores and find fresh pathways ahead. The full moon on 1/2 May will spotlight any aspects of your work you feel are outdated. Pluto's retrograde phase beginning on 6/7 May will encourage you to review aspects of your daily schedule that require a tweak. There is no immediate rush to alter your circumstances, but rather to register what is and isn't working and work accordingly.

LEO · MAY

June

WEEK 1: 4–10 JUNE

Key decisions and developments are likely: for some Leos these will be in your career and work life and for others regarding health and/or your past. You may feel uncharacteristically emotional, so it will be in your interest to gain perspective and take a step back if necessary so you are able to see things clearly. Be methodical and practical above all.

WEEK 2: 11–17 JUNE

Prepare to turn a corner in a work or personal context this week as you begin to see communications in a fresh light. You'll be drawn to take action in new directions. If you encounter an obstacle you may be surprised later in the week as fresh options arise. Close relationships from your past may become very much present, and you may enjoy a spontaneous catch-up with someone fun.

WEEK 3: 18–24 JUNE

Intense people could lead to drama and distractions, so plan to enjoy a diverse schedule but avoid conflict. Overindulgence will appeal, so be careful with money. Take the initiative at work and health-wise as you could make progress. Key talks could produce a new arrangement or agreement with someone either at work or play. Use your intuition: you are insightful at the moment.

WEEK 4: 25 JUNE–1 JULY

As Jupiter enters your sign you will appreciate the potential for joy and abundance to return to your life over time. You may already experience a lucky development this week. Key discussions are likely to revolve around love and money. Monday/Tuesday's full moon will spotlight a fresh daily health or work schedule, and for some who and what is most important to you.

HEALTH

You are likely to be particularly emotionally led both at the beginning and the end of the month, so if you have found that your emotions can get the better of you sometimes this will be a good month to find ways to manage them. It is a good time too for self-development, especially psychic and psychological development, so be sure to take the initiative and research options.

FINANCES

You are one of the most extravagant signs of the zodiac, and this month you are likely to be drawn to overindulge once Venus has entered your sign on the 13th. Your predilection for a little luxury and comfort may peak towards the 17th and 18th. This is also when you're likely to wish to spend more than usual on your favourite activities and people. If you have the money, why not, but if you're in debt it's time to be careful.

HOME

Decide where your priorities lie, as you may be led by your desires rather than your needs now. In particular, your attention may actually be more focused on your work and activities than your home life yet your home life will demand attention, especially towards the end of the month. A family member or housemate may need more focus then and you may need to make a tough call regarding your long-term plans.

LOVE LIFE

Mid-month is likely to be a fairly intense time for you as you look at ways to maintain a sense of spontaneity, individuality and freedom within your relationship while also enjoying the closeness of a relationship. Finding the balance will be key to avoiding the necessity to navigate potentially tense circumstances. Singles may find this a particularly upbeat month, especially mid-month once Venus has entered your sign and when meeting people will keep romance alive.

WORK

The new moon supermoon on the 15th will be a perfect time to consider whether you are still invested in the groups and organisations you are currently with. Developments that could put you in a vulnerable position may actually be obstacles in disguise, as you are likely to encounter a surprise development that could actually place you in a better position. Be sure to keep an open mind should you encounter some swings and roundabouts this month.

LEO · JUNE

July

WEEK 1: 2–8 JULY

A friend, group or organisation has news for you that is likely to be unexpected. Developments will snowball, so find ways to slow them down if possible. Keep talks and negotiations on an even keel or you may be liable to get caught up in restlessness or even dramas and turmoil this week. A change of schedule or at work could be beneficial but will need adapting to.

WEEK 2: 9–15 JULY

You will enjoy indulging in the arts and romance towards the weekend and may also enjoy a financial or ego boost. However, some arrangements that are outside your control will need careful navigation as plans may alter rapidly, either towards the end of the weekend or early next week. You will enjoy a reunion and/or the chance to review both your working week and health.

WEEK 3: 16–22 JULY

This is a good week to make headway with your career and status. You are likely to experience unexpected or unusual changes in this field, so the more you can work with developments the better it will be for you. Ask yourself where you would ideally like to bring more of your favourite activities into your daily life and work towards accomplishing this.

WEEK 4: 23–29 JULY

Now that the sun is in your sign you are likely to experience gradually improved energy levels over the coming weeks. The full moon in Aquarius on the 29th/30th is likely to be fairly intense for you, and a personal or business decision will figure as part of developments. Consider circumstances this week to be therapeutic in the long run, even if some aspects are triggering.

HEALTH

There are many therapeutic aspects to the month that will initially potentially appear as the opposite. If you discover you have a vulnerability in your health, be this physical, mental, spiritual or emotional, this will be your opportunity to set yourself on a better path. Sometimes it is possible to outgrow a particular health practitioner, and if you feel this is the case now you may be drawn to research a different expert in your field.

FINANCES

There are certain non-negotiable aspects to some of the financial arrangements you've made, and this will become evident during July. However, this does not mean that you cannot improve your finances and you have excellent stars for doing just that, especially mid-month. Be prepared to work with organisations and/or experts who can help you. The full moon on the 29th/30th may spotlight a quirky or different financial option due to work progress.

HOME

A key to working out your priorities in July is to ask yourself where you feel you belong. If you are happy in your current home and/or with a property investment you can be sure that your investment is likely to work out. However, if you feel the opposite – that there are aspects of your home life you would like to change – then this will be an ideal month to set the ball rolling, especially mid-month.

LOVE LIFE

July-born Leos will find the first week of July a particularly transformative time in your relationship. If you are single you're likely to be socialising a fair amount this July. A change in work routine could also provide you with more time and space to devote to that special someone in your life. Some Leos will be drawn to reconnect with someone from your past, and this could in the long-term bring considerable change your way.

WORK

The first week of July is likely to bring considerable news your way at work. It will be in your interest to see the glass half full as opposed to half empty as developments arise. You are in the position to move into fresh territory, and developments may even be unexpectedly positive. Be prepared to discuss your options with those they concern as opposed to digging your heels in. The new moon supermoon on the 14th will prove to be revitalising.

August

WEEK 1: 30 JULY–5 AUGUST

You'll gain the motivation and potential to make considerable changes that bring more stability and security to your career, direction or status, so be sure to take practical yet proactive steps to build the outcome you want. There is still a degree of tension in the air post the full moon, so keep an eye on communications to avoid these becoming intense.

WEEK 2: 6–12 AUGUST

This week's total solar eclipse will be in Leo, so it will be more intense for you than for most other star signs. If you were born before the 12th–13th this eclipse brings considerable change to your personal life, and if you were born after the 13th you will experience changes in your daily schedule such as an alteration in your usual work or health routine.

WEEK 3: 13–19 AUGUST

This week's conjunction between Mercury and Jupiter in Leo will bring key news, especially in your personal life if you were born in July and at work or regarding health if you were born in August. You have the ability to boost circumstances in all areas and may even attain a fresh sense of status as a result. This will depend on previous decisions and, for some, on your ability to evolve.

WEEK 4: 20–26 AUGUST / WEEK 5: 27 AUGUST–2 SEPTEMBER

WEEK 4: developments this week could involve a tough call for you regarding either your home or work and general direction. However, a reunion or inspiring discussion could improve one or all areas, so be sure to take the initiative.
WEEK 5: the partial lunar eclipse on the 28th will spotlight your shared duties, responsibilities and finances, as a fresh way to configure these may appeal.

HEALTH

Keep an eye on your health as it would be easy this month to place your attention everywhere but your well-being. However, your health is your main driver for vitality and productivity, so be sure to factor a self-nurturing schedule into your routine. You'll gain the opportunity towards the 12th to transform your usual health routine so it better suits you. If you experience health issues at this time it's better to be inquisitive than to ignore them.

FINANCES

August is an excellent month to build wealth and stability and the key lies in undertaking research, so that during the intense phases around the 12th and 28th you will be in a stronger position to navigate key financial decisions. As the end of the month sails closer it will be important that you focus also on joint finances: think shared household expenses and taxes. You may be easily influenced now so keep an eye on the facts.

HOME

Important decisions regarding finances, your home life and direction will arise this month, not least because of the total solar eclipse in your sign on the 12th/13th. If you were born before 12 August you are likely to need to make changes in your personal life, and if you were born afterwards at work. Both these scenarios can have flow-on effects on your home, which will deserve focus as you may otherwise neglect this area and restrict future options.

LOVE LIFE

There is still a little tension at the start of the month. However, some relationships thrive on romantic tension and this may actually create a passionate, enjoyable framework. However, if you find some interactions stressful find the time to established common ground as opposed to entering conflict. The total solar eclipse on the 12th/13th brings a fresh chapter if you were born before 13 August in your personal life. Communications may be tense at this time, so be patient.

WORK

The start of the month is ideal for making progress at work. You may need to be super careful with conversations with colleagues and/or groups and organisations to avoid misunderstandings. The total solar eclipse on the 12th/13th brings a fresh circumstance if you were born after 13 August and all Leos may also experience intense conversations and developments at work mid-month and towards the 28th, so be sure to maintain good relationships.

LEO · AUGUST

September

WEEK 1: 3–9 SEPTEMBER

You'll appreciate the increasing sense that your career, status and general direction are becoming clearer and that you can, at the very least, see the rhyme and reason for events. Persevere with your plans, because when you do you are likely to see positive results even if at first you must overcome an obstacle. You may even receive a boost to your self-esteem or finances this week.

WEEK 2: 10–16 SEPTEMBER

You will enjoy reconnecting with someone special. If you have a negotiation or agreement to undertake ensure you stick with facts and avoid basing decisions on expectations, as mistakes could be made as a result. However, if you initiate talks, especially to do with work and your favourite projects, you are likely to succeed with your ventures. You may need to choose between work duties and domestic duties, so choose wisely!

WEEK 3: 17–23 SEPTEMBER

A plan, venture or project is likely to take a concrete step forward this week even if in the process you feel the opposite. There will be positive progress nevertheless in a health, travel or well-being context. Be sure to discuss your options with experts, as they will prove super insightful. You will appreciate the opportunity to reconnect with someone special.

WEEK 4: 24–30 SEPTEMBER

Mars enters your sign now, and over the coming weeks will contribute to improved energy levels. However, it may also make you prone to tempers, so be sure to avoid allowing intense feelings destroy your peace of mind. This weekend's full moon will spotlight a travel, overseas, legal or educational matter, and you may be surprised by particular news in one or more of these areas. A fun break may appeal.

HEALTH

September is the best month of the year to devote time to this important aspect of your life as you could potentially positively transform your health. Be sure to invest in fun activities and healthy options. The new moon on the 11th will help you kick-start fresh initiatives. Be prepared to consider the interface between mind and body to maximise this therapeutic phase. A friend or organisation may be particularly influential. Just avoid rushing and overexertion on the 27th.

FINANCES

There is as much potential for a financial breakthrough as there is for financial obstacles in September. The key to success revolves around your ability to be diligent and persistent without being obsessive about money. Once you set your eyes on a goal you will gain the opportunity to reach it and as a result you may even experience improved finances in September, especially around the 10th and at the end of the month.

HOME

You'll gain the motivation to put energy into your home and immediate environment, especially after the 11th. Whether you decide to spruce up the décor by adding pops of colour or make more serious changes to your environment, you are likely to be drawn to experience more comfort at home with the people you love. If you do decide to travel you'll gain a sense of belonging at your destination and bring that essence back into your home.

LOVE LIFE

You will enjoy deepening your ties with someone special and communications are likely to run more smoothly after the 10th. Romance can thrive towards the 12th and 14th, but you must avoid misunderstandings towards the 15th, 17th, 22nd and 27th. Avoid rushing or pressuring someone who may not appreciate it. You have a wonderful opportunity to improve your relationships at work and socially. Be prepared to invest that little bit extra into your love life to see it flourish.

WORK

You can make a great deal of progress this month at work and career-wise that will revolve around your ability to be a self-starter and initiate changes. Be prepared to negotiate and discuss your options. The new moon on the 11th and full moon on the 26th/27th may bring in a fresh opportunity that could be ideal, but if you experience a setback be positive as something new waits in the wings.

LEO • SEPTEMBER

October

WEEK 1: 1–7 OCTOBER

A change of pace or of place may involve complex logistics but could be delightful despite the effort involved. Certain discussions and arrangements could even set in place a fresh commitment that could bring long-term stability. Avoid arguments, especially this weekend, and look for great ways to boost your health and well-being. You may be drawn to re-evaluate aspects of your home life, family or property over the coming weeks.

WEEK 2: 8–14 OCTOBER

This weekend's Libran new moon advocates you to establish peace, especially within relationships that have seemed tense of late. You may decide that your peace of mind is important and will focus on your happiness now. However, you or someone you interact with may feel feisty, so be sure to de-escalate differences or they could spiral into conflict. You may need to renegotiate an arrangement.

WEEK 3: 15–21 OCTOBER

Work, a shared project and finances could blossom, so take the initiative. Prepare to feel more energised over the coming weeks. Avoid overstepping boundaries or you may appear to be a little bossy. Domestic, family and property matters can also progress well. However, next week you will need to be careful with negotiations, especially concerning work, health and your home life.

WEEK 4: 22–28 OCTOBER / WEEK 5: 29 OCTOBER–4 NOVEMBER

WEEK 4: key discussions either at work or home will merit a patient approach, as you could stride forward with fresh direction as a result. Above all avoid a battle of wills, as it will escalate. **WEEK 5:** Mars in your sign makes a tough angle with Mercury, bringing the need to review some personal and domestic matters. Be positive as you could make inroads towards Wednesday.

HEALTH

There are therapeutic astrological aspects, especially early in October, that could help you improve your health, so reach out to friends and organisations. A change in your usual schedule could be intense, so be sure to provide yourself with extra time and space to adapt to a fresh routine. If you feel that some aspects of your life are painful or you simply feel vulnerable, be sure to consider the help of an expert who can help you maintain high self-esteem.

FINANCES

Your financial circumstances may seem unavoidable, as your situation stems from past actions such as financial arrangements. There are nevertheless therapeutic ways you can move forward; for example, if you are in debt. For some lucky Leos this month brings the opportunity to create more financial stability and security. Developments towards the 16th will provide insight into your true position. You may even experience a financial boost towards 4 November.

HOME

Retrograde Venus will encourage you to quietly re-evaluate aspects of your home life, family or a property. This is certainly a very good month to improve décor or even for a restructure at home. However, some arrangements may take longer than you hope, so be patient and work towards a resolution, especially towards the 10th, 20th and 30th. You may need to choose between work and/or your status and domestic decisions towards the end of October.

LOVE LIFE

You become aware already early in October about the importance of the soul-based, also known as karmic, connections you have with others, and this is comforting on many levels and also therapeutic. When making considerable decisions ensure that you take others into consideration as discussions of your plans and hopes for the future are best undertaken with those they will affect. Avoid a battle of wills towards the end of the month as this could derail the best-laid plans.

WORK

The opposition between Mars and Pluto early in the month may bring intense developments at work or at least within your daily routine. Be sure to avoid allowing these to disrupt your peace of mind or, worse, to disrupt your relationship with colleagues, employees or employers, especially towards the 2nd, 20th and 26th. This aside, you have a wonderful opportunity towards the 16th and at the end of the month to make considerable progress at work so take the initiative.

LEO · OCTOBER

November

WEEK 1: 5–11 NOVEMBER

Monday's new moon will kick-start a fresh chapter in your domestic world. Developments may feel a little intense, but if you invest time and energy into your home life you are likely to appreciate the outcome. This could also mean a change with family or regarding property. For some, though, developments will revolve around your deepening spirituality. Be sure to avoid arguments for the best results.

WEEK 2: 12–18 NOVEMBER

This will be a super-significant week as you gain the opportunity to boost your self-esteem and finances. For some, though, this week will all be about the connections you make, both in your personal life and at work. You can make great strides ahead in both areas. A get-together will be super significant and could also be therapeutic for your status.

WEEK 3: 19–25 NOVEMBER

You may be surprised by developments this week, so the more grounded and practical you are the better will be the outcome for you. You'll again the opportunity to improve both your personal life and status. Some developments may even be therapeutic; for example, a holiday or favourite activity could take off. However, you must avoid impulsiveness, especially towards Friday. You will appreciate a lovely reunion.

WEEK 4: 26 NOVEMBER–2 DECEMBER

You could gain a commitment from someone and, at the least, feel you are in a stronger position, so be sure to take the initiative both at work and in your personal life. However, some conversations may bring out your sensitivities, so pace yourself and avoid arguments. You may experience a financial or work improvement, but if the opposite occurs be diligent as a fresh option will bring more stability.

  2026 **HOROSCOPES**

HEALTH

Mid-month and towards the 29th may be stressful. For some Leos this will nevertheless mean a great deal of positive change, but even positive change can feel overwhelming. It will therefore be important for you to maintain your physical health routine, especially at super-stressful times. It will also be in your interest to look for other ways, such as emotional, spiritual and mental health routines, to maintain a positive outlook and manage stress.

FINANCES

You may enjoy a financial improvement towards the new moon on the 9th that may be connected with developments regarding home, a property or family. Once again, mid-month and towards the 29th it is possible that developments either at work or home will boost your financial circumstances. Avoid making impulsive investments or financial transactions at this time and, if necessary, consult an expert, especially if you feel under pressure.

HOME

The new moon on the 9th signals a fresh chapter at home, with family or property. In the lead-up avoid unnecessary arguments and consider how to invest constructively to find peace, calm and harmony at home. As a result, this is what you will find. Changes at home, with family or someone special mid-month will put you on a fresh track, and you'll gain a sense of clarity. Developments towards the 29th may bring out your vulnerabilities, so remain positive.

LOVE LIFE

Singles will appreciate the synchronicity or seemingly haphazardness of a meeting with someone mid-month that may in fact have karmic elements to it. Be discerning as you meet new people rather than simply assuming that a karmic connection will equal happiness. You may tend to be a little impulsive. You may even be drawn to reunite with an ex, but must carefully consider this. Couples will appreciate a therapeutic development that enables you to rekindle romance and a sense of security.

WORK

You are moving towards considerable transformation at work, so the more aware you are of this the more likely you will make the most of opportunities. You'll gain the chance to turn a corner within your career towards the end of the month, so in the lead-up the more realistic and less impulsive you are the better for you when opportunity knocks. You may need to sacrifice one goal for another.

LEO • NOVEMBER

December

WEEK 1: 3–9 DECEMBER

Prepare to turn a corner at home, with family or in your domestic life. You'll enjoy being more outgoing but may unintentionally tread on someone's feet, so be careful with communications both at home and work. You may benefit by sharing key duties or finances in a new way. Be prepared to think outside the box about your options. A trip or holiday will appeal.

WEEK 2: 10–16 DECEMBER

You'll get the chance to review some of your ideas about a domestic, family or personal matter. If you work with property or property matters have been on your mind you may receive key news. This will be a lovely week to deepen your connection with someone special, so be sure to take the initiative as you will appreciate the outcome, not only in the relationship but also in your self-worth.

WEEK 3: 17–23 DECEMBER

You will appreciate the therapeutic influence of similarly minded people in your environment, and a fast pace also suits your mindset now. However, developments may predispose you to forgetfulness and an inability to focus on important details such as finances, so be sure to keep an eye on spending and overindulgence to avoid debt. Some lucky Leos will be embarking on a holiday, while others may experience a financial or career boost.

WEEK 4: 24–31 DECEMBER

The full moon supermoon this Christmas Eve will encourage you to adopt a caring approach to a social and family setting. Your relationships will take an upturn as a result and you'll feel more light-hearted going into 2027. However, you will need to demonstrate patience, especially if you are travelling or undertaking projects and ventures that are outside your comfort zone. You'll feel more in your element towards New Year's Eve.

HEALTH

You will be drawn to approach life from an idealistic point of view, which in many respects could lead to wonderful outcomes as you may enjoy travelling, the arts or spiritual self-development. A holiday or trip could also be ideal. However, in the process it will be important to keep an eye on your interactions as you may tend to inadvertently ruffle feathers. This will lead to stress, the opposite of having a perfect time.

FINANCES

You'll have the opportunity to improve your financial circumstances through careful management. Mars in the meticulous sign of Virgo in your money zone until mid-July 2027 will certainly help with planning. However, in the short term you may need to manage overspending as the festive season approaches. Be sure to put a careful budget in place to avoid debt. That said, some Leos will experience a financial boost towards the 12th and 18th.

HOME

December is an excellent month to be adventurous with your home life. Developments may go well towards the 12th. Some Leos will be drawn to travel and others to invite guests over. A change of environment or even a move will be uplifting but inevitably comes with a little upheaval, so factor this into your plans. A patient approach to those you share space with will be advantageous, as otherwise a battle of wills could mar an otherwise festive month.

LOVE LIFE

The new moon on the 9th kick-starts a fresh chapter in your personal life. If you live with your partner this new chapter could take you into exciting territory; however, you must avoid arguments, especially towards the 5th, 8th, 9th and 21st. You'll gain the opportunity on the weekend beginning the 18th to enjoy the therapeutic company of someone you love. This weekend and New Year's Eve will be excellent for singles to meet like-minded people and enjoy romance.

WORK

The big-picture process for you is one of transformation and success. Be positive and maintain sight of your goals because you may undergo circumstances that try your patience or even willpower, especially at the start of the month. However, around the 18th you are likely to experience a positive development within your career or status, but if you experience disappointments at this time rest assured that development will ultimately take you to a better situation.

LEO • DECEMBER

January

WEEK 1: 1–7 JANUARY

A key relationship such as your connection with an organisation or friend will be in the spotlight. You may find that someone close is more sensitive than usual and you'll need to tread lightly. It's a good week to consider joining new organisations or circles. Some Virgos will begin a fresh cycle in your status or career so prepare to alter domestic circumstances if need be, especially on Tuesday.

WEEK 2: 8–14 JANUARY

Your creativity and relationships could blossom. A fun and dynamic approach to your favourite projects may boost your circumstances, so take the initiative! A change of focus could require you to adapt this weekend or on Monday, as the concerns of someone close or a key project takes your focus. A change in a personal agreement or arrangement is worth considering.

WEEK 3: 15–21 JANUARY

You may wonder whether it's you or other people who seem to be missing the point: in conversations and in the bigger picture. Avoid contributing to muddles by keeping your feet on the ground, as this could otherwise be a confusing week. Sunday/Monday's new moon will kick-start a fresh phase with family or someone special, and you'll feel inclined to embrace fresh projects. An unexpected career boost or personal success will delight.

WEEK 4: 22–28 JANUARY

You'll enjoy feeling creative over the next few days. If you're in the mood for dancing and romancing this week could be ideal, but look out: someone's opinions may prove to be intense. You may feel strongly about a personal matter yourself. If you're single you may meet someone attractive, so be sure to organise events, outings and dates. Creative Virgos could produce great work.

HEALTH

The plethora of planets in the sign of Aquarius from the 20th will encourage you to look outside the box at your options to maintain a healthy lifestyle. You may even surprise yourself with some of the activities you choose, and if you have been drawn to complementary medicine and activities such as meditation and spiritual development you are likely to experience a boost in mental, spiritual and emotional well-being.

FINANCES

This month will bring opportunities to improve your daily work life, so be sure to keep an eye out for options and be prepared to negotiate so you are able to receive adequate remuneration for your hard work. This is certainly a good month to consider where you would like to see yourself financially this year, and the end of the month is particularly conducive to finding something new or potentially even gaining a promotion.

HOME

The new moon on the 18th/19th will be conducive to begin something new at home, especially if you were born mid-September. You may be ready for a move, renovation or new housemate. If you're travelling you'll love bringing some of the unusual aspects from your destination back into your home to improve your home life. You may even be inspired to move but must plan carefully and avoid making impulsive actions.

LOVE LIFE

Love can thrive early in the month so be sure to invest in this important aspect of your life, especially around the weekend of the 10th and 11th. If you're in a couple the concerns of your partner must be factored into your decisions to avoid complexities; you may be asked to take their opinion into account. The conjunction of Mars and Pluto towards the 27th will ignite passion, so be sure to organise a date but avoid arguments.

WORK

If you're in a creative field you'll be busy early in the month, as you'll gain the opportunity to broaden your interests in practical ways. However, if you work with others it will be in your interest to be diplomatic and tactful, especially during the second week of the month up until the new moon on the 18th. You may receive an unexpected offer of promotion, and if you're looking to move jobs this is the time to do it. Be positive!

VIRGO • JANUARY

February

WEEK 1: 29 JANUARY–4 FEBRUARY

Get set to turn a page as you will be ready to let go of a chapter. This may arise via a change of routine, work or your health or simply because you realise more about what and who mean the most to you. News at work or concerning health may require an innovative approach, and developments will provide a sense of direction.

WEEK 2: 5–11 FEBRUARY

A change of routine will boost your mood but you must be well prepared, have a plan of action and be able to adapt to a new environment, as otherwise abrupt schedule changes could derail even the best-laid plans. A financial or work boost could be on the way, and at the very least a work or health matter will draw your focus. You are in line for surprising news.

WEEK 3: 12–18 FEBRUARY

Get set to turn a corner at work. You may be ready for something quirky or different: something involving your imagination or a new daily routine. For some this week's developments will revolve around a better health schedule, more time to enjoy life or a fresh diet. However, watch out for impulsiveness or even mistakes, especially around St Valentine's Day.

WEEK 4: 19–25 FEBRUARY / WEEK 5: 26 FEBRUARY–4 MARCH

WEEK 4: this is a good time to make plans with those you love. Base decisions on facts, not assumptions, especially with shared finances and long-term investments. You'll enjoy socialising towards the 22nd. **WEEK 5:** for some the end of February will involve focus on commitments or a work opportunity. The lunar eclipse on 3 March in Virgo will help you turn a corner in your personal life, especially if you were born in August.

HEALTH

Be prepared to think outside the box about your health and well-being in February, and use your intuition to guide you with regard to better health. A change of routine or specific health news will help you improve your well-being. You may be drawn to consider a fresh look as well, which may even be something you wouldn't normally choose but it will provide a sense of the changing tides.

FINANCES

There is a degree of unpredictability about your general status, especially in connection with your work and finances. For this reason it is in your interest to secure a bottom-line financial safety net so you know you have a small kitty available in the event of a rainy day. However, you are just as likely to enjoy a financial boost as you are a setback, so be sure to take the initiative with work opportunities to ensure your finances stay afloat.

HOME

February kick-starts an eclipse season, which are invariably intense. The second of the series of two eclipses will be in your sign on 3 March, and it will focus attention on your personal life if you were born in August and your work and health life if you were born in September. Both scenarios could have an impact on your home life and family, so be prepared to see this important aspect of your life as a part of any choices you make now.

LOVE LIFE

You'll appreciate the opportunity to consider fresh ways to relate with someone special and this could add sparkle to your love life, especially for August Virgos. If you are single be prepared to try new ways to meet people; for example, if you have up till now rejected online dating, the plethora of planets in Aquarius may help you see the benefits. If you are tired of online dating you'll be ready to consider meeting people through other means.

WORK

A flexible and upbeat attitude to the changing face of your everyday schedule will help you stay on top of a changeable routine. It's a good month to be open to learning new skill sets and investing in your work life with an inquisitive mind, as new opportunities will present themselves. If you have a choice regarding how you configure a fresh schedule be sure to factor in the relative merit of a safe and healthy routine.

March

WEEK 1: 5–11 MARCH

You'll appreciate the chance to reconnect with someone you admire or love. You may be drawn to be more sociable and will enjoy networking. It's a good week for communications, so be sure to take the initiative with important talks both at home and work. A collaboration such as a work relationship could go well; just avoid making rash decisions based on expectations rather than realities.

WEEK 2: 12–18 MARCH

This will be a good week to decide how you'd like to move forward in your personal life, such as with a love affair or family. Creative Virgos can make great headway with your projects but you must keep communications clear, especially towards mid-week next week. Singles may meet someone you feel a close affinity with, especially if you were born at the end of August or early September, so be sure to organise dates.

WEEK 3: 19–25 MARCH

Singles may be drawn to a fresh personal relationship at this time and couples to bringing more inspiration and fun into your relationship. It's a good weekend for socialising. You may also be drawn to make a commitment to a venture or person but you must avoid being super idealistic. Check the facts, and if everything lines up you may experience a wonderful opportunity that may even be unexpected.

WEEK 4: 26 MARCH–1 APRIL

A healthy boost or outdoors activity will raise morale. Someone may unexpectedly ask for your help. You will appreciate the opportunity to devote at least some time to your health and well-being. You may enjoy a visit somewhere therapeutic. A change of routine or unusual event may surprise you next week or will represent a change of schedule.

HEALTH

March is a favourable month for you to look at ways you can improve your health and fitness regime. You may be particularly drawn to self-development and spiritual understanding this month and will find the end of March, especially towards the 26th, particularly healing. A change in your usual working schedule or daily routine could also be revitalising, so be sure to schedule a short break if possible.

FINANCES

As a perfectionist you like to stay on top of your budget, so in comparison with other zodiac signs you tend not to experience too many surprises financially due to negligence. Keep an eye mid-month, however, on some of your joint expenditures such as household expenses you share with others or family duties. You may need to adjust which organisation or business you depend upon for utilities, for example, to maximise your budget.

HOME

An adventurous and outgoing approach to your home life in March will certainly reap rewards. Be sure to seek the collaboration and cooperation of those within your home as this will also be productive. As it is possible that you begin to see your direction in life in a slightly new light or simply that a career or shared circumstance changes, rest assured you will be able to organise your home life accordingly.

LOVE LIFE

You're stepping into a fresh chapter in your primary relationship. For some this will be because your partner is feeling more positive and outgoing, while some Virgos may be feeling more outgoing yourself as you look for more diverse activities and fun in your love life. If you're single and looking for a commitment you may experience one now, although it will take you into fresh relationship dynamics so be sure you're ready, especially mid-month.

WORK

This is an excellent month to step into fresh territory both work-wise and with your ambitions and general direction. You may even experience a lucky break, so if you're looking for work be sure to circulate your résumé and meet people as you could step up now. You may be surprised by some developments towards the 18th. Keep communications clear as best you can as new opportunities will arise.

VIRGO · MARCH ✦ 139

April

WEEK 1: 2–8 APRIL

Mercury and Mars in Pisces puts the focus on your relationships. You'll enjoy socialising at the end of this week and at the weekend. However, some people may seem less reliable, more idealistic or vague or even feistier, so be sure to maintain an even keel in your relationships where possible. You may be drawn to reconfigure some of your financial arrangements.

WEEK 2: 9–15 APRIL

Ask yourself which activities and people you most wish to invest in. This will be a good week to bring favourite activities and people whose company you truly enjoy to the forefront of your life. If you are single you may meet someone alluring this weekend or on Monday. A social event or project is likely to go well on Monday but it's always good to be well prepared.

WEEK 3: 16–22 APRIL

The more you believe you will succeed the more you will! Avoid feeling overwhelmed by developments by organising your week in advance. You'll feel re-energised by turning a corner with a business or personal venture. You may be prepared to make a commitment. This is a good week to focus on your health and well-being and that of someone close.

WEEK 4: 23–29 APRIL

You'll appreciate a change of pace and may also enjoy a change of environment, either at work or in your spare time. You may even be surprised by developments towards Friday. This is certainly a good week to focus on your favourite activities and people. Romance can also thrive towards the weekend and mid-week next week, so be sure to organise a treat.

HEALTH

This is a good month to find a group or organisation with a health focus, so if you've been looking for a sports team, gym or martial arts group, for example, be sure to reach out early in the month as you are likely to find a group that suits. The new moon on the 17th has a strong link with health, so beginning anything new in the second half of April is likely to be therapeutic.

FINANCES

The full moon on the 2nd will spotlight a financial matter that will benefit from information from a friend or organisation. This matter may be particularly connected with shared aspects of your finances; for example, a mortgage or taxes. Look for the most balanced way forward. Avoid gambling, especially on the 4th, 5th and 24th. You may need to pay attention to your budget towards the 25th and must avoid arguments with people you share finances with.

HOME

There will be various activities or aspects of your life that will be up in the air by the end of the month. As an earth sign you prefer to know where you're heading and keep your feet on the ground. Your home life needn't be an uncertain aspect of your life, but to avoid this occurring it will be in your interest to minimise arguments and conflict between the 23rd and 27th as these could snowball.

LOVE LIFE

This is a good month to establish a stronger relationship with someone special, particularly regarding the long-term security you are looking for. However, you must avoid allowing this wish to morph into a degree of controlling or controlled effort as control issues could arise, especially around the 4th. Aim to find a balanced way to establish more stability in your love life. You will find out a little more towards the 12th whether you have over- or underestimated someone.

WORK

The start of April has excellent stars for communications, so this is a good time to boost your work relationships as you could create better camaraderie, especially around the 12th and 13th. This is also a good time to build on your strengths, especially if you are looking to make considerable changes in the long term in your career. The new moon on the 17th could kick-start a fresh venture, and you may also commit to a new agreement.

VIRGO · APRIL

WEEK 1: 30 APRIL–6 MAY

Friday/Saturday's full moon will spotlight the importance of good communication skills, and while your skills may be wide ranging, news will spotlight the need for a different approach or arrangement regarding study, travel or negotiations. You may need to update digital devices or repair a vehicle, for example. For some Virgos this week's developments will highlight the importance of careful sharing of information or finances.

WEEK 2: 7–13 MAY

You'll enjoy a social event and being with like-minded people. This is also a good week to commit to a particular project or venture that resonates with you. Financially, there will be incentives to put in place a budget or arrangement with someone with whom you share finances. You may be repaid a debt or will manage to repay one yourself.

WEEK 3: 14–20 MAY

You'll gain reassurance that your plans and activities can work, especially at work and with someone special. If you've been planning a trip, study, spiritual development or simply just have a long-term desire for more stability in your life, this is the week you're likely to see progress. However, you must avoid allowing a difficult circumstance to linger and find ways to progress constructively.

WEEK 4: 21–27 MAY / WEEK 5: 28 MAY–3 JUNE

WEEK 4: you'll enjoy the opportunity to deepen a relationship: for some this will be at work and for others at home. You'll need to adjust to a change of routine or in your direction, career or status. **WEEK 5:** a fresh phase in your domestic life around the full moon on the 31st will be exciting, but you must ensure agreements you undertake are super clear to avoid making mistakes.

HEALTH

A holiday or short trip and time spent engaging with your favourite activities will certainly revitalise your energy levels. May's two full moons will help you organise something special. Be sure to take the initiative and plan activities you love and that you know are good for the soul. You may even be drawn to something different towards the 22nd. Ask yourself whether your current health routine works for you and, if not, it's time for a change.

FINANCES

The full moon on 1/2 May will spotlight important financial or business-related matters that deserve attention. It'll be important to decide where your priorities lie with a person or project, for example. Aim to organise finances so you are able to best support your aims without adding fuel to the fires of conflict, especially early in the month. The second week of May will be an excellent time to put in place new financial arrangements concerning shared finances.

HOME

The prevailing mood in May is one of change within your relationships and communications. You are likely to be drawn to activities that take you out of your home such as travel, but for some Virgos and especially August-born Virgos the focus towards the end of the month will be on revitalising your home and interpersonal dynamics there. It's a good month to be adventurous, whether you are drawn to travel or home transformation.

LOVE LIFE

As Pluto begins a retrograde phase you may discover there are aspects of your close relationship you are ready to learn from and transform. A partner or someone you love may need more time or space than usual or even a degree of care and attention you hadn't until now realised they needed. You may discover a vulnerability in them or the relationship. If so it will provide an opportunity to overcome differences.

WORK

Be prepared to step into fresh territory within your career and at work. The new moon supermoon on the 16th/17th will encourage you to be practical about any changes you make and also to follow your heart and engage in activities you love. You may even be drawn to make a commitment to a project or career move. Towards the 22nd you're likely to experience a surprise or the upshot of developments in your work and projects. Be prepared to innovate.

VIRGO · MAY

June

WEEK 1: 4–10 JUNE

This is a lovely week for socialising and get-togethers with dynamic people whose company you enjoy or admire. You could make valid work agreements and commitments but you must research terms and conditions to avoid disappointment further down the track. Ensure you carefully consider developments towards next Tuesday and avoid taking adverse developments personally.

WEEK 2: 11–17 JUNE

Prepare for a fresh chapter in your status, general direction or career that will be more in line with your upbeat, busy and sociable personality. Your interests and even love life could blossom: for some Virgos in unexpected ways, as you may enjoy an impromptu date or social event. If a friend or organisation lets you down be prepared to see the situation for what it is: a lack of dependability.

WEEK 3: 18–24 JUNE

A fairly intense weekend and a change of circumstance could bring out your inner drama queen, so be sure to maintain perspective. A lovely health or beauty treat will appeal in preparation for a change of routine or social event. Romance could flourish, so plan a date. A favourite activity will be therapeutic. For some, a busy week at work means projects will blossom.

WEEK 4: 25 JUNE–1 JULY

This will be a good week for collaborations, especially at work, although you may also enjoy a reunion with someone special. Monday/Tuesday's earthy full moon could create a feeling of more stability where your home life, family or property-related matters are concerned. Both work and health could benefit from decision-making that provides more security in your life.

HEALTH

Developments currently would make it easy for you to ignore your health and vitality, largely because you have a relatively free pass this month in this respect. However, if you're not careful you will be living off your nerves, as opposed to pools of reserve energy. For this reason it's important to take regular breaks during the working week and schedule fun events that replenish your happiness.

FINANCES

Keep an eye on your finances towards mid-June, as you may be inclined to see some of your commitments in an idealised way as opposed to in a realistic light. However, if you are able to put in place a stable budget in June you can make a great deal of headway this month. You may experience a positive development at work towards the 18th that could also improve your finances.

HOME

Your attention is likely to go more towards your career and activities and home life in the first part of the month. However, important decisions or developments connected with family, a property or your home life are likely to bring your attention back to these important aspects towards the full moon on the 29th/30th. Be prepared to make important decisions, especially in relation to overheads, expenses and shared duties.

LOVE LIFE

It is possible that some communications are more stressful or difficult than you may prefer within your close relationships, especially mid-month, so be sure to avoid making assumptions should some developments be intense. If you are single the period around the 9th and 18th will be perfect for meeting upbeat and interesting people, so be sure to socialise or organise events. Once again, however, avoid taking people's random comments personally.

WORK

For some Virgos developments already early in June concerning your work and career may feature tense communications, so be sure to be clear about your intentions. If you are drawn to a new project or job, ensure the terms and conditions are very clear to avoid misunderstandings further down the line. The new moon supermoon on the 15th and developments towards the 18th may bring a surprise development your way that opens doors.

VIRGO · JUNE

July

WEEK 1: 2–8 JULY

You'll achieve a lot by focusing on chores and making time for your favourite activities. Be spontaneous, as a change in your usual activities could help you gain self-esteem and happiness. If you've already planned a holiday it'll take you somewhere different. A difference of opinion with someone special or an organisation is best handled diplomatically to avoid matters escalating. Avoid focusing on what's not working; focus instead on what is.

WEEK 2: 9–15 JULY

Venus enters your sign and will bring your attention to love and money. You will find your attention goes to someone you have a fated link with, either in your love life or family. If you're single you may meet someone significant, so be sure to organise dates! Just be careful to avoid misunderstandings early next week and make a wish on the new moon.

WEEK 3: 16–22 JULY

Whether you're looking to change your personal life, activities or status this is an excellent week to take the initiative. Just ensure that you have done adequate research rather than jumping into new situations, as impulsiveness could set you back several steps. Ensure you are also not seeing life through rose-coloured glasses as this would be a true pitfall.

WEEK 4: 23–29 JULY

The sun in Leo will add a spring to your step this week and it is a good time for socialising and taking your favourite projects seriously, as you could make great headway. The full moon on the 29th/30th will spotlight your personal life and specifically your feelings towards someone special. It's likely this is an intense time, so be sure to pace yourself.

HEALTH

Many Virgos will have the opportunity to do something different such as travelling somewhere you have never been before or finding the time for your favourite activities. If you have been meaning to attend a self-development class, for example, or visit a family member, the start of the month and mid-month are particularly conducive for securing plans. Be sure to focus on your own happiness, as in this way you will find ways to boost it.

FINANCES

Be prepared early in the month already to make necessary arrangements financially with those you must rely on, such as partners and banks, to ensure that you have a smoothly running cash flow. Be prepared to keep lines of communication open with a friend or organisation so you do not limit your options. Shared finances will require additional focus as you may discover you have an idealistic view of taxes or shared household expenses, for example.

HOME

Changes in your domestic and family life will prove to be long term, so be sure when you make decisions that you keep an eye on your goals as you otherwise will tend to see only short-term scenarios, especially if you're under pressure. A personal situation will drive change in your status and this will have an impact on the areas you share such as your home, so be sure to research your situation before taking action.

LOVE LIFE

It's a mixed bag at the start of the month: you have as equal a chance to enjoy a super-romantic start to July if you focus on your romantic life as you do that you argue with someone special and it becomes a prolonged conflict. The choice, to a degree, is yours. Mid-month and towards the 27th are ideal for romance and if you're single to meet someone compatible, so ensure you organise dates then.

WORK

Be innovative and investigate new ideas and even the chance to broaden your horizons, as it's all change for you career-wise and within your usual activities. For some Virgos this will mean a change in your career and for others simply the chance to take a well-earned break. If you have had communication difficulties with someone at work these may come to a head. It's far better to fix differences early in the month rather than allow them to escalate.

VIRGO · JULY

August

WEEK 1: 30 JULY–5 AUGUST

You'll experience intense interactions with people unless you ensure you find common ground and avoid conflict. This is not always possible as you cannot be responsible for someone else's reactions; however, you can build careful and steady relationships with those you cannot avoid interacting with such as colleagues. This is a good time to work towards a business or personal commitment.

WEEK 2: 6–12 AUGUST

The solar eclipse on the 12th/13th will stimulate a need to turn a corner in practical ways, especially concerning the past, work and health. You'll do well to research your circumstances as opposed to taking a leap and making enquiries afterwards. For some Virgos developments this week will spotlight a change in your social life. Some interactions are likely to be intense while others will be truly romantic.

WEEK 3: 13–19 AUGUST

You'll be reminded of the past, and a reunion or simple nostalgia will draw your focus. News to do with health or a change of schedule at work may mean you must adjust to circumstances. Rest assured that when you do you will gain a steadier foothold within your projects, even if at first there is a little disruption. You may be pleasantly surprised by unexpected developments early next week.

WEEK 4: 20–26 AUGUST / WEEK 5: 27 AUGUST–2 SEPTEMBER

WEEK 4: your energy levels will improve and you may also gain the opportunity to indulge in activities that raise your spirits. It's a good week to make a financial commitment as long as you have researched the facts. **WEEK 5:** be prepared for a fresh chapter at work or regarding health. If you were born before 27 August you may experience key developments in your love life.

HEALTH

This is a good month to create a strong health schedule. Be prepared to look into collaborations with experts, medical professionals and sports teams to improve your fitness. You may experience a build-up of energy and wonder where it all comes from, and if you do not have fitness routines already to hand that help you channel this energy you may feel a little frustrated, so be sure to put in place energetic health routines.

FINANCES

You'll gain the opportunity in August to embrace positive financial developments, largely due to changes either at work or in your status. Be prepared to embrace new ventures, as they are likely to be beneficial and will bring financial security in the long term. It is a good month to plan long-term financial stability as your endeavours are likely to be productive, but you must seek correct information and avoid acting simply on trust or hunches alone.

HOME

The eclipses this month on the 12th/13th and 28th will primarily affect your work and daily routine. For some, though, additional focus on your health will be necessary. These areas are the most prone to change in August. However, a change in your usual schedule will impact so many different areas of your life, especially your home life, so it's in your interest to keep an eye on maintaining the status quo at home.

LOVE LIFE

The first week of the month culminates with Venus entering Libra, the sign it rules. You may find romance thrives at the start of August but you must be careful with communications to avoid misunderstandings. Mid-August is a truly romantic phase for you and will be a good time for couples to organise a break or some treats and reconnect romantically. Singles may meet someone alluring.

WORK

If you would like a commitment from someone such as a work colleague or employer this is possible towards the 7th and 21st. The total solar eclipse on the 12th/13th could kick-start a fresh commitment in a work capacity; you may even be surprised by offers that come your way. News towards the 17th will mark a turning point and could bring more stability at work. However, you may also be very busy at this time so be prepared.

VIRGO • AUGUST

September

WEEK 1: 3–9 SEPTEMBER

The sun in Virgo will encourage you to be more outgoing and practical in your personal life and communications. Someone will prove helpful regarding matters you must plan at work and you may even receive positive news at work. However, you must avoid assuming all relationships will go well and may need to be more patient with some collaborations. You'll enjoy a reunion or news from the past.

WEEK 2: 10–16 SEPTEMBER

This week's Virgo new moon signifies the chance to turn a corner in your personal life, especially if it's your birthday on Friday or Saturday. This is also a peak week for romance and improving your status in general, so if you are single this will be a good time to socialise and couples could deepen their relationship. Avoid misunderstandings, especially from the 10th to the 12th.

WEEK 3: 17–23 SEPTEMBER

Where your opinions differ to those of others it is an opportunity to explain your thoughts and position. Ensure you're diplomatic if someone's ego is at stake. Be sure to carefully approach a financial matter. If you need to make a new arrangement this is a good week to do so, but you must ensure you adequately research your circumstances and do not simply take someone at their word.

WEEK 4: 24–30 SEPTEMBER

Negotiations, trips and agreements that take you into new territory will be exciting and could also improve close relationships. Someone may be ready to commit to a new arrangement or agreement, making shared duties or finances easier to manage. If you get stuck on certain ideas, ensure you think laterally as you may discover a wonderful solution to an old problem.

HEALTH

This month you have the opportunity to improve your status, which includes your health. Your career will demand a large amount of energy, so be sure to pace yourself. Consider a health and fitness routine you can engage in with someone close; for example, a colleague or personal partner. This may initially seem as something that could be challenging, but it may in fact add another positive quality to your relationship.

FINANCES

You will find out in September whether some of your spending habits have created debt as opposed to creating enjoyable situations in life, especially towards mid-month and between the 17th and 22nd. During these phases it will be important to be circumspect around finances, especially if you must make a fresh arrangement. This arrangement may be via work or a new living circumstance. In all eventualities, be sure to gain professional financial advice if necessary.

HOME

You have positive opportunities in September to create a steady sense of progress in your personal life that will reflect in a more stable and comfortable feeling at home. However, Uranus does bring a degree of financial uncertainty as you develop and broaden your scope career-wise. Your career largely comes in growth spurts, so finding ways to stabilise your income so you feel safe and secure at home is a goal.

LOVE LIFE

Someone you rely on may be less vivacious than usual and less likely to take the initiative. It's your turn to step up and shine and bring a little fun and enjoyment to your love life: you are likely to succeed. If you are single you may meet someone attractive towards the 10th and at the full moon on the 26th. However, misunderstandings abound from the 10th to the 22nd and on the 27th, so take things carefully then.

WORK

The key to successful collaborations at work lies in good communication skills. Avoid taking inevitable restrictions and limitations or lack of empathy in some work colleagues personally. Be prepared to work hard, and you will gain ground at work and perhaps even in unexpected ways. The Virgo new moon on the 11th will be particularly favourable for those born after mid-September for beginning new projects. The full moon on the 26th will highlight the true potential of a key collaboration.

VIRGO · SEPTEMBER

October

WEEK 1: 1–7 OCTOBER

News or a trip or meeting could unexpectedly put you on a fresh path. Your sixth sense will alert you to the best way forward this week, so be sure to consult your intuition should you be unsure of decisions, especially concerning finances, a commitment and collaborations. Avoid arguments and intrigue, especially on Friday. Romance could blossom, so be sure to organise a date.

WEEK 2: 8–14 OCTOBER

You're known to be a good communicator, but even you can find communications complex if others are unclear or misunderstandings occur. If some interactions have been intense find ways to establish more balance, especially this Friday and Saturday; your efforts will have unexpected gains when you do. You'll appreciate the opportunity to find time to consider how to more effectively manage finances and personal resources.

WEEK 3: 15–21 OCTOBER

You may begin to see your energy levels return if vitality has been lacking. Look for new ways to feel energised such as enjoying a good diet and exercise. Your career and work life could thrive, so be sure to take the initiative. If you're looking for work, circulate your résumé; you may be surprised by the results. Keep an eye on good communication skills and finances next Wednesday.

WEEK 4: 22–28 OCTOBER / WEEK 5: 29 OCTOBER–4 NOVEMBER

WEEK 4: this will be an important week regarding certain discussions and negotiations. Just be sure to avoid intense interactions and look for the most therapeutic way ahead. **WEEK 5:** if you have neglected finances recently you will need to attend to these now. Be patient with a friend, collaborator or group as you could make a breakthrough as a result, with a financial or ego boost on the way.

HEALTH

You are known to be generally grounded and practical, yet even you can feel frustrated and angry. Developments at the start of the month may motivate you to find ways to have peace of mind and calm in your heart, especially if some interactions cause you to lose your usual perspective and cool. Mid-month, an activity or opportunity to spend time with like-minded people in a healthy environment will be uplifting.

FINANCES

A key financial commitment may be made early in October, towards the 10th. This may prove to be particularly lucrative as long as you have researched circumstances. Developments towards the 15th and 30th may be uplifting. However, you could easily be misled in October, so it will be important to check facts and figures. Avoid unnecessary arguments with those you must share finances with and base discussions on facts rather than feelings if you feel conflict is brewing.

HOME

Important personal and financial decisions can be made in October that are likely to have an impact on your home life. It may even be the case that you must work constructively to alter past decisions, and for this reason being constructive about domestic matters with a view to a progressive outcome will benefit you. While much of your attention will be elsewhere this month, it's important not to underestimate the importance of a steady home life.

LOVE LIFE

The first weekend of October is a romantic time, and you may be inclined to make a commitment to someone close. If you are single, socialising and romance will appeal. However, this phase does feature the likelihood of intense feelings. There is also the likelihood of tempers becoming frayed, especially towards the 1st, at the new moon on the 10th/11th and towards the 30th. You may be drawn to an ex but must evaluate eventualities.

WORK

Your key to success in October at work revolves around your ability to take the initiative, and not only to be brave and venture into fresh territory but also to manage strong emotions or difficult communications. You may experience an unexpected promotion or positive business success early in the month around the 7th and mid-month and then towards the 30th, but you must be careful with negotiations to secure the financial aspect of work.

VIRGO • OCTOBER

November

WEEK 1: 5–11 NOVEMBER

This is an excellent week to find ways to improve communications and avoid misunderstandings; you'll experience better relationships as a result. A new device may boost communications, and you'll enjoy the opportunity to meet and greet new people. Towards Tuesday you may receive positive work or financial news and will at least experience an ego boost. You'll enjoy a reunion.

WEEK 2: 12–18 NOVEMBER

When you look at developments at work or health-wise you may see that they have been a long time coming. However, you may also feel that developments have come very suddenly despite this, so you will need to be on your toes. Avoid misunderstandings, especially on Friday. For some lucky Virgos this week's developments signal the opportunity to change your usual working schedule and take a break.

WEEK 3: 19–25 NOVEMBER

The full moon supermoon will help you turn a corner within your career, and if you are not working there will be a change either in status or direction. Work towards your goals, as you can achieve them; they may even be therapeutic. For some Virgos a holiday is on the cards, and for others improvement in your daily routine and health. You'll enjoy romantic or domestic improvements mid-week.

WEEK 4: 26 NOVEMBER–2 DECEMBER

Now that Mars is in Virgo you're likely to experience improved energy levels over the coming weeks. However, you may feel restless sometimes and may be seen as aggressive, so keep your temper in check. You will appreciate a change of pace or of place and may also enjoy a reunion or return to an old haunt. A positive development at home or with someone special will raise morale. Avoid overspending.

HEALTH

Health and well-being will be a focus early in the month, mid-month and towards the end of November, and you'll gain the motivation to look more deeply into a particular health circumstance of your own or of someone close. Be prepared to take action to improve your health, and be sure to research and reach out to experts as their input will measurably benefit you. A holiday or at least a short break will also improve your health.

FINANCES

You may experience a financial improvement, as you'll gain the opportunity to create an environment at work that better suits you. This in turn will impact your finances positively, so be sure to negotiate terms tactfully and diplomatically should the opportunity arise to improve your work circumstances. If money has been an issue during the first two weeks of the month, rest assured things will begin to improve with due diligence. You must avoid overspending, especially towards the 29th.

HOME

The key to a happy home revolves around good communication skills and the willingness to adapt to circumstances. The full moon supermoon on the 24th/25th may even bring a surprise your way that will have an impact on your home or family life. Keep channels of communication open so you are able to negotiate and collaborate with those concerned. You'll gain the opportunity to create a more stable environment at home without losing the sense of fun and adventure.

LOVE LIFE

Developments in your love life could include a change in status; for example, from single to married or single to dating. You will gain the opportunity to move your circumstances forward in whichever direction you like. Particularly romantic times will be towards the end of the month but this is not to say that you cannot build towards romance, as you will certainly find your efforts succeed: if not this month, then next month.

WORK

You may receive good news concerning work already towards the 9th or 10th, and if you have been looking for something new both the start and end of November may bring options. Be careful with your communications, especially on the 13th and 19th. A change of pace mid-month may be as simple as a holiday. Some will gain the opportunity to turbocharge your working life, and when the opportunity arises be sure to take the initiative.

VIRGO · NOVEMBER

December

WEEK 1: 3–9 DECEMBER

You'll enjoy getting into the seasonal festive mood and making changes at home due to receiving guests or taking a trip. You will appreciate and enjoy being in touch with someone close such as a family member. It's in your interest, however, to avoid contentious topics as arguments are possible either at work or at home, particularly on Friday and Wednesday.

WEEK 2: 10–16 DECEMBER

This is an excellent time to engage in tactful conversation with someone who is unavoidably in your life such as a colleague or partner. You're likely to enjoy a lovely get-together this weekend, and if some matters have been stressful you'll manage to establish a practical solution to conundrums, so be sure to build bridges. Developments at home could deepen your understanding of someone you love.

WEEK 3: 17–23 DECEMBER

Mars in your sign is bringing out your determination and willpower. However, you must be careful, especially towards the 21st, to avoid arguments as it's far better to maintain sight of your goals and achieve them. You are likely this week to enjoy considerable success, especially in relation to your domestic life and at work if you work with property. Be careful with details towards the 23rd to avoid misunderstandings.

WEEK 4: 24–31 DECEMBER

You will enjoy the seasonal festivities and the chance to deepen your links with those you love. However, someone close to you may surprise you, and this may present initially as an inconvenience or challenge. However, if you remain diligent you can still achieve your goal this week: enjoying a break. Avoid entering into conflict with someone who can be infuriating, as this would become long-standing.

HEALTH

You may be prone to overwork, especially early in the month. A change in your circumstances may create a little stress, so it's important that you manage this by timetabling stress-busting activities right at the start of the month and then stick to the schedule. There are therapeutic aspects in December, especially around the 18th and 23rd, and these will enable you to alter your usual routine so you enjoy the season all the more.

FINANCES

Venus in the passionate sign of Scorpio this December will be in your money box, suggesting you will be prone to overspend. It is likely, however, that you will also gain a financial boost but you must then be careful not to spend more than what comes in. You will also have a tendency to speculate this month and this could lead to disappointment. It's far better to plan financially than to gamble.

HOME

You'll appreciate the opportunity to make changes at home that provide a sense of freedom and adventure. You may be drawn to travel or to receive visitors and will enjoy improving décor to suit the occasion. However, you may be tempted to overspend, especially early in the month, so be careful to avoid debt. You will enjoy bringing the seasonal atmosphere into your home, and the weekend beginning the 18th may see developments that turbocharge happy circumstances.

LOVE LIFE

Romance can thrive, especially towards the 7th, 11th, 14th, 25th and 28th, so be sure to make plans to enjoy this romantic time. Early December is an excellent time to plan a holiday or trip. A change at home could bring a more settled yet proactive feel to your relationship. Changes domestically towards the 18th create a busy time, which you'll enjoy. However, if you are missing someone be sure to find ways to nevertheless enjoy the season.

WORK

Uranus at the zenith of your chart brings a variable and changeable month work-wise. Be sure to schedule in your favourite activities and projects, as otherwise you may be at the beck and call of everyone. Aim to delineate what is your duty and what is that of other people to avoid overwork. If you work in property you may be particularly busy this week, so be sure to pace yourself.

VIRGO • DECEMBER

January

WEEK 1: 1–7 JANUARY

As the new year begins this week's full moon on the 3rd brings a fresh chapter within your career or direction and within your status, and this will have an impact on your home life or family. Someone has surprise news for you or will reveal their failings or weaknesses. It's a good week for home renovations, gardening or even a move. Romance can flourish, so organise a treat!

WEEK 2: 8–14 JANUARY

Domestic developments could be ideal, and you'll enjoy being hands-on with circumstances to bring the best out in them. You'll appreciate a little touch of luxury in your home. Be prepared to enter fresh territory with your various domestic arrangements. A visit or holiday will be enjoyable but you must pay attention to details. A change in your usual routine will merit attention to details in your communications.

WEEK 3: 15–21 JANUARY

This is an excellent week to focus on practicalities, especially at home and work, as otherwise frustrating delays may distract you from your priorities. Changes at home should be enjoyable, but a trip, visit or news will mean a change of environment and the necessity to keep an eye on your health and a fresh schedule. Someone will surprise you, but you're ready to adopt a fresh attitude to them.

WEEK 4: 22–28 JANUARY

This is a good time to press ahead with your various ventures, but you must avoid tempers and tantrums and inflexible talks with those you share space with as an intense event at home with family or property may be on the cards. That said, developments at home could be ideal, especially if you'd like to invest more in your domestic circumstances. Powerful Pluto may contribute to a restless feeling.

HEALTH

Your home is your haven with regard to your health in January, so be prepared to feather your nest to make the most of the opportunity to nurture your body and mind. If you're travelling, a little luxury will certainly appeal. You must avoid overdoing activities as these will lead to fatigue. Mid-October–born Librans will be in a position to devote more focus on your health early in January, and you'll welcome the help of an expert.

FINANCES

A great deal of financial focus will be on your domestic and shared expenses. Some of your decisions and expenditure will depend on the financial circumstances of someone you share your space with. It is as well to be optimistic that you will meet your budget; however, you must be sure to maintain clear communications with those you depend on to pay your wages on the one hand and who share your domestic expenses on the other.

HOME

Your home life will demand a great deal of your attention in the first few weeks of the month. Some Librans will also be super busy at work, so it'll be in your interest to find the balance between the two areas of your life early on to avoid a conflict of interest. A business or personal partner will need your attention towards the 10th to the 15th and the 18th and 27th, so be prepared to exercise your judgement then.

LOVE LIFE

A partner will need your focus early in January, so be prepared to pay them more attention than usual. They could simply be feeling vulnerable or more sensitive than usual and this may be due to an emotional or physical health situation. Be prepared to give them a supporting shoulder to lean on, but if you feel they are leaning too heavily then they or you may need to seek expert help.

WORK

You can make progress work-wise in January, especially towards the new moon on the 18th. Be prepared to reconfigure your usual routine so it suits you, especially your domestic choices and arrangements, and look at how you would ideally like to configure your schedule so it works well with your domestic life and those you share your work and domestic space with. You could construct a beneficial schedule now.

February

WEEK 1: 29 JANUARY–4 FEBRUARY

The full moon on the 1st puts your connection with a group, friend or organisation in the spotlight. You're ready to reconfigure who and what must come first in your life and find more value in your daily undertakings and career. Discussions will help sort out how to approach your personal life and domestic arrangements in light of fresh news from a personal or business partner or from family.

WEEK 2: 5–11 FEBRUARY

As an air sign you like to make careful, analytical choices based on facts, yet this week you may need to think on your feet and must rely on a snap judgement, largely due to the likelihood of spontaneous events arising that you can't plan for in advance. Avoid allowing intense emotions to dictate your actions, especially at home.

WEEK 3: 12–18 FEBRUARY

You may discover a hidden artistic talent as your appreciation for beauty will blossom, perhaps even in unexpected ways. Be sure to explore your creative side. For some a fresh chapter will begin in your personal life, and if you're single this could be a quirky week in your love life while couples may enjoy trying something new. Avoid gambling and making assumptions.

WEEK 4: 19–25 FEBRUARY / WEEK 5: 26 FEBRUARY–4 MARCH

WEEK 4: it's a good week to improve your personal life and spruce up your office. A change of routine or a health or beauty boost could be ideal. A friend, expert or partner will prove to be helpful, so reach out. **WEEK 5:** aim to get key plans sorted before the 26th to avoid delays. Someone you rely on may surprise you, so be adaptable. You'll enjoy a reunion.

HEALTH

Neptune in your health sector will bring either clarity to a health situation or the need to find out more. The latter will lead to transparency down the road, so be sure to research health matters in February and especially aspects of your health you do not understand or would like to heal. Consider, too, whether any aspects of your lifestyle do not support good health as February will be a good time to make any necessary changes.

FINANCES

You are in line to experience some financial surprises early in February, and these are likely to be associated with domestic, property or family costs. It will be in your interest to seek expert advice if you feel you are out of your depth. A personal or business partner will help you if you have a large, unexpected outlay, so be sure to seek the help of experts and those who support you if necessary.

HOME

Pluto is adding a sense of intensity to your domestic life, and coupled with Mars, the sun, Venus and Mercury also aspecting this important part of your life means your home life may be busier or more disruptive than usual, especially at the start of February and around the 5th and 8th. Be prepared to look at healing ways to bring more peace into your home life, family and property.

LOVE LIFE

Someone close may surprise you with their news or unpredictability early in February, and while you tend to prefer to be philosophical about your relationships the disruption that is caused may be more than you can accept. For this reason it will be important to look at the positives within your close relationships, and as long as the disruptions don't outweigh the positives be sure to maintain the status quo, especially at home, where intense feelings may arise.

WORK

You'll gain the opportunity in February to elevate your work to a new level, so look out for opportunities to explore different avenues. The Saturn–Neptune conjunction on 20 February will bring the chance both to gain more security in your work and a deeper sense of achievement. This conjunction marks a major turning point, so be prepared to look outside the box at your long-term plans to make the most of this transformative time.

LIBRA · FEBRUARY

March

WEEK 1: 5–11 MARCH

You'll feel motivated to be more productive, at work and home and in your personal life. A change of circumstance awaits. News or developments that affect your status will improve your daily routine, even if initially there are logistics to manage. A fresh scenario will develop either at work or regarding your health and well-being. You can prospectively make a commitment to a proactive new schedule.

WEEK 2: 12–18 MARCH

This will be a good week for exploration and research, especially in conjunction with work and/or health. Be open to new ideas and the wisdom of others, as you may meet someone who is particularly helpful or insightful. You may experience an unexpected or pleasant development this weekend or mid-week. Just be sure to avoid being drawn into arguments mid-week next week as these could set you back.

WEEK 3: 19–25 MARCH

Thursday's new moon will help you turn a corner, especially if you feel some areas of your life have become stale or that certain activities or people need to be reprioritised. Be inspired and consider how you could boost interpersonal dynamics, and take the initiative. A creative project begun now could be a success. Some Librans will experience a career boost.

WEEK 4: 26 MARCH–1 APRIL

A personal or work partner or colleague may need your help or will be super helpful to you, so be sure to reach out if you need advice or support. An unexpected change of circumstance in a shared situation such as in your home life or a collaborative project may be a surprise but ultimately productive. You'll enjoy an impromptu romantic get-together towards Sunday.

HEALTH

If health has been an issue recently this will be an excellent month to step into a new understanding of your health and well-being. You may even discover different treatments or fitness and dietary regimes that will support your constitution. Be positive about developments and look for experts in your fields of interest so you can find out more about how to look after your health and well-being.

FINANCES

As Jupiter again achieves influence in your career sector you're likely to also gain financially. Over the next few weeks and months and potentially already around the 21st this month you are likely to see progress at work, which will only translate as better income. Be ready to step into fresh financial territory to manage your investments and debt with a view to future expansion.

HOME

March is an excellent time to invest in your home life and family as your efforts are likely to succeed, and where you are looking for collaboration and cooperation from someone within your household or a professional this is also likely to go well, so be sure to reach out. If you have been considering a DIY project, renovation or even a move this is an excellent time to form your plans.

LOVE LIFE

Singles are in line to meet someone who has a soul connection with you. This could be someone who seems familiar, even if you have never met before, but it will not necessarily mean this will be an ideal relationship. It is in your interest to explore a little further before assuming you have found the perfect romance. Some Librans may bump into or hear unexpectedly from an ex, and it will be your choice whether or not you resume that relationship.

WORK

The conjunction in early March between Mercury, Venus, Saturn and Neptune could bring something exciting your way, so be sure to explore new opportunities. You're in a strong position to enter fresh territory. The positive aspect between Jupiter and Mars will also promote progress towards the 21st. Jupiter will gain influence in your career sector as the weeks go by, bringing the potential for expansion and luck at work.

April

WEEK 1: 2–8 APRIL

Thursday's full moon in Libra kick-starts a fresh health or work phase if you were born in October and a new cycle in your personal life if you were born in September. Be prepared to consider new ways to create more security in all these areas and reach out to experts and those you know can help you advance. Avoid a battle of wills towards Sunday and Monday.

WEEK 2: 9–15 APRIL

The entry of Mars into the upbeat sign of Aries spells a busier time for you both at work and within your personal life until at least mid-May, so this is a heads-up to pace yourself. This week you may receive important news to do with a health or work matter. A personal or work collaboration is likely to go particularly well towards Sunday and Monday.

WEEK 3: 16–22 APRIL

Friday's new moon has a strong influence over your relationships, so this is a good time to forge fresh ties or rearrange existing agreements. Romance could thrive this weekend, and a development at home will fuel good vibes for the week ahead. A fresh start on the way in a business or personal partnership may take a little adjustment, so take things one step at a time.

WEEK 4: 23–29 APRIL

A change of pace or of place will add excitement to your week. You may enjoy a short break or receive an unexpected visitor. This weekend there may be matters that need to be ironed out with a relationship or arrangement, and the more you can avoid a battle of wills the better it will be for you. Early next week you'll appreciate a positive development at home or in your personal life.

HEALTH

The full moon in your sign on 2 April will stimulate the need to find more balance in your daily life, especially for October-born Librans. September Librans may need to establish more balance within both your personal and work relationships. It will be a good time to reach out for expert advice, both in the field of physical health and emotional help. Avoid trying to be stronger than everyone else: be prepared to acknowledge when you need some support.

FINANCES

The new moon on the 17th and developments around the 24th point to the need to rearrange certain financial circumstances, especially those you share with someone close such as a business or personal partner or for household expenses. Be prepared to configure new agreements from a long-term perspective. You may discover a debt or circumstance that needs more attention. You will manage to make headway either at work or through the arrangements you make.

HOME

You have an opportunity early in April to make changes at home that support a busy daily routine, so get everyone on board so your schedule runs smoothly. However, there is also the possibility that someone – even you – is seen as controlling or domineering, so be sure to avoid this scenario. You'll gain the opportunity mid-month to make arrangements that put you in a strong position. Avoid arguments towards the end of April, as these could snowball.

LOVE LIFE

April is an excellent month to establish the kind of balance you need in your love life. However, this may come about through situations that demonstrate where balance, peace and calm are lacking, especially in the first week of the month, so be prepared to weather the dips and stresses in your love life with a view to improving circumstances and, above all, avoid a battle of wills as this could cascade.

WORK

Work, your career and duties will take much of your focus in April and May and could even create stress either in your personal life or within your health circumstance, so you must be sure to avoid allowing your work to dominate your life, especially around the full moon on 2 April. You will gain direction at work towards the 13th that will enable you to gauge whether you must make changes moving forward.

LIBRA · APRIL

May

WEEK 1: 30 APRIL–6 MAY

The full moon will spotlight a financial matter, and for some mid-October–born Librans a personal situation that requires a change. Decisions will need to be made concerning domestic or property-related matters, and the more information you can obtain the better will be the outcome of your decision-making. Rest assured you'll gain the time to reconfigure aspects of your home life you'd like to change, so avoid feeling pressured.

WEEK 2: 7–13 MAY

A collaboration in your personal life or at work could thrive, so if you have joint ventures you'd like to advance this is the week to do it! Some lucky Librans will receive positive financial news via work or the opportunity to boost your status at work. This is also a good week to focus on managing shared finances such as household expenses, as the arrangements you make are likely to take.

WEEK 3: 14–20 MAY

This weekend's new moon on the 16th will revitalise your relationships in the long term, so ensure you initiate talks and make agreements that suit you. Avoid obstinacy; find ways to collaborate instead. A commitment you make now could be long term. You're likely to be drawn to experience new events and some of these will also have a therapeutic effect on your closest relationships. Romance could thrive, so be sure to organise a date.

WEEK 4: 21–27 MAY / WEEK 5: 28 MAY–3 JUNE

WEEK 4: get set for a change of pace this weekend, as you'll enjoy excitement and trying something new. A development that could broaden your horizons, whether through travel or a fresh project or even friendship, will provide a fresh perspective. **WEEK 5:** logistics may require patience and clarity at various points, so maintain a view of the big picture and be sure to discuss your ideas before taking action.

HEALTH

It's likely that the health and well-being of someone close to you become a focus, especially at the start of the month. The health situation may not simply be of a physical nature; consider emotional, spiritual and mental health in the bigger picture of how best to care for or help someone close to you. For some Librans a health situation will impact your love life, and this will again be your cue to explore ways to find better health.

FINANCES

The full moon on 1 May will spotlight important financial matters that deserve attention, especially those to do with domestic circumstances and/or finances you share with someone else. Be prepared to discuss options with those they concern, especially where income and expenditure are concerned. The second week of May will be a good time for negotiations, so be confident and take the initiative with talks then even if you are a little apprehensive.

HOME

You'll gain a sense of the importance of a nurturing and caring atmosphere at home. You may experience a particular situation either early in May or towards the end of it that brings this realisation to mind. You may simply like to improve and/or bring into being new dynamics in your home life this month. A trip or project will take you outside your home but will again highlight the importance of a stable home life.

LOVE LIFE

Someone close may reveal a vulnerability, and this will provide an opportunity to understand them better. May is certainly a good month to work on better relationship skills, whether you are already in a relationship or single. Bear in mind that someone in your circle may need to improve their communication skills, so avoid taking personally their inability to express themselves well. The full moon on the 31st will bring an adventurous spirit to your love life.

WORK

The second week of May will be a particularly positive time to advance your career and status through careful talks and negotiations, so be prepared to take the lead with your various collaborations and projects. You may even be drawn to make a fresh commitment to a project or work situation. You are also going to be drawn to enter fresh territory, so for that reason be sure to double-check arrangements or contracts.

LIBRA · MAY

June

WEEK 1: 4–10 JUNE

This will be a good week to make a commitment to someone important, either at work or in your personal life. Working Librans could broaden your horizons as you gain the opportunity to experience fresh avenues in your career. You may enjoy news from a distance or regarding travel and study. Be proactive if health has been on your mind, as you may receive a key insight.

WEEK 2: 11–17 JUNE

You'll appreciate doing something different and may also enjoy a spontaneous event, as your career or status is set to improve unexpectedly. You may hear from someone from a distance from out of the blue or discover a fresh interest or hobby. Monday's new moon suggests travel, and the lure of the exotic or overseas will be hard to ignore. For some there will be a fresh collaboration to consider.

WEEK 3: 18–24 JUNE

Developments at home could involve a change of focus in your career or expectations in general. If you're considering restructuring a home or domestic circumstance, experts may be helpful. Travel and romance will appeal, which you'll enjoy. Your help and expertise will be in demand and someone may need a little support. If you need help yourself it will be available, so just ask for it.

WEEK 4: 25 JUNE–1 JULY

You will appreciate the opportunity to connect with like-minded people and may also enjoy favourable circumstances within your career. However, if you feel developments at home or concerning your status and direction are intense, focus on grounding yourself and being practical. A methodical approach to key conversations or a trip will work well at June's end.

HEALTH

The start of June will be ideal for discussing health and making a clear plan for your well-being, especially if you were born in October. All Librans will gain the chance to bring aspects into your life and daily routine that create a sense of well-being. You will especially find a change of routine or pace towards the 17th and 18th could open doors to a pleasant break.

FINANCES

You may receive an unexpected financial boost that may be in connection with a business or personal partner towards mid-June. Just be sure not to overspend as a result and avoid gambling, as it's far better to organise your finances rationally as opposed to leaving your financial situation open to the fickleness of fate. An expert will be useful if you must reorganise shared finances such as a mortgage or tax return.

HOME

If you have been looking for ways to transform your home life, family circumstance or even a property, developments will bring some of your views and ideas to a head, especially towards the 18th and the 29th when circumstances either at work or concerning your bigger-picture status could impact your home life. Be prepared to look outside the box at your various options for the best results, as you could make progressive changes to this important area of your life.

LOVE LIFE

You're looking for a little spontaneity and something different in your love life, and singles are likely to bump into someone different and exciting towards the new moon on the 15th. This may be in an environment that is new to you, such as through a holiday or trip. Be open to meeting unfamiliar people. Couples will also benefit from embracing the new, be this a fresh daily routine or connecting through fresh activities.

WORK

The conjunction of Jupiter and Venus on the 9th/10th will spotlight your status and career. If you have been looking for a new career or job opportunity this will be a good time to discuss options, as will the 15th and 18th. However, you may feel vulnerable or even unworthy in some way, so it will be important if this is the case to find ways to boost your self-esteem. A training course may be in the cards.

LIBRA · JUNE

July

WEEK 1: 2–8 JULY

This is a week to get things done! Get busy, but avoid being distracted by matters you can't control. Be adaptable but focused, especially regarding developments in your career and general direction. A personal or business partner may have unexpected news. Avoid taking it personally if it involves a stretch of the imagination, but consider ways in the meantime in which you can maximise your happiness at home.

WEEK 2: 9–15 JULY

In the long term you have some wonderful opportunities to create the daily and home lives you've always wanted. In the short term, however, there will be various negotiations and arrangements you will need to make that will require tact and diplomacy. Be careful to navigate someone's unpredictable behaviour. A friend or group may be particularly helpful to you so be sure to seek advice if necessary.

WEEK 3: 16–22 JULY

It's all change for you in your personal life and domestic circumstances. For many this may be ideal, but if you find circumstances intense be sure you pace yourself and find ways to let off steam. Be prepared to configure a daily routine that suits you best to avoid overcommitting to activities that you will not be able to manage.

WEEK 4: 23–29 JULY

You will appreciate the sense that your previous actions related to work are showing positive results as good news comes your way. The lead-up to the full moon on the 29th/30th may be fairly intense, but luckily you are in a position to appreciate the potential for outcomes both at work and in your personal life. A development at home or regarding family will be transformational, so think long term if you are making tough decisions.

HEALTH

You will gain direction with a health matter that will enable you to put an action or health and fitness plan in place. Some Librans will be drawn to alter your appearance, and this is something to look into carefully as opposed to jumping at the first option. If you are considering procedures such as cosmetic surgery, ensure you do your research to avoid unexpected outcomes.

FINANCES

You may receive unexpected news regarding shared finances or financial links you cannot avoid, such as those with a housemate or partner. Be prepared to work with the situation as opposed to against it, but keep an eye on your long-term goals as you may otherwise be prone to being easily influenced financially. This is essentially a transformative month, so it is important that you keep on top of finances as developments arise.

HOME

Early July is an excellent time to consider new and progressive ways to breathe life into your domestic or family life or property. You may even be surprised by a housemate's or partner's news in the first week of July that will considerably alter aspects of your domestic life. If you have already been planning a move, this is likely to take you to a better circumstance even if it creates a little upheaval in the process, especially mid-month.

LOVE LIFE

The first week of the month will benefit from a patient and constructive approach in your love life, as you may otherwise succumb to pressure that brings a sense of drama, vulnerability or even lack. If you focus instead on moving into fresh territory with your partner you could establish something that will broaden horizons for you. Singles are likely to meet someone new, perhaps even unexpectedly, on the 4th and 5th, so be sure to organise something special.

WORK

Changes in your status or career may pose logistical issues early in the month, but with a patient attitude and optimistic mindset you will see that some developments, even if they appear to be initially negative, will actually take you into fresh territory at work that is not only exciting but could also be profitable. Jupiter will encourage you to broaden your outlook work-wise, especially towards the 20th and 21st and the 29th.

August

WEEK 1: 30 JULY–5 AUGUST

You will already be aware that certain circumstances in your life do not automatically promote peace, calm and harmony. For example, someone who can be competitive will need to express this aspect of themselves. During this week you'll gain the opportunity to create a secure and steadier relationship both for yourself and someone special at work or at home that enables you to build trust and, ultimately, peace, calm and harmony.

WEEK 2: 6–12 AUGUST

Venus enters Libra on the 6th/7th, bringing your attention to love and money. This is also a super-romantic week in which someone special is likely to surprise you. If you are single the days around the solar eclipse on the 12th/13th may even bring a fun social networking opportunity your way. Be sure to avoid intense communications at that time at home and at work as these could escalate.

WEEK 3: 13–19 AUGUST

A changeable atmosphere may lead to indecision about activities and what events will be undertaken for the best results. Trust your instincts. Towards the weekend a get-together with those you love will make your heart sing. You'll enjoy a reunion and the chance to deepen your bonds with those you love. Work-wise, be prepared to discuss your options to avoid making assumptions.

WEEK 4: 20–26 AUGUST / WEEK 5: 27 AUGUST–2 SEPTEMBER

WEEK 4: you may need to make a tough call this week regarding a personal or work collaboration. A choice could create more stability and security for you, but on the other hand you must avoid limiting your options moving forward.
WEEK 5: the partial lunar eclipse on the 28th will kick-start a fresh phase in your personal, creative or family life. This is a good week for health appointments.

HEALTH

You will be drawn to focus on your appearance and health. A fresh look such as a new hairstyle or wardrobe will appeal. You will find out during the days around the solar eclipse on the 12th whether you have over- or underestimated your health situation. The good news is that this will allow you to reset your health schedule. This is a good time to enlist the help of experts and join groups of like-minded people.

FINANCES

It's important this month to evaluate and be certain about exactly where your joint financial responsibilities lie. This applies not only at home and with family but also regarding taxes and work. This is largely because otherwise mistakes can be made this month that could trip you up financially. Be sure to take advantage of opportunities to research your options and shared finances where possible, especially if you are considering making key commitments.

HOME

Be prepared to step into a new understanding of your home life, especially with regard to how you share it with family or housemates. The eclipse season that is at its most intense from the 12th to the 28th will bring a fresh chapter in your personal life that will invariably affect your home life, so be sure to factor your domestic circumstances in your big-picture decisions in August.

LOVE LIFE

This month's eclipse season, which begins with a total solar eclipse on the 12th/13th depending on where you live, will bring a fresh phase within your personal or family life. You will gain the opportunity to turn a corner, so singles may be enticed to make a commitment to someone special and couples may be drawn to invest more in the fun and creative side of your relationship. If you have been planning a family, a turning point in this respect will arise.

WORK

You will gain insight into your best way forward as you are either in a position to proceed more dynamically within your working life or must make a tough decision to favour one or other aspect of your life; for example, your home life. Developments around the 12th and 17th will spotlight your true options, so be sure to evaluate circumstances carefully. The opportunity to discuss details in your working life is not to be missed.

LIBRA · AUGUST

September

WEEK 1: 3–9 SEPTEMBER

Someone you rely on either at home or work may be delayed or not as supportive as usual. Avoid being derailed by uncertainties and remain optimistic, as this week you'll gain the opportunity to put in gear some of your plans and options. Once you do you'll gain strength as opposed to being reliant on others. You'll enjoy a lovely social or work development towards Sunday or Monday.

WEEK 2: 10–16 SEPTEMBER

As Mercury enters your sign communications will be busy and you'll gain the opportunity to deepen key personal and/or family relationships. Romance also abounds this week but, unfortunately, some Librans will find this time a little disorienting if not intense, so do avoid a battle of wills and/or conflict as this is likely to escalate rapidly. Friday's new moon will kick-start a fresh health or work schedule.

WEEK 3: 17–23 SEPTEMBER

The sun enters your sign on the 23rd, which is the equinox, and you'll find over the coming weeks that your usual optimism and ability to find peace and happiness in life returns if it has been lacking lately. Meanwhile, a financial or personal decision will merit care and attention. If a change of environment seems challenging, take breaks and spend time replenishing your energy levels. Someone close has your back.

WEEK 4: 24–30 SEPTEMBER

This weekend's full moon is a super-romantic full moon, and it could bring new parameters to your love life. For some a fresh work schedule, shared project or business relationship will change. New agreements could be binding or hard to get out of, so ensure if you're making a commitment that you're happy with the terms. For some Librans there will be a change of a daily or health schedule.

HEALTH

You will find out whether you have been labouring under an illusion regarding your health and fitness. For example, if you do not exercise you will discover the merits of physical movement, while active Librans may discover that all your hard work is paying off. Either way, you'll gain insight towards mid-month and be able to make informed choices as a result. You'll also be drawn to improve your appearance. A fresh look may appeal.

FINANCES

Venus in your finance sector will bring your focus to money, at least until the end of October. You are best to get major financial decisions shipshape by the end of this month before Venus turns retrograde in early October. Be careful with financial decisions in September, especially towards the 10th and 12th and around the 27th, as mistakes and miscommunications could occur. This aside, you have excellent prospects for improving your financial circumstances as long as you avoid gambling.

HOME

You'll gain a wonderful opportunity in September to make long-term and beneficial changes to your home, family life or a property. If you have been considering moving or other major changes at home your efforts are likely to culminate in decisions now as you consider the pros and cons both personally and financially of a change at home. You'll gain a sense more specifically towards the 26th to the 28th as to the true nature of transformational home dynamics.

LOVE LIFE

Good communication skills are the backbone of all relationships and especially in your love life. In this case communication skills include not only verbal communication but also non-verbal. This month you may need to be a little patient with one another and will also need to avoid a battle of wills, as this is likely to escalate, especially mid-month. Be sure to avoid misunderstandings as these will be prevalent as well, especially towards the 10th to the 22nd and the 27th.

WORK

A positive social and networking scenario can help you in the workplace. During the first two weeks of the month your communication skills will either smooth over work circumstances or contribute to obstacles. Be prepared to take the initiative at work as you may experience a breakthrough towards the 7th. The new moon on the 11th and events around the 17th to the 22nd and the 26th will kick-start a fresh daily schedule for you.

LIBRA • SEPTEMBER

WEEK 1: 1–7 OCTOBER

Your sign's ruler turns retrograde and this could bring a retrospective or nostalgic week for you. However, it is important that you maintain focus on current circumstances, especially those concerning your status, career and home life, as these are all likely to need important consideration. A key decision will be necessary involving either a business or personal partner. This could elevate your status but you must avoid unnecessary disputes.

WEEK 2: 8–14 OCTOBER

If you're working you're likely to be busy and it could be a lucrative time. A change of circumstance may be appealing, but be prepared to adjust to new conditions. If disputes arise these may be due to a difference in values, so avoid taking them personally. This weekend's new moon will be in Libra and is an excellent chance to revitalise your love life, health and appearance.

WEEK 3: 15–21 OCTOBER

You'll see how well your past hard work is beginning to pay off, whether financially or purely through feeling more contented either in your personal life or at work. Some may receive a debt repaid. You'll enjoy a get-together and socialising towards the weekend. However, some talks and developments mid-week next week will merit patience to avoid arguments and hard feelings.

WEEK 4: 22–28 OCTOBER / WEEK 5: 29 OCTOBER–4 NOVEMBER

WEEK 4: as Venus enters Libra your attention will go increasingly to love and money. A surprise development may ask that you make new arrangements in your personal life or shared resources such as finances. Avoid a battle of wills and instead look for constructive ways forward. **WEEK 5:** tough communications towards the 30th are best navigated carefully, especially at work. Your efforts will be rewarded by 4 November.

HEALTH

You'll find out in October whether you have been labouring under an illusion concerning your health. For example, if a particular diet has promised you better energy levels but has not delivered, you will gain the opportunity to find something different. The new moon on the 10th/11th can help you turn a corner health-wise, both with your appearance if you were born before the 10th and your constitution if you were born afterwards.

FINANCES

Your sign's ruler Venus will be retrograde in your finance sector for most of the month, which will bring the opportunity to review your circumstances. If you have overspent in the past you will need to establish a fresh budget that enables you to repay debt. Be careful towards the 9th and 10th with financial transactions, as mistakes could be made. If you are making fresh arrangements, be careful with the details.

HOME

You may discover you need to make a tough call between your career and home life and, for some, regarding your health and/or personal life. You may even question whether to kick-start a fresh relationship or end an existing one. Before you make snap decisions be sure to discuss all your options, as you could make some valid changes now that may truly enhance your home and happiness. Be sure to carefully manage flashpoints towards the 20th and 26th.

LOVE LIFE

Some aspects of your love life are fated, such as the fact you crossed another's path, but your future is always dictated by your choices. This month be sure to prioritise that someone special where possible if you feel your paths align. Singles may be drawn to a therapeutic relationship, but if conflict becomes too frequent it will impact the longevity of your relationship. Be super careful with conversations towards the 10th, 16th, 20th and 30th to avoid arguments.

WORK

You have a wonderful opportunity at the start of the month, towards the 15th and at the end of the month to improve your work circumstances. Be positive and optimistic about your options. Some discussions may be intense, especially around the 10th, 20th and 30th, but if you remain practical and logical you could overcome nerves and needless arguments. The new moon on the 10th/11th will kick-start a fresh work cycle, especially if you were born after the 10th.

November

WEEK 1: 5–11 NOVEMBER

A brand-new financial cycle is about to begin for you and it may feel intense. You'll diminish the amount of tension surrounding finances by avoiding arguments with a friend or organisation. Be prepared to step into different territory in your earning and investment strategy. Some Librans will be ready to begin a fresh chapter in a close business or personal collaboration, but you must research the details.

WEEK 2: 12–18 NOVEMBER

Key meetings may seem serendipitous and you may need to take swift action to engage someone's attention. If you love socialising this is likely to be a busy week. Singles will gain the opportunity to meet an upbeat and varied crowd and romance could certainly thrive, so be sure to take the initiative. For couples, there is a likelihood that a therapeutic development will boost the fun factor in your life.

WEEK 3: 19–25 NOVEMBER

Be careful with communications, especially with a friend, group or organisation, towards the weekend to avoid unnecessary misunderstandings or arguments as these are likely to arise unless you are careful. The full moon supermoon brings a fresh chapter with your favourite activities. You may be drawn to travel, study, self-development or spiritual matters. You will enjoy reconnecting with someone you love.

WEEK 4: 26 NOVEMBER–2 DECEMBER

You'll enjoy socialising this weekend. Venus in your sign makes a wonderful link with Jupiter, which could help boost your vitality and also may encourage you to review personal circumstances. Enjoy the chance to relax this weekend. A misunderstanding or sensitive topic may arise so be prepared to manage discussions and look for a therapeutic outcome, which is possible. You may experience a financial or ego boost towards Monday.

HEALTH

A group, friend or organisation will prove particularly beneficial health-wise, so if you've had certain health issues on your mind this is the month to investigate organisations and practitioners who could be particularly helpful as you are likely to find someone suitable for you, especially towards the 12th, 14th and 29th. You will appreciate a positive change in schedule or health routine towards the 23rd that could truly lift your spirits.

FINANCES

You'll begin a fresh phase financially and this will be determined by past investments and where you would like to continue to invest your money. You may already see signs of financial growth, but if the opposite occurs you will find an organisation particularly helpful due to the advice they provide. The full moon supermoon on the 24th/25th could spotlight an unexpected financial development that for many Librans will be positive. However, you may need to tactfully discuss shared finances.

HOME

You are moving towards considerable changes in your domestic life, and these are likely to work out for you for the best. Be prepared to make changes and avoid fighting against these, as conflict will make your life more difficult than it needs to be. Be prepared to work with those in your family from common ground as opposed to looking only at factors you dislike. It's far better to feel encouraged than demotivated.

LOVE LIFE

November brings a fresh chapter for you, especially regarding your values and principles. You may feel particularly intensely about your ethics or certain points, which could affect your relationship, so be careful to avoid arguments this month and look for common ground as opposed to differences. Couples will find developments mid-month therapeutic, while singles may meet someone significant mid-month or towards the end of November and may even hear unexpectedly from an ex. Consider bringing more fun into your relationship.

WORK

This is an excellent month to work towards your goals, as you are likely to achieve them by the end of the month at the least. You certainly are in a position to show off your skill sets, both with groups and organisations and especially after mid-month, and you may even experience positive feedback and developments towards the 23rd and 30th. For some this could involve a surprise financial improvement.

LIBRA • NOVEMBER

December

WEEK 1: 3–9 DECEMBER

Get set for fresh dynamics in your communications and relationships. You may be inclined to approach people with a more upbeat attitude, and plans for travel point to a welcome break. You may be drawn to update a communications device or vehicle. Just be careful towards the weekend and on Wednesday with communications both at home and socially, as there may be misunderstandings.

WEEK 2: 10–16 DECEMBER

This is a good week to get on top of chores at work. Some lucky Librans may even be able to take a break from work. You may enjoy a boost at work or health-wise. You are likely to appreciate a financial improvement, or you may be repaid a debt or can repay one. You will enjoy a social event this weekend and reconnecting with someone you love.

WEEK 3: 17–23 DECEMBER

Therapeutic developments will bring you closer together with those you love. For some this will involve travel and for others receiving visitors. A sociable weekend will be enjoyable; however, you are likely to need to collaborate well with others to achieve your goals, so be sure to sharpen your communication skill sets. There may be traffic delays towards Wednesday, so give yourself plenty of time for trips.

WEEK 4: 24–31 DECEMBER

While so much of your attention goes into keeping the peace in your life, paradoxically you can feel tense as a result. This week someone's erratic behaviour may be a challenge, but if you are able to avoid ruffling feathers you will be so much happier. You will enjoy socialising and being with those you love. A domestic or family circumstance can thrive. You will enjoy short trips or visitors.

HEALTH

A positive mindset is known to improve health and well-being, and this month you may be drawn to investigate ways to be more upbeat, adventurous and self-confident. Some Librans will be lucky enough to begin the holiday season early, with developments towards the 11th and then the 18th and 23rd bringing a change of pace and also improved energy levels as a result. Be sure to take time out with someone special to achieve a truly relaxing environment.

FINANCES

Venus in Scorpio this month will predispose you to overspending during the festive season, so be sure to put in place a budget that is realistic enough for you to stick to. Luckily, you may experience a financial boost towards the 11th to the 14th that will largely be contingent on your past actions; for example, the result of hard work well done or of good investments.

HOME

You have many positive aspects regarding your home life this December that mainly involve a change of environment or pace. You will appreciate a change of pace that has an impact on your domestic circumstances; however, it is in your interest to avoid overspending on your home or a property and you will gain insight into whether you already have around the new moon on the 9th.

LOVE LIFE

The key to a happy love life revolves around looking for and establishing peaceful ways to get on with everyone. This will involve good communication skills, as you may otherwise disengage or feel that you must acquiesce to everyone's demands. Beware of a battle of wills, especially on the 5th, 8th and 9th, and aim to defuse this before it grows. Singles will enjoy the festive season and socialising will appeal, especially on the 7th, 8th, 11th, 12th, 18th and 23rd.

WORK

This will be a good month to discuss your year at work with those your activities involve such as employees, employers and colleagues. Reviews may be particularly beneficial and talks especially around the 11th and 21st could even put you in a strong position, so be sure to take the initiative with work discussions. However, you'll need to be prepared to be careful with communications to avoid any misunderstandings.

January

WEEK 1: 1—7 JANUARY

Saturday's full moon points to a fresh interest, project or venture, and this could mean a change in your primary relationships due to the need to travel or work more closely with someone. You may receive news to do with a favourite activity, travel or study. You'll enjoy a lovely get-together this weekend or early in the week.

WEEK 2: 8—14 JANUARY

Key news or a trip or visit will bring changes in your environment. You'll enjoy getting together with someone close to your heart and romance could blossom, especially this weekend. During the week some communications will require additional tact at work for the best results. You may require the help of a professional or expert to come to a different work agreement or schedule.

WEEK 3: 15—21 JANUARY

You'll appreciate a change of environment or pace even if it means adapting to fresh circumstances. Mid-November—born Scorpios will enter a new financial phase that could be uplifting or lucrative and that also signals changes at home or with someone special. First, however, logistics will merit care and attention. Avoid being careless financially; ensure you are clear with communications to avoid mix-ups.

WEEK 4: 22—28 JANUARY

You may be surprised by someone's dramatic ideas or actions and may surprise someone with your own thoughts. A trip could open new horizons. Avoid outbursts, misunderstandings and gambling, as you'll regret it! That said, you can shrug off adversity like water off a duck's back, and this weekend you'll enjoy romance but must avoid some intense situations becoming too hot to handle.

HEALTH

January will be a good month to pay extra attention to your health, especially in the second week of the month, as you may feel more under pressure than usual. This will not necessarily be due to a gruelling work schedule; it could simply be due to the need to adapt to a fresh daily routine. Even if the new schedule is more relaxing in the long term it may also take a little time to adjust to.

FINANCES

Mid-January will be an excellent time to consider how best to reconfigure your financial arrangements. However, first it is in your interest to avoid gambling of any nature; for example, by investing in a scheme that has not been proven to be successful. You may be drawn to being super generous with travel and your activities this month, so do keep an eye on expenditure to avoid overspending.

HOME

You will gain insight and a deeper sense of the importance of a stable yet inspiring home life in January and will have the opportunity to enjoy time with family and all those who make your home life all that it is. Be prepared to invest in this invaluable part of your life in January and you will reap the rewards. Nevertheless, a trip and travel in general will appeal, especially towards the end of the month.

LOVE LIFE

You'll enjoy the opportunity to do something different if you're in a couple, such as a trip somewhere beautiful, or make changes at home. If you're single you'll be drawn to meet a fresh group of people. Mid-January and the end of the month may bring someone different into your realm. The new moon on the 18th/19th will spotlight an unpredictable aspect of your love life, and for many this will be due to the spontaneity inherent in your relationship or partner.

WORK

This will be a good month to broaden your scope at work or in your career. However, you may find that domestic demands or simply being busy puts you in the crosshairs so be sure to pace yourself, especially in the second week of the month. If you're on holiday the change of pace will suit you, but you will need to summon extra resolve to resume your work schedule after the break.

SCORPIO · JANUARY

February

WEEK 1: 29 JANUARY—4 FEBRUARY

Intense talks or a trip this week will contribute to a fresh perspective in your personal life. A new chapter is about to begin that is likely to affect circumstances such as the activities you undertake in your spare time, including your pastimes. You may find that your home life or relationships change as travel, study or key people become more important to you.

WEEK 2: 5—11 FEBRUARY

A change of circumstance could be tied up with your home or a business or personal partner. You may be surprised by someone's reactions to events; avoid being swayed by their inconsistencies. A change in your domestic circumstance or family will benefit from care and attention. Avoid allowing strong feelings to boil over; instead, find a safety valve, especially on Thursday and Monday.

WEEK 3: 12—18 FEBRUARY

Prepare for a fresh chapter to begin in your personal life. For some this will revolve around changes at home that take you into fresh territory, and for others the circumstances of the people around you will change and stimulate discussion. To make decisions that produce the best results do your research and avoid impulsiveness and secrecy.

WEEK 4: 19—25 FEBRUARY / WEEK 5: 26 FEBRUARY—4 MARCH

WEEK 4: you'll enjoy music, dance and romance but must avoid overspending. Someone from your past may need your help or advice, and you'll enjoy getting together with those you love. **WEEK 5:** a family or domestic development is best approached from a long-term viewpoint as opposed to resorting to short-term measures. You may be surprised by news towards the 26th. Be practical, but also inspired.

HEALTH

February is an excellent month to look at ways to improve your health as you will gain the opportunity to find the right help specific to your medical or well-being needs, so be sure to reach out and find the right practitioners for your circumstances. There are healing aspects to make the most of towards the end of the month, so be sure to look for avenues that promote both your and your family's well-being.

FINANCES

Looking for stability yet being open to growth are important values to consider during February, as you will gain the opportunity to experience a sense of progress financially and therefore also a sense of security. However, you must avoid gambling as this will chain you to a course of events that will be outside your control. Be prepared to seek expert advice if a domestic commitment overshadows your ability to grow.

HOME

An adventurous and progressive approach to your home life will certainly help you move forward with respect to unpredictable or uncharted waters in this area. Be prepared to look outside the box at your options, especially in early February. The solar eclipse mid-month adds a quirky aspect to your domestic life or concerning a property, and those close to you will prove to be an invaluable help.

LOVE LIFE

The start of February will put your focus on your love life and especially on aspects of your relationship that you do not understand, so it will be in your interest to find common ground to discuss differences. If an expert can help you understand each other's idiosyncrasies then, again, the start of February will be excellent for finding help. Singles may discover that some people cannot be relied upon, and in that case your likely take-out from that will be to avoid them.

WORK

Consider the practicalities in your daily work life, as this will help you find the balance between your work and home lives. Finding work-life balance will be super necessary in February, as you may discover that your home life commands a great deal of your attention. Your work life may, in fact, have a therapeutic quality because you are able to get on with things without distractions.

SCORPIO · FEBRUARY

March

WEEK 1: 5–11 MARCH

You'll enjoy a sociable end to the week and weekend. Someone may even surprise you, or an impromptu event will be fun. It's a great time to lavish family and friends with love, and it will be reciprocated. You can make progress at work too, with a key meeting or news that buoys your position or kudos. Some Scorpios will be making considerable changes at home.

WEEK 2: 12–18 MARCH

Investment in your home, family or a property will bring a sense of accomplishment your way. A little home decoration or DIY project may appeal. You could experience a personal or financial boost, even if a conundrum needs sorting out mid-week. For some Scorpios a change of environment either due to a holiday or changes at home will be refreshing. However, you must pay special attention to logistics mid-week next week.

WEEK 3: 19–25 MARCH

You may be drawn to spruce up both personal and domestic dynamics, or to renovate or even move. The Pisces new moon on the 19th will inspire you to invest more in your personal life, and a trip or fun venture will revitalise relationships. This is a good time to make decisions regarding personal and domestic matters, but you must avoid making snap decisions or changes because things seem too limiting for now.

WEEK 4: 26 MARCH–1 APRIL

There is a therapeutic or healing aspect to the week's events. It's a good time for a health appointment. A creative or family project could produce an unexpected outcome. Someone may ask for your help. Sunday and early next week are ideal for romance and the arts, so be sure to organise a treat then. You may unexpectedly bump into an old friend.

HEALTH

Your sense of contentment and well-being will come from feeling secure in your work life and at home in March, so be sure to find the balance between the two areas and avoid burning the candle at both ends. The conjunction of Venus and Chiron on the 26th/27th will bring the focus on either your health or that of someone close to you. This can be a particularly healing time, so be sure to pay attention to good health.

FINANCES

Jupiter will bring any debt to light at the moment, and right now this is likely to be predominantly to do with domestic or household expenses. If you are starting a fresh chapter domestically be careful not to go too deeply into debt. If, however, you are able to clear past debts, especially those associated with domestic or family matters, this will be the month to achieve this.

HOME

You will appreciate the opportunity to invest in your home life and family early in the month already and mid-month. Someone special such as a family member or expert will help you if you are considering a little DIY project or a move. However, there is also the potential for you to overspend on household expenses, so be sure to keep your household budget on an even keel where possible.

LOVE LIFE

You like adventure and excitement in your love life, and in March you are certainly going to enjoy at least some of these qualities. The period from the 5th to the 9th will be particularly conducive to romance. You may enjoy a change of environment via a trip or visit, and someone close may surprise you. The new moon on the 19th will revitalise and inspire your love life; just avoid being super idealistic about your relationships at this time.

WORK

For some Scorpios the end of March will bring changes to your usual work schedule. This may be due to the fact you will be taking a holiday; however, for all Scorpios March is an excellent time to organise your working day and week so it is as efficient as it can be. This is so you then have the time and opportunity to spend with those you love on the activities you enjoy and on relaxation.

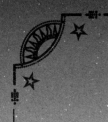

April

WEEK 1: 2–8 APRIL

You'll enjoy a trip or visit but must avoid a change of schedule that creates stress, so be sure to organise yourself in advance. Important work or personal developments will need focus. A dynamic yet tactful approach to both areas of your life will be productive. Be prepared to instigate change, as a workable arrangement can be found that will suit everyone concerned at work and at home.

WEEK 2: 9–15 APRIL

Romance, the arts and creativity will thrive this week, so these are productive areas on which to put your energy. If you have been trying to make changes with your family or home life you are likely to see transformation take off over the next few weeks, so be sure of the direction you are taking. Sunday and Monday are good days for romance or at least a change of pace.

WEEK 3: 16–22 APRIL

This week you'll enjoy taking your work life up a level. If conflict has been simmering, though, you must find ways to establish peace. A health situation may need more focus than usual. Take your time to adjust to circumstances, as some talks, conversations or communications may seem intense. Romance could blossom this weekend, so be sure to take the initiative.

WEEK 4: 23–29 APRIL

A chance encounter may turn aspects of your life upside down. You may receive news that means you must alter some of the agreements you have either at work or in your personal life. Luckily, you'll gain the chance to iron out various details within your commitments towards the people you love in your life such as friends and family. Be careful this weekend to avoid travel delays by planning ahead.

HEALTH

A change in your usual schedule or work routine may add a little extra pressure on you, so be sure to take things in your stride. A trip somewhere beautiful or being able to welcome someone lovely at home will be relaxing but you must ensure, especially at the start of the month, to avoid allowing other people to destroy your peace of mind. The new moon on the 17th is a good time to develop a fresh health schedule.

FINANCES

Keep a close eye on shared expenses such as utilities and overheads, as these may blow out or will need paying early in the month. If you undergo changes in your work routine be sure to stay on top of payments, as these can be forgotten when you're on holiday. Extracurricular activities such as travel or holidays this month are also liable to blow your budget, so try to head off debt before it accrues.

HOME

You'll enjoy a change of scenery in early April that may come in the shape of a holiday or visitor whose company you enjoy. Your creative side may come out in April as well, and it will be a good time to look at ways to beautify your immediate environment. It's likely that in mid-April a work or health schedule will require focus, so do ensure your home life provides a progressive yet solid base for the best results then.

LOVE LIFE

Mid-April will be an excellent time to invest in your love life, as your efforts will be successful. If you have been trying to make changes recently without much luck you are likely to see more success over the following weeks up until at least mid-May, so take the initiative to create more of a sense of romance in your love life. The weekend of the 11th and the 13th, 17th and 18th are particularly conducive days for romance.

WORK

There is stress in the stars at the start of April, especially regarding communications, so if you feel certain people at work do not understand you or that you do not understand them try to find ways to smooth over differences to avoid conflict later in the month. The full moon on the 2nd and developments towards the 26th may spotlight changes at work that are best taken in your stride as long as your finances are covered.

May

WEEK 1: 30 APRIL—6 MAY

The full moon will be in Scorpio and signifies the chance to turn a corner in your personal life, especially if it's your birthday in October. November-born Scorpios may begin a fresh daily, work or health routine. Key news towards the weekend will enable you to make plans concerning your usual daily work or health routine. It's a good week to look for new expert advice if it's needed.

WEEK 2: 7—13 MAY

Take the initiative with your projects as you could make great progress, especially with study, travel and your favourite activities. You may experience a boost in your personal life and may be inclined to make promises; just be sure that you can keep these. It's a good week for discussions and getting closer to those you must collaborate with, both at home and at work.

WEEK 3: 14—20 MAY

This weekend's new moon signals a fresh start in a business or personal partnership. If you were born after mid-November expect a fresh phase to begin soon, if it hasn't already, at work or health-wise. You may need to act swiftly but also intelligently with a health or work matter this week and must ensure you are well-informed if you're making considerable changes to your daily life.

WEEK 4: 21—27 MAY / WEEK 5: 28 MAY—3 JUNE

WEEK 4: you may be surprised by developments concerning your key business and personal relationships, so maintain an open mind. Do keep an eye on your principles, beliefs and values but equally be prepared to adopt new beliefs in line with changing circumstances. **WEEK 5:** be adventurous and prepared to step into fresh territory both in your personal life and at work.

HEALTH

During the first week of May and towards mid-month health and well-being are likely to be at the forefront of your mind. This may be due to your need for a health boost, and for some Scorpios it will be due to someone close needing health-related advice or at the least a morale boost. It's certainly a good time to look for expert help if it's needed. You may be asked for help.

FINANCES

Be prepared to discuss your finances with those they affect, such as family and those you share expenses with. If you realise you must devise new arrangements you'll find 11 to 13 May particularly beneficial for this process. The new moon on the 16th/17th involves the chance to improve your work and therefore your income, so keep an eye open for opportunities then. Developments towards the 31st will encourage you to try something new financially, with expert advice.

HOME

Where do you feel you belong? This question may be difficult to answer right now due to a changing scenario in your personal life; however, it is an important question and one that holds the key to your progress over the coming months and years. If you feel you have idealised various aspects of your home life, property or domestic circumstances, this month will help you get your feet back on the ground and put practicalities first.

LOVE LIFE

Good communication skills will be necessary in May, especially during the first week. This is largely so you can avoid miscommunications and mix-ups, which would be frustrating. You will gain the opportunity over the coming weeks and months to improve your communication skills and review best practice when it comes to being clear with your own intentions and feelings. It's certainly a good month to look at motivation and the psychology behind some of your self-expression.

WORK

This is a good month to take positive steps in the direction you wish to go. Be prepared to take the initiative with negotiations and talks, especially between the 11th and 13th, as you are likely to succeed. The conjunction of Mars and Chiron on the 16th/17th may bring noticeable developments at work. There is a therapeutic aspect, so even if you experience a setback it is likely to suit you in the long term.

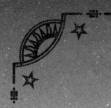

June

WEEK 1: 4–10 JUNE

This weekend is particularly good for improving health via fitness. This is also a good week to decide where your priorities lie, especially in connection with your favourite activities, self-development and if necessary legal matters. Be decisive and make the necessary commitments to ensure you can achieve a sense of stability. You'll enjoy a trip, sport or the chance to boost your health. Just avoid fatigue and minor bumps and scrapes.

WEEK 2: 11–17 JUNE

You will enjoy the lighter atmosphere in your love life, especially as the weekend approaches, as you'll gain the opportunity to enjoy favourite activities. If you are single you may spontaneously meet someone attractive. Consider approaching those with whom you share space and duties in a new way: you may find you are more adaptable than you believe and that it's possible to breathe fresh air into relationships.

WEEK 3: 18–24 JUNE

This is the kind of weekend you love as it will include your favourite pastimes and the chance to indulge in the people you love. A trip or fun event will bring your emotions to the surface, however, so keep an eye on intense interactions, overspending and mix-ups. Plan travel ahead to avoid delays. There is a therapeutic aspect towards the 21st that you will appreciate.

WEEK 4: 25 JUNE–1 JULY

You will appreciate the opportunity to bring more activities you enjoy into your everyday life such as travel. You may dream of faraway places and find inspiration in hobbies. You may be forgetful or prone to making mistakes, so aim to focus more than usual. Monday/Tuesday's full moon suggests a fresh agreement or arrangement that could provide stability.

HEALTH

A trip or the opportunity to broaden your horizons via a course or self-development, for example, will appeal. If health has been an issue for you or someone close it will be important to prioritise this. Be sure to schedule enjoyable activities and fun events, as these will encourage you to relax and will also reintroduce elements of joy into your life. Focusing on your health towards the 13th and 21st will provide insight into where you stand.

FINANCES

The new moon on the 15th and developments towards the 21st will bring your focus to shared finances such as household expenses, joint financial investments and tax matters. It is in your interest in June to avoid gambling, as this will only complicate matters. You may nevertheless experience an improvement either in your work life or finances around the latter part of the month, especially towards the full moon when new arrangements can be made.

HOME

Developments towards the 17th could bring positive changes at home. However, if you have inadvertently idealised some of the aspects of your home life, family or property you may need to return to a more realistic approach to the issues at hand. Be prepared to discuss your various ideas and options with those they will affect and avoid making snap decisions as these could backfire, especially once Mercury has turned retrograde from the 29th.

LOVE LIFE

This is an excellent month to devote time to love, and specifically the health of your love life. Ask yourself where the joy is. If you feel that some of the fun or spontaneity has been lacking, consider scheduling activities that will revitalise the fun factor in your love life. If you are single you may be in line to meet someone who has a refreshing character so ensure you schedule dates, especially around the 9th and 17th.

WORK

There is a sense in June that you will need to focus on exactly what it is – apart from money – that you want from your work life. Developments between the 13th and 15th will spotlight your best path forward. If you experience a disappointment at this time, bear in mind that it may open the door to fresh options that will in fact suit you better. A new agreement towards the full moon on the 29th/30th could provide stability.

SCORPIO · JUNE

July

WEEK 1: 2–8 JULY

A trip or activity may be delayed or frustrating, and as you prefer to stride ahead you must be patient. You can certainly get a great deal done, especially if you have done your groundwork, but you must avoid impulsiveness. A business or personal partner has unexpected news, and a change of environment could prove to be exciting or exhilarating despite delays.

WEEK 2: 9–15 JULY

The new moon on the 14th will be in Cancer and the run up to that is an excellent time to turn a page, bringing more activities and people into your life whose company you truly enjoy. A reunion or return to an old haunt will bring this in sharp focus. A change either within your career or personal life will need careful management to avoid fallout.

WEEK 3: 16–22 JULY

The key to success this week revolves around good communication skills: this more so than usual, because a personal relationship will involve new, different or even unprecedented variables. A trip or project may bring a little intensity into your everyday communications, so to avoid fallout remain realistic. This may be one of the most romantic weeks of the year as long as you do not succumb to pressure.

WEEK 4: 23–29 JULY

You will appreciate get-togethers with like-minded people and an opportunity to network and boost your status or general feel-good factor in life. This is also a transformative week in your key relationships, when many of your plans, discussions and ideas will take form. If you are single this is a key week for socialising, and you could meet someone who has a transformative effect on your life.

HEALTH

Being such a passionate sign, patience is not one of your virtues and unfortunately at the start of the month this is something you will need to learn. This may simply be due to delays with travel, for example, but if you find you are laid up due to health issues it will provide you with the opportunity to develop a better health plan moving forward. The full moon on the 29th/30th will spotlight your true circumstances health-wise.

FINANCES

Your communication skills are in demand in July because you will need to be on the same page as people with whom you share finances: think your home life, work and pay, for example. Mid-month may be a flashpoint when disagreements could arise in any of those areas mentioned, and it will be important at this time to ensure you do not lose out financially. Focus on security as opposed to adopting a scarcity mindset.

HOME

Certain relationships and duties connected with your home life will come into sharp focus in July and merit careful attention so you do not drop the ball or overlook any necessities that require your input. There are therapeutic aspects to the month that require you to be patient but also clever about how you navigate your long-term options. This is certainly a key month that can transform your life.

LOVE LIFE

You will receive unexpected news or may see a partner as quirky or less reliable than you'd prefer early in the month already. While you may enjoy spontaneity in your love life, if you dislike unpredictability in a partner this could rock the relationship boat. However, if you are more open-minded and can adapt to someone's need for self-expression and growth in the relationship it could bring a more exciting phase your way. Singles could meet someone positively transformative.

WORK

A change in your usual schedule may initially feel like a let-down; however, you may discover therapeutic aspects to a change at work over time. There will be certain discussions and activities over which you feel you have no control, so developing patience will certainly help you overcome any work obstacles. Be sure to keep communications as calm as possible for the best effect, especially towards the 20th and 29th.

August

WEEK 1: 30 JULY–5 AUGUST

The Leo sun makes a beautiful aspect with Saturn, and this can be a time of great accomplishment. You'll be drawn to invest in your favourite activities and people. It's a good time to plan a holiday and make the most of your hobbies by scheduling them into your weekly timetable. If events bring conflicting feelings, it's time to align your actions with your priorities.

WEEK 2: 6–12 AUGUST

Communications are likely to be intense, so be prepared to take a deep breath when you're under pressure. The total solar eclipse on the 12th/13th will kick-start a dynamic phase as you gain the opportunity to spend more time doing activities you love such as spending time with someone special. You may feel that your ideas or projects are admired or at least validated.

WEEK 3: 13–19 AUGUST

You'll appreciate the opportunity to take a trip or indulge a little more in your favourite activities such as sport or self-development. This will also still be a romantic time, so be sure to organise dates. However, there is the likelihood that some arrangements, discussions or relationships are built on assumptions, so to avoid misunderstandings be sure to establish common ground.

WEEK 4: 20–26 AUGUST / WEEK 5: 27 AUGUST–2 SEPTEMBER

WEEK 4: this will be a good week to focus on improving your usual daily routine to incorporate more of what you love in life. You may be fortunate to enjoy a short holiday and, at the least, a therapeutic activity. **WEEK 5:** the partial lunar eclipse on the 28th will spotlight developments in your personal life and especially at home. This may be due to developments or news concerning projects that take you into fresh territory. News may surprise you.

HEALTH

Be prepared to prioritise your health. You will gain the opportunity over the coming weeks to find more time for the activities you enjoy, which will naturally boost your mental, emotional and spiritual well-being. Differences of opinion, however, can do the opposite. Sometimes it is impossible to change someone's opinion, but it is possible to alter your reaction to their inflexibility or ideas. Be sure to create a balanced mindset that enables you to retain your peace.

FINANCES

Uranus in your eighth house of shared finances is creating a situation where you need to be able to balance joint finances such as those you share with people you love and with groups and organisations such as employers or employees. The eclipses will be highlighting your career and home lives, and this indicates considerable changes occurring in both areas and the likelihood that shared finances need attention.

HOME

This is potentially a sociable and adventurous month that will lead you to spend more time outside your home. However, a sense of belonging is never far away and this is something that contributes to a sense of well-being and even good health. For these reasons be sure in August to factor your home life into major decisions. The lunar eclipse on the 28th could bring key change in this vital area of your life in any case.

LOVE LIFE

Be prepared to step into new territory. This is potentially a super-romantic week. For couples this will involve a little innovation, adventure and excitement, which will take you outside your comfort zone. Discuss your options with your partner for the best results. Singles may be drawn to make a commitment to a particular activity or hobby that brings you in touch with like-minded people, some of whom may resonate with you more deeply than others.

WORK

The eclipse season will bring a change within your work or career direction and at the least important decisions that affect your career or general direction. If you have been making tracks to extend your skill sets, this is an excellent month to continue doing so as you could build a strong platform for yourself. However, you may need to make an important decision towards the 21st and 28th, and to ensure it is correct consider all the variables.

SCORPIO · AUGUST

September

WEEK 1: 3–9 SEPTEMBER

People's quirkiness may become more apparent now as will their inability to understand others, especially at work or in your daily life. Avoid taking random comments personally. Focus, instead, on taking your goals towards success. Once you overcome minor obstacles this week you could attain a goal; you may even be pleasantly surprised by the praise you receive. You'll enjoy a trip or favourite activity towards Sunday and Monday.

WEEK 2: 10–16 SEPTEMBER

As Venus enters Scorpio your attention goes increasingly to love and money. The opposition with Chiron may illuminate someone's vulnerabilities, so be careful with communications to avoid conflict. Keep a close eye on health and work schedules as you can improve both now. This is potentially one of the most romantic weeks of the year so be sure to schedule in treats, which you'll enjoy.

WEEK 3: 17–23 SEPTEMBER

A group, friend or organisation may present an interesting offer that merits careful thought. A change of circumstance at home or in your general status will need a careful approach, using tact and diplomacy. You may have to make a tough choice and you could even hear surprising news from a business or personal partner. However, this may help you make up your mind in the bigger picture.

WEEK 4: 24–30 SEPTEMBER

You'll appreciate reconnecting with friends and being with like-minded people this weekend. You may find developments are therapeutic or have a health-related theme. A healing approach to someone or yourself will be effective. This weekend's full moon will shine a light on family, your creativity or a domestic matter. Romance, music and the arts could thrive, so be sure to organise a date.

HEALTH

You like to know where you stand with the people close to you. The situation of someone close either at work or in your personal life may mean that you feel you are slightly in limbo this month. For this reason it will be important to focus on your sense of stability and security via such activities as meditation and yoga, which will help you gain a sense of peace regardless of someone else's circumstance.

FINANCES

Venus in your sign will make you partial to the luxuries and creature comforts in life, even if only because you will wish to enjoy the arts, music and romance more. Be sure to factor in the expenditure to avoid a financial shortfall or debt later in the month. Keep an eye on shared finances such as household expenses and taxes to avoid a shortfall towards the end of the month.

HOME

You will appreciate a get-together with someone close to your heart towards the 10th, and the new moon on the 11th will help kick-start a fresh phase socially. If you have been socialising too much recently you will gain the opportunity to slow down and focus more on those you love and your home life. If you have recently felt you've been housebound you will gain the opportunity to be a little more flexible, which you will enjoy.

LOVE LIFE

The second week of September and the full moon on the 26th/27th have all the hallmarks of romance, so be sure to plan special events. However, misunderstandings and conundrums are also possible so communicate well to avoid misunderstandings, especially between the 10th and the 15th, the 18th to the 22nd and the 27th. If you have been looking for a commitment from someone or must make a commitment, you may find this to be therapeutic.

WORK

Be prepared to put in hard work, especially at the start of the month, as your hard work will pay off. Don't be put off by obstacles. You may even achieve a long-term goal. The new moon on the 11th and developments towards the 18th could bring fresh opportunities at work or within your favourite activities, so be sure to explore new ideas then. You may need to make a tough choice, so you'll need to carefully research the options.

October

WEEK 1: 1–7 OCTOBER

Venus, the planet that rules both love and money, turns retrograde in your sign this week, which suggests you may reconnect with someone from your past or may even experience a nostalgic phase when the grass always seems greener elsewhere. Avoid falling into this trap and maintain a solid, optimistic outlook, especially regarding a trip, work and health. Avoid arguments towards Friday, as these could escalate.

WEEK 2: 8–14 OCTOBER

Tact and diplomacy are your keys to success this week, especially at work. While Jupiter in your career sector signals the chance to broaden your horizons some conversations will require delicate handling, especially on Friday and Saturday if you are working then. The Libran new moon this weekend could bring more balance to your everyday life, although you must be careful with travel and communication this weekend.

WEEK 3: 15–21 OCTOBER

You'll enjoy a group get-together or favourite activity. You're likely to feel some of your usual joie de vivre resurface. A change of environment or an exciting fresh venture will appeal towards the weekend. Just be sure to keep an eye on good communication skills, as you may otherwise inadvertently give or take offence in a social or work circumstance.

WEEK 4: 22–28 OCTOBER / WEEK 5: 29 OCTOBER–4 NOVEMBER

WEEK 4: as the sun enters Scorpio you'll appreciate elevated energy levels over the coming weeks, starting now! The full moon in Taurus points to a fresh daily routine or health schedule. It's time to focus on your well-being or that of someone close. **WEEK 5:** be tactful with communications to avoid giving or taking offence. You'll enjoy a change of pace such as a break or work improvement.

HEALTH

The conjunction between Mercury and Venus on the 7th and developments towards the full moon on the 26th/26th could bring key news your way regarding your health and well-being or that of someone close, especially if you were born in October. All Scorpios will enjoy the opportunity to change your daily schedule so it incorporates more opportunity to invest in your health and well-being in October and to pursue your favourite activities, especially around 7 October and 4 November.

FINANCES

Financially, this will be a good phase throughout the month to review your finances with the perspective of considering fresh parameters that could take you into new territory financially towards the end of the year. Try to get important plans and budgets on the table before the 24th when Mercury turns retrograde, unless you feel you need more time to ponder your financial circumstances and could wait until the end of November to make firm decisions.

HOME

You will appreciate the creature comforts early in the month already. If you've been considering a move or bringing someone new into your environment this could proceed as long as you have made the necessary checks and balances. A change of pace or environment towards mid-month or at the end of the month could prove to be therapeutic, but you may need to be patient with communications throughout October to avoid simmering unrest.

LOVE LIFE

This is an excellent month to make your partner your focus, as you could truly infuse your relationship with a sense of fun and excitement. A trip, favourite activities and collaborations will all put you on a solid footing. Just avoid unnecessary arguments towards the 2nd, 3rd, 9th, 10th and 20th. Be prepared to embrace a fun and spontaneous outlook towards someone special. A health or well-being focus towards the end of October will be rewarding.

WORK

Your sign's rulers Mars and Pluto could bring inner conflict and even arguments and dissatisfaction at the start of the month, so be careful to maintain perspective, especially around the 2nd and 3rd. Another hotspot will be towards the new moon on the 10th/11th and the 20th, 26th and 30th, when a battle of wills could arise. This aside, mid-October and 4 November could bring a wonderful opportunity to boost your work circumstances, so keep an eye out.

SCORPIO • OCTOBER

November

WEEK 1: 5–11 NOVEMBER

Monday's Scorpio new moon signals a fresh start in your life, especially if you were born on 9 or 10 November. For some this will take place in your work arena and for others in your personal life. Take the time to work on improving relationships, especially with loved ones. A reunion may be ideal. Consider circumstances from a fresh perspective and avoid being inflexible about your options.

WEEK 2: 12–18 NOVEMBER

Key developments that could transform both your career and status are best taken one step at a time, because developments are likely to be fast. Be sure to consider your big-picture wishes and goals before being swept up in developments. This aside, you could make great progress both at work and within your projects and ventures. Someone significant will play a part in your enjoyment of developments.

WEEK 3: 19–25 NOVEMBER

You'll gain the opportunity to turn a corner in a shared circumstance; for example, a personal relationship, household chores or duties. You may even be surprised by some developments that will alter either your career or status. You may even experience a therapeutic development work-wise. Just avoid knee-jerk reactions towards Friday. You'll enjoy a lovely reunion towards Sunday or Monday.

WEEK 4: 26 NOVEMBER–2 DECEMBER

You may experience an uplifting development that either changes your usual daily routine or improves your career or status in some way. You may need to review domestic and financial matters and how to embrace these as your general direction, career or status change. You will have the opportunity to create more stability in all of the above areas. It's a good weekend to improve your health.

HEALTH

You have a wonderful opportunity this month to improve your health. For many this will come about through a wonderful trip or opportunity that enables you to relax, while for some a holiday or simply a change of schedule at work will provide the variety and well-being you enjoy. Developments will provide the opportunity for a well-earned break or fresh environment that will help boost your health and well-being, especially towards the end of the month.

FINANCES

You may experience a surprise towards the end of the month, so it's in your interest beforehand to ensure that you feel you are wholly on track financially and that you have not left any of your bases uncovered. Avoid making rash financial decisions. It is likely that you'll experience changes within your career this month, and although these are likely to be positive you must not jump the gun financially and above all must avoid gambling.

HOME

Important developments within your big-picture progress will predispose you to focus on opportunities in your status and career, and your home life may be something you need to re-evaluate in line with these. This does not mean you necessarily move or change location, but it is in your interest to evaluate domestic circumstances. You will enjoy a return to an old haunt towards the end of the month as a reunion either with family or to a place that warms your heart.

LOVE LIFE

The Scorpio new moon on the 9th brings a fresh chapter in your love life, especially if your birthday is before 9 November. Consider your family commitments laterally and avoid putting them second. You may even need to choose between priorities at work or in your status or domestic life. Someone may surprise you towards the full moon supermoon on the 24th/25th. For many this will be pleasant, but if a disappointment arises you'll gain perspective and turn a corner.

WORK

You are about to begin a fresh chapter in your work schedule; you may even receive a good offer towards the 10th to 14th or the 28th. Be prepared to consider opportunities as there may be more to them than initially meets the eye. You will have the opportunity to broaden your horizons and enter fresh territory should you wish to do so. However, you must avoid rushing your options without due forethought.

SCORPIO • NOVEMBER ✦ 207

December

WEEK 1: 3–9 DECEMBER

Your usual lust for life returns in full force, and you will enjoy celebrating early in the lead-up to the festive season. Just be careful with some communications at work, especially on Friday and Wednesday, to avoid arguments. The new moon on Wednesday brings the chance to put in place a fresh agreement, and this will merit discussion with those with whom you must share finances and duties.

WEEK 2: 10–16 DECEMBER

You will appreciate the opportunity to get together with a friend, family or someone else whom you are close to. Some Scorpios may enjoy a particularly romantic and creative week as a project comes to completion or at least provides you with a sense of progress. Positive developments either at work or within your status and well-being will provide incentive to enjoy life more.

WEEK 3: 17–23 DECEMBER

A change in your circumstances will be invigorating, although you will need to be fully focused to avoid forgetfulness and making mistakes. You're likely to enjoy this festive season but may also be predisposed to overspending or even misplacing objects such as keys. Your duties will mean that your focus must be on family, work or those you care for, so be careful to prioritise these areas.

WEEK 4: 24–31 DECEMBER

You'll be in your element, enjoying festivities largely due to the opportunity to relax. The full moon supermoon on Christmas Eve will, however, spotlight shared duties and finances, and you may need to be careful with some interactions to avoid upheaval or unnecessary upset. Towards New Year's Eve you will once again enjoy being in your element. Just avoid overspending and overindulging then as you're likely to regret it.

HEALTH

A break in a busy work schedule will do you the world of good, so even if you can only get a few days off at Christmas be sure to make the most of it so you can unwind. Some developments early in the month will ask that you draw on your inner resources. Find ways to replenish your energy levels throughout December, as you will not only be in demand at work but also socially.

FINANCES

The new moon on the 9th brings a fresh financial cycle. You may be surprised by developments and careful discussion could strengthen your position, but you must avoid a battle of wills as this could make waves. Positive astrological aspects towards mid-month could provide financial improvement, and this will largely be due to your efforts in the past. Keep an eye on spending, especially on domestic matters, because you may be liable to overspend towards Christmas and the new year.

HOME

You'll enjoy the time of year as it brings you closer to those you love. You'll also enjoy organising reunions. However, if you have either taken a domestic situation for granted or someone has taken you for granted you may be drawn to discuss these feelings. For many there's an upbeat atmosphere in the week before Christmas, but if you feel you're missing out it will be important to address this situation rather than allowing resentment to boil.

LOVE LIFE

You will enjoy Venus in your sign this month as it brings your passions to the surface, and you will certainly appreciate the seasonal festivities. Romance can thrive: singles may meet someone exciting towards the 11th and couples will enjoy ramping up passion. Just be careful with communications between the 5th and the 9th and again towards the 21st, as arguments could flare up for no apparent reason. Your diplomatic skills will be in demand towards Christmas.

WORK

The idea that you get out of life what you put into it resonates now, especially from the 11th to the 14th and then again from the 18th to the 23rd, when it is possible positive developments at work and/or financially arise. This will largely be due to past hard work well done, which you are now rewarded for. However, if you are a workaholic you must be careful to prioritise those you care about towards Christmas to avoid making waves.

SCORPIO • DECEMBER

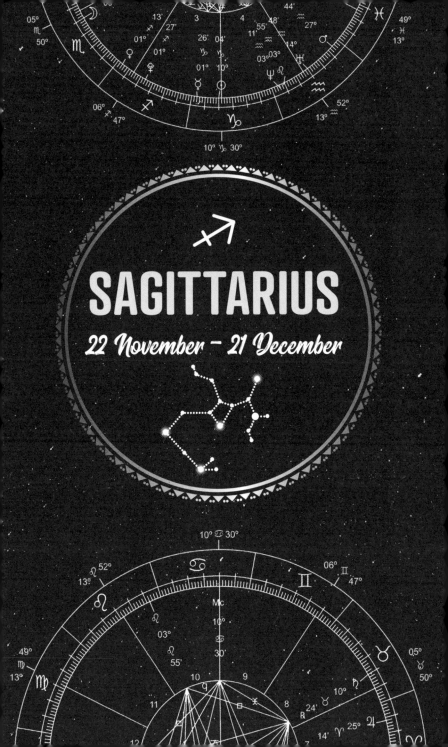

January

WEEK 1: 1–7 JANUARY

You'll gain the opportunity to review your finances and set up a fresh budget if necessary, especially with regard to shared finances such as joint accounts. You'll embrace the chance to reunite with a friend or someone special if you have been estranged. Avoid financial and emotional gambling, especially at home or regarding property, as it is likely to backfire.

WEEK 2: 8–14 JANUARY

This is a good week to make changes both in your personal life and financially, as there is potential for success in both areas and you are ready to consider your personal and financial investments in a new light. However, this largely depends on obtaining someone's agreement, and at the least in managing shared concerns. Be prepared to look outside the box at your options for the best results.

WEEK 3: 15–21 JANUARY

This weekend you'll enjoy a reunion or get-together with someone special. Be patient, as some people may be unpredictable or will need to unexpectedly alter arrangements. Financially, you may be predisposed to spend big so keep an eye on overspending. Sunday's new moon will help you turn a corner in your personal life, and some events may surprise you.

WEEK 4: 22–28 JANUARY

You're not afraid to speak honestly, yet tact can serve a purpose. You may feel strongly about an issue such as finances or personal matters; be open to new options but don't compromise healthy values. A financial matter is best approached philosophically and practically to avoid impulsive reactions. Similarly, a personal matter or one to do with self-esteem is best approached calmly to avoid a snowball effect.

HEALTH

A change of pace will certainly improve your health, so simply doing slightly different activities this month will have the same effect. Be prepared to invest in your health and well-being in January, because your efforts will pay off and you will be glad you did. You may be drawn to a new look mid-month that promises to help you express aspects of your personality in your appearance.

FINANCES

The first two weeks of January will be ideal for reviewing and potentially re-organising your finances. It's important in January to avoid gambling: whether literally (think slot machines) or, for example, buying an expensive item on a hunch that the value will increase. Both could lead to disappointment. That said, you may enjoy a financial boost towards the 6th, 8th, 14th, 18th and 27th. Be careful with household expenditure at the end of the month to avoid debt.

HOME

Whether you're travelling or at home your domestic situation can thrive in January, so be sure to revel in a little luxury whenever you can. If you're planning a move, some DIY projects or a renovation, your efforts are likely to go well. Just be aware of overspending on trends that will not stand the test of time, such as décor, paint colours or even in construction. You may be tempted to overinvest in your home so keep perspective.

LOVE LIFE

The focus early in January will be on who and what you value the most. When you look at your love life from this perspective you will be able to prioritise the people you truly love. A reunion or the opportunity to reignite a past relationship may present itself, but you must evaluate whether it would in fact be more painful than pleasant. At the end of the month you may feel differently about a relationship, so avoid impulsiveness beforehand.

WORK

A change in your usual routine is on the cards, and this could be truly enjoyable. If you're on holiday you'll appreciate the change of routine. If you're looking for fresh work opportunities these will arise. Some Sagittarians may experience an unexpected boost at work in mid-January and at the end of the month, and this will improve your finances. Be prepared to evaluate the relative value of making changes at work.

SAGITTARIUS • JANUARY

February

WEEK 1: 29 JANUARY—4 FEBRUARY

An exciting new chapter is waiting in the wings, and events now will already provide you with an idea of the changes to come. For some, developments will revolve around a thrilling relationship and for others around travel, a venture, study or plan that comes to life. A change of routine and environment may involve some teething problems, but developments will provide direction.

WEEK 2: 5—11 FEBRUARY

Changes at home or the chance to do something different such as take a trip somewhere new will add a sense of excitement to the week. However, a change of routine or environment may be tiring or require extra focus, so be sure to factor in downtime. For some Sagittarians this week's development will put the focus on finances and the necessity to adopt a stable budget.

WEEK 3: 12—18 FEBRUARY

Your communications will become quirkier and different and you may meet all kinds of interesting people. Because you will be in a fresh environment or will meet new people, be sure to focus on good communication skills. For some this week's solar eclipse will kick-start a fresh financial circumstance.

WEEK 4: 19—25 FEBRUARY / WEEK 5: 26 FEBRUARY—4 MARCH

WEEK 4: there's considerable movement in areas such as travel and personal relationships. A reunion could be ideal. If you're renovating at home or moving this should turn out well, as long as you have researched circumstances. **WEEK 5:** a financial transaction may be significant and the key to success lies in not gambling; it's far better to research valid sure-fire results. Key information around the 26th will stimulate conversation.

HEALTH

A stop-start aspect at the start of February will mean you need to dig deeper than usual to maintain a sense of status quo and direction so be sure to organise activities such as sport that help you maintain a steady flow of energy, otherwise you may find the beginning of the month draining. You'll be drawn in two conflicting directions: either work versus home, or how best to invest in yourself. Be prepared to find peace of mind.

FINANCES

You're liable to overspend now so must be careful not to exhaust your budget at the start of February. You may discover bills or charges that you had overlooked, and these will require payment. The solar eclipse mid-month will help you turn a corner financially, and an expert, friend or family member will be helpful. An unexpected development towards the end of February suggests you must maintain a steady keel, so avoid gambling in investments and increasing debt.

HOME

There is a refreshing atmosphere surrounding your domestic life. However, you must avoid being idealistic about the best way forward. If you can focus predominantly on creating a nurturing, caring atmosphere both for yourself and those you share your home with this will provide exactly what you need. The conjunction between Saturn and Neptune, which is growing throughout the month, could take you into fresh territory, so be prepared to branch out. You'll be glad you did.

LOVE LIFE

The last two weeks of the month will be ideal for boosting your love life, as you'll wish to communicate your thoughts and feelings. Beforehand, though, you may find this month stressful so you must avoid taking your stress out on your partner. If you feel you have important matters to discuss, ensure you get these on the table by the 22nd as otherwise the issues will simmer over the coming two months and could add to stress.

WORK

You may be surprised by developments at work at the start of February, and these will require you to be adaptable and innovative. A progressive approach to your work life and career will pay dividends. However, you must be careful to avoid looking only at the financial side of your work. To truly gain a sense of accomplishment you must also feel truly motivated to get up and go to work every day.

SAGITTARIUS • FEBRUARY

March

WEEK 1: 5–11 MARCH

You'll enjoy a trip or reunion and the chance to indulge in your favourite activities. A new opportunity may arise, so be prepared to at least consider it as you may discover your luck is in this week. You'll appreciate good company such as family or friends. You may also enjoy romance or a financial improvement.

WEEK 2: 12–18 MARCH

You'll enjoy a trip or change of environment and will appreciate the chance to spend time with your favourite people. A reunion or spontaneous get-together will be equally enjoyable. Pay attention to details with communications and finances towards mid-week next week (the 18th) to avoid making mistakes. An impromptu change of routine could be refreshing then too.

WEEK 3: 19–25 MARCH

Your wish for a deeper connection with someone may kick-start a fresh chapter in your personal life, either at home or with family. You'll be drawn to share confidences or at least to invest in communicating better with someone special. You may be drawn to upgrade or change a communications device, travel route or vehicle. A key financial decision may be made.

WEEK 4: 26 MARCH–1 APRIL

A change in your usual schedule may bring unexpected benefits. A visitor may be a surprise but a welcome one. Someone may need your help. Considerable focus will also need to be directed to your home life this week. If you need support around the house it will be available, so do ask. Your home can become a relaxing haven, so be sure to organise it that way.

HEALTH

Sometimes to feel well you can help the process simply by improving your mindset and appearance. This month you may discover innovative ways to improve your well-being. A change in environment or of pace will certainly help at the start of the month and mid- to late March. A change in your usual routine or fitness schedule will certainly be inspiring and keep you in top form, so be sure to look out for opportunities to experience something new.

FINANCES

This is likely to be a busy month so it will be important to keep an eye on expenditure, especially spending in connection with travel, short trips and get-togethers at mid-month. If you are investing in property – anything from sprucing up décor to moving – you must avoid overspending and going deeply into debt, especially towards the 21st and 26th. Be sure to carefully plan domestic expenses.

HOME

You will be entering a new chapter in your domestic life that may involve having to make a fresh commitment either to yourself or someone close. You may even be signing a new contract, especially if you were born in November. Be prepared to be adventurous with your domestic plans. If you have been hoping to add to your family or move this is certainly a good time to take steps down these paths.

LOVE LIFE

You'll find that the areas you share in life can truly bring a sense of satisfaction between yourself and your partner, so it will be in your interest this month to organise events that you both enjoy. Singles may meet someone new or deepen an existing connection, especially between the 5th and the 9th, so be sure to be outgoing. You may even be prepared to make a commitment to someone.

WORK

Positive opportunities will arise at work, so be prepared to recognise them as and when they do occur. Avoid seeing yourself as less able than you are and be sure to take the initiative with communications. You may be drawn to make a fresh business commitment that helps you break into new ground. Mid-March is an excellent time for talks and meetings, so be sure to take the initiative.

April

WEEK 1: 2–8 APRIL

This will be a good week to make a commitment to a person, project or domestic matter, especially if it could bring your way a positive transformation that involves a sense of increased security. Developments may arise due to a fresh chapter beginning that could alter your career, status or direction. Be sure to choose your options carefully and avoid being influenced. Make up your own mind.

WEEK 2: 9–15 APRIL

A trip, visit or change of pace will bring a sense of freedom and spontaneity to your week. This weekend may be particularly busy, and family and romantic activities will appeal. If you are involved in the arts, dance, music or film you will experience better flow in your activities. All in all, this week the pace picks up, which you will appreciate.

WEEK 3: 16–22 APRIL

You'll appreciate the chance to meet someone you love or admire, but if logistics are too complex ensure you carefully approach thorny issues. Friday's new moon will feel revitalising in your personal or domestic life and also creatively, which will enable you to gain a sense of progress. You're prepared to make a commitment to a person or project, so you must thoroughly check the details.

WEEK 4: 23–29 APRIL

Be prepared to look at your usual daily routine from a fresh perspective. You may receive surprising news that alters your work schedule or will be embracing something different over the coming days. An opportunity is not to be missed, but you may need to discuss your various options with loved ones and negotiate those options this weekend. You may reach a positive outcome next week.

HEALTH

You may be surprised by developments health-wise this month, especially towards the 24th to 26th. Be prepared to look outside the square at your various options regarding your health. If you receive news concerning someone else's health, bear in mind this will be an opportunity to be productively engaged in helping where possible. If you need the help of an expert it will be available, so be sure to reach out.

FINANCES

You are likely to experience a meeting or receive news early in the month that could be encouraging in relation to collaborations that could boost your finances further down the line. A fresh look at your career and big-picture direction will certainly help put your financial options in perspective. Just be sure to avoid gambling, especially around the 4th and 5th. You may receive good financial news towards the end of the month.

HOME

You'll gain the opportunity to create a more stable situation for yourself at home already early in the month, but you may need to evaluate options regarding your career or status first so you don't limit your domestic peace of mind by overcommitting to work duties. You'll discover closer to mid-April whether you have over- or underinvested emotionally in your home life, and as a result you will be able to plan better moving forward.

LOVE LIFE

You are communicating well at the start of the month, so if there have been issues on your mind be sure to take the opportunity to discuss these with an open mind. Just avoid a stalemate towards the 4th and 5th, as this may kick-start a stubborn phase in your relationship that will take some time to overcome. If you are single you will enjoy socialising but you must avoid emotional gambling, especially around the 4th and 5th.

WORK

The full moon on 2 April will spotlight fresh circumstances in your work options. You may be easily seduced into something new by the promise of money, but you must be careful to thoroughly research your options. It is quite possible that you will in fact receive a financial boost, but you must be sure of your options. Meetings towards the 13th and 24th are likely to provide direction regarding work projects if you are unsure of your situation.

SAGITTARIUS • APRIL

May

WEEK 1: 30 APRIL–6 MAY

You'll appreciate the opportunity to clear a backlog of chores at home and improve your domestic relationships, especially if they have been strained. You'll enjoy focusing on boosting your mental and spiritual well-being through creative projects. Friday/Saturday's full moon will spotlight your social life or loyalty to a friend or organisation. It may be time to alter some arrangements.

WEEK 2: 7–13 MAY

You'll appreciate the sense that you can make progress. For most this will be readily apparent in your personal life and for some at work. Be optimistic and take bold steps towards your goals. Romance could blossom now, so if you've been meaning to ask someone out then take the initiative. Couples will gain closeness. It's a good week to make changes at home or with family.

WEEK 3: 14–20 MAY

This will be an excellent week to consider how you might bring more stability and security into your daily life, and this will include considering how to enjoy a steadier daily schedule and a more settled personal life. You may discover who has your back and who unfortunately doesn't. Be prepared to navigate fresh waters, bearing in mind that your self-esteem and principles need to come first for now.

WEEK 4: 21–27 MAY / WEEK 5: 28 MAY–3 JUNE

WEEK 4: you'll enjoy a change of pace towards the 22nd that may involve pleasant surprises. Changes could also arise at work so be sure to check communications and arrangements, especially if you're travelling, to avoid mistakes. **WEEK 5:** the full moon on the 31st will encourage you to turn a corner in your personal life if you were born in November and at work if you're a December Sagittarian.

HEALTH

You may find that May brings a more introspective phase your way, which could predispose you to feeling less energetic, but if you are aware that the many aspects of who you are do rely on strong physical, emotional and mental health you will manage to maintain high energy levels. The end of May will be ideal for making a change of routine or pace that helps boost physical and mental health.

FINANCES

Pluto will begin a retrograde phase that will offer you the chance to reconsider some of your long-term financial investments. Over the next few weeks you'll gain the opportunity to reconfigure some of your financial arrangements from a long-term point of view. Avoid quick-fix remedies if you are in debt; look for expert advice if necessary. The phase from 11 to 13 May will be ideal for making commitments.

HOME

The first week of May will be ideal for creating the kind of atmosphere you like at home, with family or with housemates. A degree of conversation and discussion may be necessary and it will be important to avoid a Mexican standoff and, instead, work towards positive collaboration and cooperation. The second week of May will also be conducive to creating a settled atmosphere at home and potentially make arrangements that everyone can agree to.

LOVE LIFE

The full moon on 1/2 May is going to spotlight differences of opinion. Be prepared to look at a partner's big-picture motivation as opposed to how they explain their actions. You may need to re-evaluate whether you are both on the same page regarding your principles and values, as these do change over time. This aside, the start of the month is ideal for making a commitment, especially regarding domestic matters.

WORK

Creative work is particularly well aspected this month and collaborations with like-minded people are likely to go well, especially in the second week of May. The new moon supermoon on the 16th/17th will spotlight a fresh opportunity at work, mostly for November-born Sagittarians, and you will have the opportunity to collaborate. In addition, you'll gain insight into how best to innovate changes within your work schedule towards the end of the month.

SAGITTARIUS • MAY

June

WEEK 1: 4–10 JUNE

You'll appreciate the opportunity to get together with like-minded people towards the weekend. Key financial and shared matters such as joint responsibilities and even space at home will come under discussion. Be prepared to make a solid commitment to a venture or person and find common ground. Avoid sensitive topics unless they are the key to a breakthrough, in which case tact will be your most useful tool.

WEEK 2: 11–17 JUNE

You're likely to experience a busier week than usual as you hear unexpectedly from friends or family or enjoy an impromptu get-together towards the weekend. Monday's new moon could revitalise your business and personal partnerships, but if some developments, especially at home, prove to be more difficult than they are pleasant then take steps to rediscover your peace of mind.

WEEK 3: 18–24 JUNE

There will be a focus this week on your love life and finances. There is so much to be happy about, yet a feeling of intensity or other people's dramas could overshadow your contentment unless you maintain a happy stance and remain optimistic. Avoid overspending. A business or personal get-together may prove to be therapeutic, so be spontaneous. You may turn a corner with someone close.

WEEK 4: 25 JUNE–1 JULY

You can gain a commitment from someone either at work or in your personal life that brings you a sense of stability this week so be sure to initiate discussions, preferably before the full moon on the 29th/30th, which signals that a fresh arrangement or agreement with someone could provide you with a sense of security. However, you must ensure you do not restrict your options too severely.

HEALTH

A change of pace will benefit your vitality and well-being, and if you have had to be careful health-wise you may even consider fresh ways to bring a sense of healing into your life such as a nutritional diet or relaxing fitness program. A friend, family member or colleague may provide information that could be helpful in this respect. Mars in your health sector from the end of the month will help pep up your energy levels.

FINANCES

Your shared finances such as those with family or your housemates will deserve careful focus, especially towards the 9th and 18th. You may be drawn to make a considerable investment. Some lucky Sagittarians may even receive a lump sum, and it will be important to find ways to invest this carefully and discuss your shared finances with those they concern such as housemates or marital partners, as otherwise arguments could arise.

HOME

June is an excellent month to be constructive about your various home plans and hopes for family and/or property. A financial arrangement to do with your home will deserve a careful approach to ensure that everyone is on the same page and that any major financial arrangements are clear cut. For this reason, if you are making considerable investments financially you must ensure you have carefully checked the terms and conditions.

LOVE LIFE

Good communication skills will be in demand over the first two weeks of the month so be sure to use tact and diplomacy, especially if some delicate matters or sensitive topics need to be discussed. You'll gain the opportunity to celebrate your love life and enjoy fun developments. Singles may meet someone particularly young at heart and fun. However, you must use your discretion when necessary to circumnavigate sensitive issues.

WORK

A change of pace towards the new moon on the 15th and on the 28th could breathe fresh air into your usual working experience. If you have already organised a break or holiday this will certainly bring you a sense of variety in your usual schedule. The full moon on the 29th could precipitate a fresh arrangement either at work or financially that will provide new options for you, so be sure to research opportunities as they arise this month.

SAGITTARIUS · JUNE

July

WEEK 1: 2–8 JULY

You do like adventure in life; however, some developments may put you outside your comfort zone. November-born Sagittarians are likely to receive unexpected news from someone close, while December-born Sagittarians will experience a change in your usual daily routine. Be prepared to discuss your options with colleagues, business partners or employers. There are likely to be various positives connected with developments; you may simply not immediately see them.

WEEK 2: 9–15 JULY

The new moon supermoon on the 14th will usher in a fresh chapter in a key business or personal arrangement. For some this will revolve around your home life or at least will affect your home life, so it is important you are careful with communications. Unexpected news dictates it will be in your interest to maintain an even playing field as opposed to subscribe to drama.

WEEK 3: 16–22 JULY

It's all change this week, and for most Sagittarians this will involve a change of routine in your usual daily schedule. For some Sagittarians there will be a considerable change in your financial situation that will merit a level-headed and practical approach. Be sure to keep a realistic perspective of your home life and family. Some lucky Sagittarians will enjoy an ideal trip.

WEEK 4: 23–29 JULY

You'll enjoy favourite projects and activities with like-minded people in the lead-up to the weekend. You may also enjoy a trip to an old haunt. Early next week a surprise turnaround either at work or within your personal life will keep you on your toes. This is certainly a transformative time for you, so be sure to embrace new opportunities.

HEALTH

A change in your usual routine will benefit your health and well-being, although this may be in unexpected ways. An impromptu trip or visit will bring out spontaneity in you. Changes at home may involve a little hard work initially but could in fact benefit your health: think feng shui, energy clearing and eliminating dust, for example. The pace will speed up towards the end of July, so find ways to slow things down if this is an issue.

FINANCES

You may experience unexpected financial improvements, but you must avoid overspending as a result. However, if you have overspent in the past it is likely that debt becomes your focus and, specifically, how to manage it. Insurmountable financial circumstances must be addressed if necessary, and you will find the advice of an expert particularly helpful. The new moon supermoon on the 14th will help you put in place a fresh budget, especially regarding joint finances.

HOME

The key to a happy home lies in good communication skills. It is likely in July that you will need to go over old ground with previous arrangements or agreements already made regarding your home or family. It will be important this month to avoid allowing small details to become the centre of conflict. It's far better to look at the big picture and be prepared to build on common ground as opposed to differences so you can reach an ideal circumstance.

LOVE LIFE

Non-negotiable aspects of some relationships are likely to rear their heads early in the month. Ask yourself whether these are actually deal breakers, or whether as you step into new territory in your relationship some of your values and principles can change. Couples will find ways to relate differently with partners. Singles may meet someone unexpectedly and romance could peak in the lead-up to the intense full moon on the 29th/30th, so be sure to organise dates.

WORK

A change in your working routine could be beneficial, even if it takes a little initial adjustment on your part. Be prepared to bolster your self-esteem, as certain developments that are outside your control may initially seem to damage your ego. If you maintain a positive outlook you will find that developments this month could actually put you in a stronger position over time, but you must be prepared to put in the hard work and embrace the future.

SAGITTARIUS · JULY

August

WEEK 1: 30 JULY–5 AUGUST

This will be an excellent week to build strength and resilience within your personal and work-related relationships. Be adventurous but also willing to compromise and listen. A domestic or personal process will likely show signs of progress. How can you feel more stable and secure in your circumstances? If an intense topic is under discussion, ensure you remain calm.

WEEK 2: 6–12 AUGUST

A new agreement or understanding is waiting in the wings that may well encompass work or your favourite activities and daily routine and duties. This may be a progressive agreement so think big, but also be practical. Be prepared to look at your financial situation both realistically and from a long-term point of view so you are able to constructively plan ahead.

WEEK 3: 13–19 AUGUST

Key discussions and get-togethers could put you in a strong position, but this will depend on your communication skills and research. If you are ready to make a financial or personal commitment to someone special or with a property and in your domestic life, it's likely that your endeavours will flow. However, this will depend on having the correct information, so ensure you are on the same page as others.

WEEK 4: 20–26 AUGUST / WEEK 5: 27 AUGUST–2 SEPTEMBER

WEEK 4: this will be an excellent week to discuss your big-picture plans concerning work and your home life. It's likely you'll make a considerable investment or commitment to either or both areas. **WEEK 5:** the partial lunar eclipse on the 28th will bring key developments in a favourite business or personal relationship. Some Sagittarians will be drawn to travel and others to invest more in your projects and favourite activities.

HEALTH

Consider looking at new ways to boost your health and vitality this month. You are in an enviable position in which some of your favourite activities and pastimes can feed into a healthier outlook. However, there are some habits you have become accustomed to that are counterproductive, making this month an excellent time to marginalise these or even set them aside and maximise positive health habits.

FINANCES

The Mercury–Pluto opposition that coincides with the total solar eclipse on the 12th/13th puts the spotlight on shared finances such as joint bank accounts, household expenses, investments and also taxes. You may undergo significant financial developments in August, so it will be in your interest to seek professional advice if necessary. You could potentially gain financial security, especially mid-month and towards the 17th.

HOME

The beginning of the month will be perfect for discussing your domestic, family and property circumstances with those they concern, as you are likely to come to arrangements or a commitment that can provide you with more of a sense of security and stability moving forward. Be sure to take the initiative with discussions but avoid feeling that everything must be purely on your terms. Be prepared to negotiate.

LOVE LIFE

A tough aspect between Venus and Mars early in August could add a little tension to your love life. This may be due to different approaches to activities you'd like to undertake together or separately. Look for ways to build stability at home. If you are single, ensure you are spending time with those who have similar values. Developments towards the 10th, 17th and 28th could be significant, so be prepared to connect with those you love then.

WORK

As you step into new plans and embrace fresh territory work-wise there will be a lot to learn and discuss, so keep an open mind as opposed to having a set mindset about things. Collaboration and co-operation are the secrets to success now, especially around the 15th when Mercury conjuncts Jupiter and towards the lunar eclipse on the 28th. Important news or developments may involve someone else, so your communication skills must be sharp.

SAGITTARIUS • AUGUST

September

WEEK 1: 3–9 SEPTEMBER

This is a good week to ask yourself exactly where your priorities lie, largely because you may experience a conflict of interest between your duties at home and with family on the one hand and on the other a favourite activity or learning opportunity that you would like to take part in. As long as you have duties covered, whichever you choose you will enjoy some lovely get-togethers.

WEEK 2: 10–16 SEPTEMBER

This will be an excellent week to surge ahead with your projects, both at home and work. The new moon on the 11th favours activities that broaden your horizons, such as travel, study, self-development and even legal matters. Just be careful to keep communications super clear to avoid misunderstandings. Avoid taking other people's opinions personally, as a battle of wills could quickly escalate.

WEEK 3: 17–23 SEPTEMBER

Romance could blossom this weekend, perhaps even in surprising ways. A key choice – for many involving your bigger-picture life direction, including major domestic decisions – will merit careful consideration so you avoid limiting your options in the future while also seizing opportunities to gain more stability in life. Be positive and prepared to make considerable investments either to your favourite projects, work or home life.

WEEK 4: 24–30 SEPTEMBER

Prepare for a new chapter in your home or family if you were born in November. If you were born in December you'll appreciate a fresh arrangement with someone such as a new commitment to a venture, organisation or even legal matter. Luckily, your activities this weekend are likely to whisk you into different pastures that you'll enjoy. A trip or get-together could be ideal.

HEALTH

As an adventurous and energetic person you do like to venture out into nature and enjoy developing your health and fitness, and the new moon on the 11th will encourage you to do just that. A holiday or fitness club will truly boost your energy levels this month, so be sure to engage in activities you love. Developments towards the 18th and 28th may bring unexpected opportunities to improve your health schedule. Be prepared to embrace fresh and exciting activities.

FINANCES

This is an excellent month to get on top of the changing face of your financial circumstances, largely because your actions in the past will come home to roost now. If past spending has led you to debt this will be your opportunity to put a fresh budget in place and establish ways to repay debt. If you are in the enviable position of having accrued wealth you will also need to find ways to manage your finances.

HOME

Duties associated with your home or family will require extra attention early in the month, and once you completely manage your responsibilities you will be able to enjoy your spare time all the more. Once again towards the 18th and 26th you may discover that key decisions regarding your level of commitment at home need to be addressed. You may need to make a fresh arrangement regarding financial circumstances that impact your home life.

LOVE LIFE

You will appreciate the opportunity to deepen your links with someone special in September. However, some communications may be more complex than you would hope and will require a patient outlook, but if you realise that there are more serious disparities within your relationship you may need to uphold some of your values. This will merit careful communication to avoid conflict, especially mid-month and towards the 27th. Consider a change of pace to bring more fun into your relationship.

WORK

This month's positive stars could boost your work and career, so be sure to take the initiative with your projects and ventures. You may even be surprised by some initiatives or developments, especially towards the 20th and 26th; however, you may need to balance exciting work projects with domestic commitments so you are able to cover your bases in both areas. Consider being innovative also and be prepared to step into fresh territory.

SAGITTARIUS • SEPTEMBER

October

WEEK 1: 1–7 OCTOBER

Get set to consider a fresh approach to finances and someone close. This is the ideal time to consider new ways to budget. You may need to review an arrangement with a friend or organisation to reconfigure your financial arrangements. Be patient, as some conversations may be intense. This is also a good time to boost domestic circumstances, as your efforts are likely to succeed. You'll enjoy a trip.

WEEK 2: 8–14 OCTOBER

Keep an eye on communications, especially with a friend or organisation, as misunderstandings can arise. Be sure to be practical and research options, especially financially. This weekend's new moon will encourage you to turn a new leaf at work or in your status or general direction. However, you may need to overcome a challenge to do so, but it'll make it all the more worthwhile.

WEEK 3: 15–21 OCTOBER

This is a lovely week to truly feel inspired either by the people around you or by your activities, including aspects of your career. It's also a good time for romance, so ensure you organise a special event. However, you will need to be careful with communications towards mid-week next week and may even need to make a tough call between work and domestic duties. Choose wisely.

WEEK 4: 22–28 OCTOBER / WEEK 5: 29 OCTOBER–4 NOVEMBER

WEEK 4: a change within a project, family or in your personal life will command your attention. Decisions and developments will revolve around personal choices and core values. Consider your choices carefully, and avoid gambling and a battle of wills. **WEEK 5:** evaluate your options carefully, especially in relation to your work life and domestic choices. Avoid arguments and look for positive outcomes, which you may achieve through careful negotiations.

HEALTH

A firm and upbeat approach to your health will encourage you to look outside the box at ways to boost your feel-good factor. You may be drawn to a holiday or altering your usual daily schedule to factor in team sports, for example. Be prepared to stick with regimes that work and avoid stopping and starting, as you will undo all your good work. Developments mid-month may mean that you need to alter your health routine. Put your health first.

FINANCES

The opposition between Mars and Pluto early in the month brings the likelihood that you must carefully focus on finances to avoid the necessity to curb spending moving forward. Avoid gambling and speculation; it's far better to research tried and trusted methods to grow wealth. Be super careful with major investments, especially towards the 20th and 26th, and beware of being easily influenced by others and feeling coerced to follow their lead.

HOME

If you have been looking for a commitment from someone at home or considering making an important investment in your home this will be possible early in October, and may even lead to a sense of stability and security. This will depend on your due diligence regarding finances and the people in your home. Be careful with communications towards the 9th and 26th, as a hastily spoken word without forethought could disturb the peace.

LOVE LIFE

You will appreciate the opportunity to bring a little spontaneity and fun into your love life, especially towards the 7th. If you are single you may bump into someone who brings a sense of freedom your way. Be sure to make co-operation and collaboration the catalysts for good relationships, otherwise you may find yourself at loggerheads with the person you love the most, especially around the 9th, 10th, 20th and 30th.

WORK

This is an excellent month to look at ways to boost your work, career and status, as the stars will support your efforts. However, you must be careful towards the 2nd to avoid unnecessary arguments. Towards the 4th and 5th, 9th and 10th and the 15th and 26th you will gain the opportunity to make a commitment either to a work or career path or someone at home, which will impact your work life, so be careful with the commitments you make.

SAGITTARIUS · OCTOBER

November

WEEK 1: 5–11 NOVEMBER

If you were born in November you're likely to enjoy a fresh daily work or health routine this week, and December Sagittarians a fresh social and networking phase. A new chapter may even be a little intense, so be sure to pace yourself. You may experience an improvement in your status and you'll enjoy a reunion or, at the least, planning one. Your finances could improve.

WEEK 2: 12–18 NOVEMBER

Developments this week will proceed at a fast pace, which you are better equipped for than many other zodiac signs. However, you nevertheless risk rushing into something without forethought, so be sure to carefully weigh your options. For some, developments represent the chance to step into fresh territory via travel, for example, while for others significant developments with someone special either in your love life or at work will arise.

WEEK 3: 19–25 NOVEMBER

The sun enters Sagittarius this weekend, bringing improved energy and motivation over the weeks to come. If you were born at the end of November, towards the 24th, a business or personal partner is likely to have unexpected news for you. All other Sagittarians are likely either to experience a change in daily schedule or news at work. A domestic development may be ideal; just avoid overspending.

WEEK 4: 26 NOVEMBER–2 DECEMBER

You'll appreciate a work, personal or financial boost this weekend. You'll establish more of a sense of security and stability either at home or at work, which you will appreciate. However, if communications seem more complex than usual this weekend, take the time to consider how best to move ahead with less confusion in the mix. Avoid taking the random comments of other people personally.

HEALTH

As a fun-loving person you'll gain the opportunity mid-month to engage in activities that raise spirits, which you will enjoy, so if you have nothing planned yet be sure to organise something special. You may appreciate the opportunity to develop your spiritual side, which will prove particularly therapeutic. Later in the month, whether you visit someone or they visit you you'll gain the opportunity to reunite with someone who is dear to your heart, which will raise your spirits.

FINANCES

You're likely to reap the rewards of work well done. A shared financial investment or opportunity may catch your eye. As with any financial opportunity it's in your interest to investigate, at the least. Towards the end of the month you'll gain more of a sense of the long-term and transformational change occurring both at work and therefore within your finances, and you'll gain deeper understanding of any tweaks or changes you're best to make within your budget.

HOME

You'll appreciate the opportunity to build more stability and security in your home life as the month goes by and may see particularly good outcomes for all your efforts at the end of the month, when your home provides you with a sense of nurturance and even has a healing influence. A change in your circumstances around the full moon on the 24th may indicate travel, which will also feel therapeutic.

LOVE LIFE

You'll enjoy the opportunity early in the month to reconnect with someone special. Singles may even bump into someone unexpectedly. You may also be drawn to someone mid-month with whom there is a fated connection, but you must nevertheless exercise discernment. Couples will appreciate the opportunity to relax or engage in fun activities that are therapeutic in nature. Singles may be prepared to make a commitment, and this will bring a sense of stability and nurturance into your life.

WORK

All systems are full steam ahead towards the end of the month for a change in your usual schedule and routine. This is likely to bring improved circumstances within your work schedule, and these may be ideal for you. However, you will gain insight into the part that you can play earlier in the month already, so it will be in your interest to put your best foot forward in meetings and get-togethers during the month.

SAGITTARIUS • NOVEMBER

December

WEEK 1: 3–9 DECEMBER

Tenacity and diligence will help you attain your goals, so if you feel some developments are outside your comfort zone then rest assured you can succeed. Wednesday's new moon will be in your sign and signals the time is ripe for a fresh phase. If you were born before 9 December change will manifest in your personal life, for others at work and for some with a fresh, healthier lifestyle.

WEEK 2: 10–16 DECEMBER

For many Sagittarians this is an excellent weekend for get-togethers and socialising. You may review or revise a decision and begin to see it in a more practical light. Be prepared to see someone in your life as quirky yet loyal, and as someone whom you click with. Some Sagittarians will experience a boost at work that could translate to a financial improvement as well.

WEEK 3: 17–23 DECEMBER

You will appreciate the opportunity to indulge your adventurous spirit a little this week. Whether you're travelling, being more outgoing or investing in your home or someone you love, you will at the very least gain the impression that life is exciting. Some matters may be a little tense early next week, and the more patient and understanding you can be the better it will be for you.

WEEK 4: 24–31 DECEMBER

The full moon supermoon on Christmas Eve will spotlight an important relationship. Someone close may feel passionate, and you may need to provide more emotional support than usual for this reason. Misunderstandings and delays and even unexpected changes to your plans are possible. Nevertheless, you may experience a financial or ego boost. You'll appreciate the sense that once again life gets on an even keel towards New Year's Eve.

234 ✦ *2026* **HOROSCOPES**

HEALTH

This will be a busy month, and this is the major counter indicator to good health for you. Be careful to pace yourself, as you will otherwise be running on empty and as a result could make unnecessary mistakes at work, financially and in your personal life. A positive and open approach to your health and well-being will put you in a strong position, so be sure to reach out to experts and loyal friends if necessary.

FINANCES

You are on a generally upwards trajectory financially as changes at work and in your earning power can bring the positive results you want, so be sure to remain diligent in your pursuit of secure finances. However, early in the month you must be careful with some transactions with a friend, group or organisation, especially towards the new moon on the 9th. You may enjoy a financial boost towards Christmas and the chance to discuss shared finances at that time.

HOME

This is an excellent period to invest time and effort in beautifying your home, especially during the first 10 days of the month and again in the week before Christmas. You may even feel that your self-esteem is improved as a result of an improved ambience at home. The opportunity to visit other people's homes to socialise or invite visitors to your home will also prove to be uplifting.

LOVE LIFE

You will appreciate increased energy levels as the month goes by, and this will reflect well in your love life. You may also be drawn to socialise more than usual due to the festive season. Luckily, the transit of Venus through your social sector will bring an amiable social and networking scene your way. However, you must be careful to avoid a battle of egos early in the month, as this will only disadvantage you.

WORK

As this busy month begins you'll undertake a change of routine or pace, and this will become evident towards the 8th. If your timetable or developments seem too challenging, bear in mind that with diligence you will be able to overcome obstacles. Some negotiations may need to be undertaken to ensure you are not overworked. Some Sagittarians will experience a boost at work towards the 11th and you may need to undertake careful discussions in the process.

January

WEEK 1: 1–7 JANUARY

This week's full moon will spotlight a personal or business partnership if you were born before the first week of January. If relationships have become stale it's a good week to revitalise them, but you must avoid thorny topics if possible. If you were born after the first week of January you'll experience an alteration in your routine such as a change at work or in your daily schedule.

WEEK 2: 8–14 JANUARY

The conjunction between Mercury, Mars, the sun and Venus in your sign – all opposite Jupiter – points to an intense week, especially if you were born around 10 January. If you are single you may meet someone towards the weekend, but you must also keep an eye on domestic concerns. Conversations, negotiations and meetings this weekend are likely to be busy, so keep perspective and also avoid gambling.

WEEK 3: 15–21 JANUARY

This week's Capricorn new moon signals a fresh chapter in your personal life, and if you were born after mid-January expect a fresh daily schedule at work or health-wise. You may be surprised by some events this week and dismayed by others, so it's wise to avoid impulsiveness. Nevertheless, you'll enjoy being spontaneous this weekend and trying something new, for some at home and for others due to a shopping spree.

WEEK 4: 22–28 JANUARY

You'll enjoy socialising towards Friday and at the weekend. A meeting with a friend or organisation should be upbeat or productive, but if feelings are intense aim to work off excess energy constructively rather than start arguments. Beauty and love will blossom in your life as long as you are not distracted by challenges or negativity. Romance could thrive, so organise a date!

HEALTH

The first two weeks of January will be ideal for focusing on improving your health and well-being, as these weeks will facilitate your bringing more self-care into your daily routine. For this reason you're more likely to succeed when you instigate a fresh fitness schedule, for example, or a more nutritious diet. For some improved well-being will be due to the chance to have a break, and for others due to the need to organise one.

FINANCES

You may experience a boost in finances in January. For many this will be in connection with your home life, a property or family, but for many there will also be work opportunities that include options to broaden your horizons and learn something new. However, if you have been prone to gamble in the past or you are prone to gamble now you do risk losing money, so be diligent with your research.

HOME

January shows a great deal of promise in connection with your home, a property and/or your family. You will gain the opportunity to invest both financially and in practical terms in your home life and may even be surprised by some of the developments, especially towards the end of the month. If you've been wanting to increase the size of your family you may hear good news.

LOVE LIFE

If you're looking for love, the 6th, 8th, 14th and the end of the month will be excellent times to find someone compatible. You may meet someone who is larger than life and who truly creates a sense of romance. However, you will need to factor in the practicalities of your domestic or family situation. It's certainly a romantic month, so couples must organise a treat too. Just avoid intense circumstances and drama, especially in the last week of January.

WORK

If you were born after mid-January you are likely to experience the most change in your work life. This may be due to a holiday, although for some it will be due to a fresh work opportunity or schedule. Be sure to factor your domestic demands into any major work decisions. Be inspired towards the end of the month, as you may gain insight into promising new work and financial options.

February

WEEK 1: 29 JANUARY—4 FEBRUARY

A fresh arrangement with someone close will arise as you share space, finances or duties in a new way. For some Capricorns developments will occur more in line with personal or family decisions and priorities that must be attended to. A sense of destiny may prevail, and the more you can work with circumstances with a positive and logistical mindset the better it will be for you.

WEEK 2: 5—11 FEBRUARY

A change of pace or a surprise will test your mettle. If some aspects of your circumstances are unclear or require change be sure to do your research, as you'll be better able to negotiate and move forward. Avoid financial and emotional gambling. You must be prepared to deal with the situation carefully and make decisions based on facts, not feelings.

WEEK 3: 12—18 FEBRUARY

This week's solar eclipse will precipitate a fresh chapter in your financial circumstances. Be ready to try a fresh approach to your investments and expenditure, as a new budget could be the key to running a more enjoyable daily life. For some this week will create the opportunity to revitalise your personal life. Someone close may re-enter your life.

WEEK 4: 19—25 FEBRUARY / WEEK 5: 26 FEBRUARY—4 MARCH

WEEK 4: try to nip domestic disgruntlement in the bud, as this could otherwise get in the way of a happy two weeks. Be proactive instead, and find ways to move forward. **WEEK 5:** you'll enjoy lovely get-togethers, and a reunion may be particularly significant. Try to get key financial matters sorted out before the 26th, as there may otherwise be delays for some weeks to come.

HEALTH

February will be an excellent time to devote attention to stress management, largely because you may find the start of the month particularly stressful and it will be a good time to consult health experts if necessary. Self-esteem is a key to mental and emotional health now and you'll find that opportunities, especially towards the end of the month, will enable you to find more peace of mind. Be sure to organise activities that allow you to unwind.

FINANCES

As someone who likes to take life one step at a time gambling is not something that generally soothes your soul, yet this month you may be uncharacteristically drawn to engage in a tricky investment or scheme that is unproven and untested. This essentially would be a gamble and is most likely to revolve around your home life, family or business arrangements. Think twice.

HOME

Sometimes a little disruption has to take place for things to settle once again. If you feel that developments are simply too erratic for your liking at the start of February be sure to find practical ways to resolve issues. You may be surprised by developments towards the end of February, as a change or visit will precipitate unexpected circumstances: for most towards the 27th. Avoid knee-jerk reactions and look for ways to create the stability you prefer at home.

LOVE LIFE

With Jupiter in Cancer you are likely to feel fairly open-hearted towards the person you love right now. However, you and they may also have a tendency towards idealism. If you find yourself at odds with one another consider whether a more realistic approach to conundrums could be effective. Singles will be drawn to an ideal of who you believe could be a good companion as opposed to who people really are, so be real!

WORK

This will be a good month to work towards creating a better situation for yourself. If you were born after the first week of January you may even experience a financial or work boost. For all Capricorns a steady approach to developing your self-esteem and confidence in the work arena will be productive so think laterally about how you can do this, especially if you have felt a little lacking in confidence of late.

March

WEEK 1: 5–11 MARCH

This is a good time to discuss a shared circumstance such as a commitment or joint finances and space at home or work. Be adaptable, as there may be some adjustment necessary due to a fresh opportunity at home or with family. Romance could flourish so be sure to organise a date, especially between Thursday and Sunday. Key financial developments will merit careful focus.

WEEK 2: 12–18 MARCH

It's a good week to discuss your financial and work plans with those they affect. Consider seeking the advice of experts or loyal friends who can help you; you may discover someone who really knows their field. Someone close such as a business or personal partner will have news, and a little research or soul searching may be necessary towards mid-week next week.

WEEK 3: 19–25 MARCH

Thursday's new moon will be a good time to begin new ventures, especially those that involve a financial or personal investment. Be guided by your intuition, but avoid making decisions based on assumptions alone. It is likely that a business or personal partner will have an influence over your decisions, so be sure to do independent research. You may enjoy a financial boost.

WEEK 4: 26 MARCH–1 APRIL

A trip or meeting will draw on your energy reserves, so be sure to factor in extra time for travel and also be patient with communications. Your matter-of-fact approach to life will be useful, especially regarding particular information and talks. Be diplomatic and avoid taking the unpredictability of others personally. You'll enjoy an impromptu visit or domestic development at the weekend or early next week.

HEALTH

You will gain a sense of self-esteem and self-confidence by focusing a little more on your appearance and ability to communicate both verbally and non-verbally. In other words, your gestures and body language communicate as much about you as do your words. March is a good month to be more aware of how your general presentation, including your appearance and wardrobe, affects others, and this will help boost your overall feel-good factor.

FINANCES

March will be an excellent month to develop a fresh approach to your finances. This will be particularly necessary as it's likely your financial circumstances will change. For some this will be for personal or domestic reasons and for others due to work. You are likely to experience positive opportunities but must be prepared to devise a clever budget that supports you. You may experience a financial boost around the 20th and 21st. Just avoid overspending at that time.

HOME

You will enjoy investing in your domestic life, both financially and energetically, early in March. You may even be surprised by the positive effects a little extra focus on your home life makes. You may be pleasantly surprised by a visitor or unexpected change of events mid-month, towards the 18th. The new moon on the 19th will help you find the finances and motivation to make changes at home.

LOVE LIFE

Communications will thrive at the beginning of March so be sure to discuss any thorny topics, especially those to do with finances, earlier in the month. Singles will notice whether people you meet create a sense of confidence or the opposite, and you'll measure how much time you spend with them as a result. Someone is likely to have a considerable influence over you around the 21st, which will boost self-esteem. Avoid throwing caution to the wind.

WORK

This is a good month to invest in work relationships, as the more you invest in this important aspect of your workplace the more rewarding some of your joint successes will be. You may consider investing money in a work venture but will need to first research your options. During the first two weeks of March you may need to review some of your circumstances and, gradually, as the month proceeds you are likely to gain a sense of progress.

CAPRICORN • MARCH

April

WEEK 1: 2–8 APRIL

Good communication skills point to a pleasant week, especially if you look for calm and harmony, as you may otherwise find some developments a little stressful or limiting, especially at the weekend and on Monday. A trip or activity could bring you a sense of freedom and adventure on the one hand and on the other a sense of restriction, so be sure to carefully plan travel and activities.

WEEK 2: 9–15 APRIL

You will be drawn to invest in your home life, both time-wise and financially, and in those you love such as family. If you have been considering visiting someone else's home this is likely to be enjoyable. Carefully research any kind of investment in your home life or family to avoid overspending. It's a good week to put a secure budget in place.

WEEK 3: 16–22 APRIL

You may be inclined to be uncharacteristically spontaneous or even impulsive. Approach matters carefully to avoid misunderstandings and regret further down the line, especially where finances are concerned. Be patient. You're set to begin a fresh chapter domestically or make a fresh commitment. Some Capricorns will be drawn to travel or updating communications devices or a vehicle.

WEEK 4: 23–29 APRIL

You are likely to move into fresh territory in your personal life, which may entail some surprises this week either within family or at home depending on your birthday. Be prepared to look outside the box at your options and avoid being obstinate and entering conflict, as the more adaptable and forward looking you are now the better it will be for you.

HEALTH

You'll gain the opportunity early in April to enjoy some free time such as a weekend away or a holiday. This will be a welcome break and will boost your happiness and well-being. A visit to someone's house or the opportunity to improve your décor or environment will also raise morale. A fresh dynamic at home or with family may initially be a little disruptive but promises to bring more peace of mind further down the line.

FINANCES

You will enjoy a sociable time early in the month but may be prone to overspend, so early April is a good time to put in place a solid and stable budget that suits your needs. If you have large overheads – for example, domestic expenses – you may find ways to break payments down into smaller sums. A financial development towards the 13th may be ideal, but if the opposite arises you'll manage to remedy the situation.

HOME

You will enjoy the company of those you love at home. If you are drawn to visit family you are likely to appreciate the change of environment, so be sure to reach out and spend time with family and loved ones, especially around the weekend of the 11th. The conjunction of Venus and Uranus on the 24th may bring a surprise either at home or with a property or family. Be prepared to be adventurous as you enter fresh territory.

LOVE LIFE

Communications are going well at the start of the month especially, so this will be a good time to meet people if you are single and deepen your connection if you are a couple. However, the full moon on 2 April may bring out strong emotions in a partner, so be sure to maintain perspective if this arises. Singles may unexpectedly meet someone towards the end of the month, while couples will enjoy entering fresh territory at home or with family.

WORK

You can make quite an impression in April at work, so be sure to take the initiative. If you have been looking for work you are presenting well, especially early in April, so be sure to circulate your résumé and network, place phone calls and research your options. You may be tempted to overwork this month so ensure you take regular breaks if you feel under pressure, especially towards the end of the month.

CAPRICORN • APRIL ✦ 245

May

WEEK 1: 30 APRIL–6 MAY

Friday's full moon will spotlight your general direction in life, so for some Capricorns this will concern mostly your career and for others your marital circumstance: for example, if you see yourself as married or single moving forward. For others a sense of willingness to step into new territory such as through adventures and travel will appeal. Avoid making impulsive decisions if possible.

WEEK 2: 7–13 MAY

You will appreciate the opportunity to improve your financial and personal circumstances this week. It will come down to you being realistic and practical about your circumstances and taking steps to communicate and negotiate an outcome you're happy with. It's a good week to collaborate. Some Capricorns will be drawn to socialise a little more than usual and others to travel, both of which you will enjoy.

WEEK 3: 14–20 MAY

This weekend's new moon signals you are ready for changes at home, within family or a property. Spiritual Capricorns may even undergo an epiphany or find a true sense of belonging through your spirituality. A lovely event, trip or get-together is likely to be nurturing. Just be sure to avoid rushing and keep an eye on erratic drivers this weekend to avoid accidents.

WEEK 4: 21–27 MAY / WEEK 5: 28 MAY–3 JUNE

WEEK 4: you'll enjoy a surprise, and an impromptu development at home or with family will mean you must be adaptable. You will enjoy an ego boost or compliment and must be prepared for an exciting chapter that can boost your circumstances, either at work or in your personal life. **WEEK 5:** the full moon on the 31st will spotlight your true feelings about ways to improve your life.

HEALTH

Ask yourself where you feel you gain a sense of motivation: is it through work, your home life, adventure or relationships, for example? Motivation and purpose are important aspects of mental health, and this month will be ideal for you to consider how you can gain this sense of purpose for the remainder of the year. In the meantime, the second week of the month is positive for taking short trips to revitalise your energy levels.

FINANCES

You may experience a considerable development concerning finances and, if so, this will direct your attention to the need to reconfigure your budget and find fresh ways either to earn more money or spend more wisely. If you are already in debt you will gain the opportunity over the coming weeks and months to repay this, but you will need to be patient with the process. That said, the 8th will be particularly positive for financial discussions.

HOME

You are likely to feel the winds of change in your home life even if they simply manifest as the need or desire to change things for the better in this area. The new moon in your domestic zone on the 16th will provide you with the opportunity to create a sense of stability and security even if, in the process, a degree of upheaval must occur.

LOVE LIFE

Jupiter in your seventh house of partnerships puts a great deal of emphasis on your partner. Their influence on your life may be more obvious than usual, and especially in the second half of May you'll find discussions and negotiations particularly prevalent and also prospectively productive. Be sure to take the initiative and bring meaning and purpose to your relationships, as it is likely as a result you will gain exactly that.

WORK

Venus travelling through your sixth house of work until the 20th will contribute to a friendlier environment than usual, and you may appear to be more approachable as well. For these reasons May will be an excellent time to discuss some of your long-term plans to do with work, not only with friends and family but also with employers or business associates. Be prepared to socialise and network to broaden your horizons.

CAPRICORN • MAY

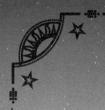

June

WEEK 1: 4–10 JUNE

This will be a good week to make a commitment to a domestic plan of action or a trip. This is a romantic time for you, and you'll enjoy spending time with someone special. Singles may even meet someone sensitive yet fun. However, you may uncover vulnerabilities in yourself or someone close, so be prepared to look after yourself and see another person's perspective.

WEEK 2: 11–17 JUNE

Keep an eye on communications, both at work and in your personal life, towards the weekend as mistakes and misunderstandings could occur. Get set to turn a corner at work or change your daily schedule so it suits you better. Some Capricorns will be kick-starting a fresh chapter in your personal life. If you're single you may meet someone chatty and fun, especially if you were born around mid-January.

WEEK 3: 18–24 JUNE

Romantically inclined Capricorns will enjoy a weekend of indulgence and love. Just avoid intense topics to sidestep drama and conflict, both at work and at play, as this could be an intense time. Developments may bring out your emotions, but there is a therapeutic quality as you will get the chance to express your true feelings. A financial matter can improve, so look for solutions.

WEEK 4: 25 JUNE–1 JULY

You'll enjoy get-togethers with favourite people, and if you need to make agreements or arrangements with a business or personal partner these are likely to go well now. Just ensure you have all the information you need at your fingertips to avoid making mistakes. The Capricorn full moon on the 29th/30th signals the start of a fresh phase in December Capricorns' personal lives and January Capricorns' work or health schedules.

HEALTH

The new moon supermoon on the 15th will help you kick-start a busier schedule that can include a certain number of hours per week devoted exclusively to your health. While this may not appeal to you, you may surprise yourself and enjoy a fresh environment. January Capricorns will again sense a different daily schedule towards the 29th, so be sure at this second opportunity to make health and fitness a regular part of your daily routine.

FINANCES

There's a philosophical aspect to your approach to finances in June, namely whether your values are dictated by other people's values or by your own. This will largely inform your response to developments that will ask you to focus increasingly on your home and those close to you. You will gain the opportunity now to decide whether finances are your main goal or whether other values are just as important.

HOME

The start of the month will be ideal for making headway with your domestic plans or family matters. It's a good time to be practical and realistic about what you can achieve at home or with the property. In June you are likely to consider fresh arrangements with someone close such as a family member or partner. It will be important to maintain an open mind and avoid restricting your options too severely moving forward.

LOVE LIFE

The conjunction of Venus and Jupiter in your seventh house brings romance your way at the start of June, with significant developments towards the 9th, 10th, 15th and 17th. This will be a lovely time to schedule romance. Singles may meet someone unexpectedly towards the 15th; however, someone may be feeling under the weather and confusion may be prevalent. Keep an eye on misunderstandings, especially around the 13th, as these could trip you up at this time.

WORK

The second week of June will be an ideal time to start a fresh work project, especially in the days following the new moon on the 15th. Be prepared to step into different territory and also to embrace new ideas and projects. A change of pace around the 18th and the 29th – the latter for January-born Capricorns – may also bring a breath of fresh air into your usual routine.

July

WEEK 1: 2–8 JULY

While Mercury is retrograde there are tough astrological aspects this week that could mean communications are particularly difficult, so it will be in your interest to be careful to ensure conversations are actually on the same ground as opposed to talking at cross purposes. This will save you a lot of time and effort. A family member or domestic circumstance may bring a surprise your way.

WEEK 2: 9–15 JULY

You will enjoy reconnecting with someone special; however, you may need to also navigate unexpected developments either within an agreement or at home. Avoid taking someone's news personally and work towards a positive outcome, especially in your personal life and financially. A positive outcome is possible but you must be able to navigate out of the extraordinary developments in the process.

WEEK 3: 16–22 JULY

You'll enjoy the arts, socialising and networking. If you're single you may meet someone a little quirky or different but who resonates, and if you have been dating for a while you may be prepared to commit. Meeting family and friends and creative projects will go well, as long as communications are kept on an even keel and someone's intense feelings – perhaps even yours? – are managed well.

WEEK 4: 23–29 JULY

Your sign's ruler Saturn begins a retrograde phase that will enable you to review some of the decisions you have made so far this year. This will help you pace yourself this week, which will potentially be very busy. Nevertheless, you'll gain the opportunity to connect with favourite people towards the weekend, and next week significant changes in your personal and financial lives will begin to sink in.

HEALTH

You are known to be a practical person and for that reason can be sensible. Developments towards the middle of July will require that you be reasonable, as some developments will defy logic. To avoid being caught in confusion or frustration, be prepared to be realistic and grounded and, if necessary, find healthy ways to maintain your mental clarity via such methods as visualisations or meditation.

FINANCES

Financial circumstances in connection with work and/or your income will benefit from special focus to ensure you are on the right track. Avoid simply going for a get-rich-quick scheme or making arrangements at work that you have not researched yet, as you will then avoid making financial mistakes. You may enjoy ideal circumstances financially this month, but if you have miscalculated in the past this month will be your opportunity to set things right.

HOME

Changes at home will merit careful focus, whether you have planned these in advance or they take you by surprise. You may welcome an unexpected visitor or must attend to domestic circumstances you had not envisaged. Be prepared to innovate and also to ask for expert help should the situation be outside your area of expertise. Changes in your domestic realm, including family, will take you into new territory, so be prepared to innovate.

LOVE LIFE

Keep an eye on clear communications early in July to avoid unnecessary misunderstandings. The new moon supermoon on the 14th will help you turn a corner in a nurturing way. However, it is likely that you or someone close feels uncharacteristically vulnerable or sensitive so you must take things one step at a time, especially mid-month and towards the 29th. Avoid knee-jerk reactions as these are likely to backfire. Be prepared to usher in fresh dynamics in your key relationships.

WORK

Be prepared to go that extra yard to ensure communications are clear at work, especially during the first week in July, as otherwise misunderstandings could prevail. If you were born in mid-January the new moon on the 14th will help you to turn a corner at work. However, you must be careful with communications at this time and especially if you are drawn to signing a new agreement or legal document. Ensure you check the fine print.

August

WEEK 1: 30 JULY–5 AUGUST

In the lead-up to the weekend remind yourself that they are made for relaxing, so make plans to de-stress this weekend to ensure you boost your health, resilience and well-being. A change of routine could be ideal for setting new plans in motion, but you must be prepared to navigate fresh dynamics within some relationships. This is a good week to build personal and financial resilience.

WEEK 2: 6–12 AUGUST

A partner, friend or work associate may propose a fresh understanding or venture, which may be exciting and could also provide more stability in your life in the long term. Some communications are going to be intense, so the more you are able to look at circumstances objectively the better you will be able to make plans. Romance could thrive, so be sure to organise dates.

WEEK 3: 13–19 AUGUST

Someone close has key news for you this weekend and you will enjoy discussing your options. You may simply enjoy a get-together with someone romantically, which will boost your self-esteem and the fun factor in your life, so be sure to organise treats this week that you know you will enjoy. Just be careful early next week at work with communications to avoid delays and misunderstandings.

WEEK 4: 20–26 AUGUST / WEEK 5: 27 AUGUST–2 SEPTEMBER

WEEK 4: a key decision concerning finances will catch your eye. This is also a good month for seeking and obtaining a commitment regarding a financial, work or personal matter. **WEEK 5:** you'll enjoy a reunion, and a business or personal partner's news may be more significant than initially meets the eye. It's a good week to make long-term plans.

HEALTH

An intuitive approach to your health will benefit you. Trust your gut instincts and make space to look after your health, as you may otherwise be easily distracted by considerable developments in your personal life. Mars in your health sector will help improve your energy levels but you must be careful to avoid overwork, as you will be busy. Avoid cutting corners, as you may also be slightly prone to minor mishaps due to rushing.

FINANCES

When you commit to building stability and security financially you will find that doing so becomes much easier than simply having a roughly sketched idea of your income and expenditure. You may find that an arrangement you make around the 7th could have a beneficial effect, and the first week of August will be excellent for building a strong and stable financial outlook. Decisions towards the 12th and 21st will also merit careful consideration.

HOME

A progressive approach to developments in your home and personal life will help you embrace them as opposed to feeling that you must hang on to the past. It is possible to build a strong domestic platform for yourself, and it will come down to realistic yet progressive and adventurous planning. The solar eclipse on the 12th/13th, depending on where you live, will spotlight whether this is possible or whether you must rethink your home commitments.

LOVE LIFE

The full moon of 29/30 July still has an impact on your personal life at the start of August, so if you found developments at the end of July particularly intense be sure to take things carefully, especially regarding shared responsibilities and chores such as joint finances and housework. The eclipses on the 12th/13th and 28th will spotlight whether your relationship is super resilient or if it is time to patch up differences. The 15th will bring additional insight.

WORK

Mars in your work sector will encourage you to work hard and feel motivated to be proactive in your daily life. In the second half of the month it will be important to keep an eye on good communication skills, as there may be a tendency to make assumptions either on your part or on the part of colleagues or employers. This could lead to misunderstandings, both in the workplace and financially.

September

WEEK 1: 3–9 SEPTEMBER

Where people's behaviour may be unreliable, changeable or even frustrating you are able to remain calm while all around you people are losing their perspective. You can make your plans stick despite the unreliability of other people. This week's difference of opinion or financial challenge will merit a practical approach. As a result you are likely to reach an amicable arrangement or agreement with someone.

WEEK 2: 10–16 SEPTEMBER

Friday's new moon will motivate you to put some of your plans into action, especially regarding how you share your time and money. There are positive stars for creative and innovative projects and events, such as those with collaborators and fun activities with family. However, you must be careful with arrangements and communications to avoid delays and mix-ups.

WEEK 3: 17–23 SEPTEMBER

A firm commitment either financially or in your personal life will put the spotlight on your ability to stick to an agreement. If you are making major financial decisions this week you must avoid overspending and overinvesting, but by the same token you must also avoid underestimating your spending power. A healing and positive environment such as a relaxing short break will boost your self-confidence.

WEEK 4: 24–30 SEPTEMBER

This weekend's full moon will spotlight important personal or financial matters. Be prepared to think outside the square as new options will come into being. This is an excellent weekend for meeting groups and friends, where you'll derive great support and direction. You may even find this is a transformative time when you enjoy the company of family and favourite activities.

HEALTH

You will gain increased motivation in September to invest a little more time and effort in yourself and your health and well-being. You may find yourself drawn either to favourite activities that raise your spirit or to travelling that broadens your horizons and provides a sense of relaxation. Take the time earlier in the month to organise something special such as a holiday or at least a short break, because otherwise towards the end of September you may be fatigued.

FINANCES

The start of the month features important focus on financial transactions. It is in your interest to research your circumstance carefully, as otherwise you may tend to misjudge your financial situation or even enter into arguments with someone who you must be able to collaborate with. Major decisions towards the 18th will once again require you to focus seriously on financial arrangements and provide stable and secure outcomes.

HOME

If you have already been considering changes at home, with family or a property you are likely to see rapid progress in September. However, you will need to be super careful with financial transactions and communications, especially between the 10th and 15th, to avoid making mistakes. You'll gain the opportunity to alter your environment towards the end of the month and may even be surprised around the 20th how a short break or visit can alter domestic dynamics.

LOVE LIFE

Mars will be in your partnership sector until the end of the month, which will bring out the fiery nature of a partner and could increase the passion in your relationship. However, it could also increase arguments. Keep an eye on misunderstandings and potentially a battle of wills towards mid-month and from the 18th to the 22nd and the 27th. During this time, however, you may also experience a breakthrough, so be prepared to work constructively to create a therapeutic outcome.

WORK

You can make a great deal of progress, especially with collaborations. You may even begin a fresh collaboration around the new moon on the 11th. Double-check financial arrangements if you make agreements as mistakes can be made, especially mid-month. This aside, an innovative approach to your work will be rewarding. You will gain insight towards the 27th about whether collaborations are working for you, then you'll be able to make relevant changes if necessary.

CAPRICORN • SEPTEMBER

October

WEEK 1: 1–7 OCTOBER

Unusual or unexpected news may arrive this week yet a lovely outcome may develop, so work towards your goals as you could truly make headway both in your favourite projects and interests and at home and in your personal life. A surprise visit or unusual domestic development may initially draw on your resourcefulness but could ultimately broaden your horizons.

WEEK 2: 8–14 OCTOBER

Certain matters are likely to come to a head in your work or personal life, and whether you feel disappointed or find the clarity you're looking for a successful resolution lies in good communication skills and the willingness to change. This weekend's new moon will stimulate renewal in the areas you share such as joint finances and household chores. Some Capricorns may need to consider a fresh budget.

WEEK 3: 15–21 OCTOBER

This is an excellent week to consider your goals and aspirations and take steps in the right direction, especially at work, home and health-wise. A trip or visit may be particularly promising. Romance could thrive towards this weekend, so be sure to organise a date. Just be careful mid-week next week with communications to avoid delays and misunderstandings.

WEEK 4: 22–28 OCTOBER / WEEK 5: 29 OCTOBER–4 NOVEMBER

WEEK 4: a trip, event or learning curve will take you into new territory. This will be exciting, and also potentially therapeutic. Some interactions will be intense, so be sure to avoid entering conflict for the best results. **WEEK 5:** this is a lovely week for romance and to plan a special event for someone you love. Just avoid contentious topics towards the weekend, and avoid delays through good planning.

HEALTH

You will appreciate the opportunity to return to an old haunt such as a holiday destination or simply the chance to indulge in spending time on your self-development and understanding of yourself. You may experience a particularly healing or therapeutic development towards the 20th and 26th that instils in you the importance of looking after your mental, spiritual, emotional and physical health. This is a good month for spiritual development.

FINANCES

Finances will deserve careful appraisal early in the month, and you may need to make a fresh commitment such as sign a contract. Ensure the security and stability of your income and savings will provide the foundation to make progress in your personal life and build wealth. Be careful with financial discussions around the 9th and 25th in particular, as you may be easily influenced or idealistic about your financial circumstances.

HOME

This is an excellent month to consider how you could pool resources with those you share your home with to improve your mutual enjoyment of your home life and joint space. You may be pleasantly surprised by developments in this regard, especially towards the 7th. However, for some discussions may be complex and you must in this case be very careful to establish common ground and common aims, especially financially.

LOVE LIFE

You'll gain deep insight into your partner and their true feelings. This may initially involve some soul searching but in the long run it will be enlightening. However, if you feel your relationship has run its course, the difficult astrological aspects early in October and at the end of the month may be the straw that breaks the camel's back unless you are careful. To overcome differences you may need to make an additional personal commitment.

WORK

Consider how you would prefer your work and career life to progress. You'll gain the opportunity to collaborate with like-minded people, be this via a learning opportunity such as a study course or via activities in your spare time. You will appreciate gaining a deeper understanding of where you feel your talents lie. Be prepared to reach out to those who you know could help you gain direction.

CAPRICORN • OCTOBER

November

WEEK 1: 5–11 NOVEMBER

Monday's new moon spells a stimulating even if potentially intense chapter in your career, status and general direction. For some, though, this new moon will help you revitalise how you appear to others through your presentation and communication abilities. Teaching, study, travel or adventure may appeal. Romance can thrive this week, especially towards Tuesday, but you must avoid arguments this weekend.

WEEK 2: 12–18 NOVEMBER

You will enjoy a reunion or two that will provide you with the motivation to be more outgoing and adventurous. A trip or get-together in nature may be therapeutic. A change of environment will certainly prove to be uplifting, and you may receive news or undertake a journey that takes you to an old haunt or someone you hold close to your heart.

WEEK 3: 19–25 NOVEMBER

You will not always agree with everyone and towards Friday it's important to bear this in mind, especially concerning shared matters such as joint finances or duties. The full moon supermoon on Tuesday/Wednesday will spotlight the chance to turn a corner with long-term projects, in your personal life or work. A family member or someone else who is close may surprise you. Romance, too, has a few surprises.

WEEK 4: 26 NOVEMBER–2 DECEMBER

You will enjoy being adventurous and may even be drawn to leave your comfort zone, which will be exciting and also potentially therapeutic. You will appreciate the sense that your business and personal relationships are improving, even if you know sometimes you need to be super sensitive to someone else's feelings. You may experience a financial or ego boost.

HEALTH

Much of your peace of mind in November will stem from good relationships. For this reason it will be in your interest to be careful with communications so you are able to achieve the peace of mind you are seeking. You may even discover by the end of the month that you are in a much stronger position than you would have been had you not devoted so much time and effort to your communications, especially in your relationships.

FINANCES

You will be drawn to be adventurous this month but will also need to evaluate whether your finances can accommodate some of your hobbies or ventures; for example, travel. If you have budgeted well you will already have funds in place, but if not consider beginning a fund now for some of your favourite activities down the line. You are likely to alter how you share certain financial arrangements and may seek expert help if necessary.

HOME

Changes in the way you share important aspects of your life such as duties, chores and even joint finances could require focus, as these matters have a considerable influence on your home life. It will be in your interest to minimise upheaval at home, especially around the 24th, unless long-term change such as a move is something you have already been planning. In this case your plans for change will begin to shape up.

LOVE LIFE

You will experience a reunion or deepening connection that may be more significant than meets the eye. A coincidence or synchronicity may add apparent meaning to the reunion. However, it is important to carefully evaluate the get-together before deciding it has relevance to your life now. For some Capricorns practicalities will mean changes within your love life. There are healing and therapeutic aspects this month, so be sure to reach out to experts if necessary.

WORK

The new moon on the 9th will usher in a transformative phase concerning your activities. For some Capricorns this will mean a change at work and for others in the ventures you undertake in your spare time. Developments mid-month will signal a changing of the guard regarding shared chores and duties, and you may need to undertake careful conversations about these at work. Avoid rushing decisions. You'll experience a more stable outlook by the end of November.

December

WEEK 1: 3–9 DECEMBER

You may receive good news at work or concerning your status. Be diligent with someone who can try your patience by being willing to go the extra hard yards this week. Being such a methodical person, Wednesday's buoyant Sagittarian new moon may feel unsettling unless you focus on its benefits. These include embracing a more optimistic approach and avoiding taking the opinions of other people personally.

WEEK 2: 10–16 DECEMBER

News from your past is likely to be positive, with a view to enabling progress at work and in your personal life at the least. A visitor will bring a change of routine to your usual week. You may simply wish to make concrete changes to your environment, so you will enjoy planning or even undertaking a trip. A sociable weekend will be fun. You will enjoy a reunion.

WEEK 3: 17–23 DECEMBER

Meetings, trips, socialising and get-togethers with someone special will prove motivating this week. You'll appreciate the opportunity to get on top of important paperwork and financial matters that deserve careful discussion early next week. Avoid feeling pressured by the mood of the season to overspend, as a debt or invoice will need to be paid. It's far better to manage your finances than throw caution to the wind.

WEEK 4: 24–31 DECEMBER

Get set to turn a corner this week and allow your inner nurturer to shine. You may be asked to help someone. It's a good week to quietly appraise your work circumstances. You may be passionate about your work, but if you feel that it's not on track then this week may offer insight into how to make changes. Avoid overspending and absent-mindedness.

HEALTH

You will appreciate the opportunity to indulge a little more than usual in your favourite activities in your spare time during December, which will result in raised spirits and more vitality. A trip or favourite hobby could take you into fresh territory and will not only be exciting but also motivating, all of which can improve your mental, emotional and spiritual health. The 12th is particularly well aspected to look after your favourite interests.

FINANCES

You may receive good news financially early in the month, towards the 7th. This will certainly be a good time to discuss your financial options with those they concern; just be sure to avoid entering a battle of wills at this time. Towards the 21st a shared financial situation will merit patience. Set yourself goals and discuss them with those they concern, and as a result you will be able to reach a positive outcome or arrangement.

HOME

A change of pace at home will merit patience, especially as news may come from out of the blue and therefore will need discussion. You may be ready to implement a plan that has been in the making for some time and, again, patience will be necessary. A trip or welcoming a visitor will also require adjustment, even if meetings and get-togethers will nevertheless prove to be therapeutic in many ways.

LOVE LIFE

You'll appreciate the opportunity to enter fresh territory with someone special. You may simply enjoy favourite activities in your spare time together more. Some lucky Capricorns will be travelling and taking time off. All the above can improve your relationship, especially towards the 12th. Singles may be drawn to favourite activities more than usual and may even meet someone friendly as a result. A sociable time in the lead-up to Christmas will improve both your mood and love life.

WORK

Conversations will flow towards the 8th at work and you may experience good news with projects or finances, so be sure to take the initiative, especially if you're looking for a new position or advancement. Just be sure to avoid a battle of wills towards the 5th, as this is likely to be counterproductive. You will gain the opportunity to reap the rewards for past hard work well done. Some Capricorns may even experience a financial boost.

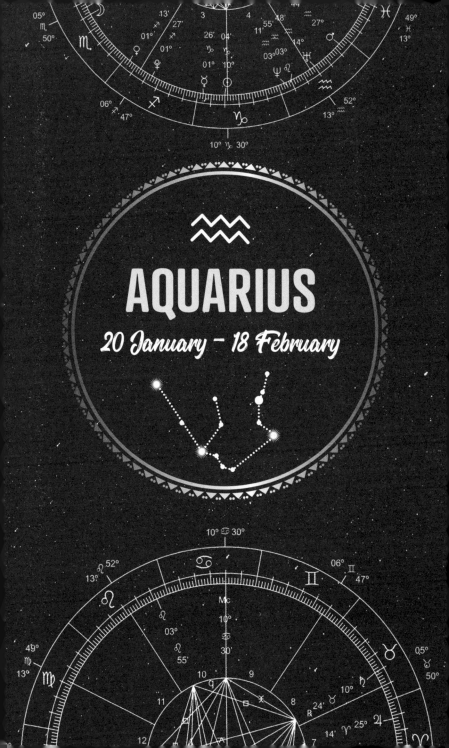

January

WEEK 1: 1–7 JANUARY

A new work or daily routine will begin if it hasn't already recently. You may see your work life or health in a fresh light and must find new ways to find the balance you're looking for in your daily schedule. It's a good week to focus on health and well-being and avoid arguments. If you're travelling, plan well ahead to avoid delays. You'll enjoy socialising.

WEEK 2: 8–14 JANUARY

As Mars and Venus align in your 12th house you'll feel drawn to revitalise an important aspect of yourself such as your health, well-being and general day-to-day routine or work schedule. A fresh interest or new relationship may begin now. Pay close attention to the dynamics and avoid a relationship where your gut simply says 'No!' It's a good time to set a fresh budget in place.

WEEK 3: 15–21 JANUARY

The entry of Venus in your sign, where it will be until 10 February, will put the initial focus on your work and health and then on your love life and finances, motivating you to improve all areas. A fresh routine or strong foundation that enables you to boost your work and health schedule will be the first step. Consider devoting more time per week to managing these areas.

WEEK 4: 22–28 JANUARY

Health and well-being are the bedrock of a happy life. This is a good week for a health appointment and to focus on improving health if you feel it's necessary. If work is your focus, ensure you reach out and discuss exciting plans. A promotion or financial boost may be in the cards. A get-together with someone from your past may be intense. A past matter may come home to roost and a debt may be repaid.

HEALTH

This is an excellent month to boost your health physically, spiritually, mentally and emotionally, as the stars will support your efforts. You may even benefit from the help of an expert or teacher so you can learn new techniques to boost your well-being. The entry of Venus in your sign from the 17th will encourage you to consider a fresh look and invest more in yourself. The end of the month will be especially good for boosting self-esteem.

FINANCES

This will be a good month to consider how you could work better financially, especially with regard to domestic expenses. You may discover a good way to make a little extra from home, even as simply as by decluttering and selling some of the items that no longer suit your needs. There is a strong connection with your past, so you may repay a loan or have a debt repaid to you.

HOME

You'll enjoy a return to an old haunt and, equally, your return to your own home after a visit elsewhere. Be careful with travel to avoid delays and plan well ahead. If you have been considering making considerable changes to your home life such as a move or renovation then January is an excellent time to research your options and take steps if you feel ready, as you may enjoy a financial boost towards the end of the month.

LOVE LIFE

Venus in Aquarius from the 17th promises to boost your self-worth and will bring your charisma bubbling to the surface. From mid-January onwards you are likely to enjoy the company of someone special more so than usual, and if you are single you could connect with someone special so be sure during the last two weeks of January to reach out and meet new people. You may be drawn to a reunion but you must carefully evaluate it beforehand.

WORK

The entry of Venus into your own sign towards the 17th will initially boost your work life, as it will motivate you to be more engaged in this important aspect of your life. If you have been looking for work this will be an excellent month to be positive that you will find the right thing to suit you. The new moon on the 18th/19th will particularly spotlight options, organisations or groups that will resonate with you.

February

WEEK 1: 29 JANUARY—4 FEBRUARY

Developments signal key changes in your personal life, so be prepared to be adaptable if necessary to avoid actions you later regret. This is a good week to put someone you care about first. If you were born in February you are likely to receive key work or health news as well and may need to reorganise your daily schedule. Be sure to think outside the box about your options.

WEEK 2: 5—11 FEBRUARY

You may be surprised by a change of circumstance or impromptu development that requires thought such as a spontaneous event or trip. Rely on your inner resourcefulness and good communication skills to maintain a calm attitude while changes unfold. For some developments may revolve around finances and for others your personal life. Developments mid-week will bring to mind what your priorities really are.

WEEK 3: 12—18 FEBRUARY

This week's solar eclipse will be in Aquarius and signals a particularly transformational time, especially in your personal life. You may be ready for a change of direction or for something new, but if you find the gears are sticking as you attempt to change gear then take the time to work out a plan. Someone close will be particularly significant.

WEEK 4: 19—25 FEBRUARY / WEEK 5: 26 FEBRUARY—4 MARCH

WEEK 4: consider your values and priorities: what would you most like to do? If you're not doing it now you must make plans to figure it into your life. Avoid overspending; look at how to create both security but also inspiration. **WEEK 5:** you may need to exit your comfort zone financially. Be practical above all else, especially in your love life towards 3 March.

266 ✦ *2026* **HOROSCOPES**

HEALTH

Find ways to calm your heart and mind to avoid taking actions you later regret. As an eclipse season kicks off it invariably points to an intense few weeks. The solar eclipse on the 17th will be in Aquarius, which will be particularly intense; then, moving towards 3 March the lunar eclipse will fall in your relationship zone. There will be considerable developments in your personal life that will merit a careful approach, especially on the 5th, 8th and 27th.

FINANCES

When life is full of change it's even more important to keep an eye on finances but, equally, to avoid allowing these to take over your decision-making process. Key developments in your personal life will merit careful financial focus to ensure you are not swept up in developments and ignore this important aspect of any relationship. Try to get important decisions or paperwork completed before the 26th to avoid having to draw out any negotiations.

HOME

There is a strong draw towards something new for you now, not only due to the solar eclipse being in your sign on the 17th but also due to the Saturn–Neptune conjunction that builds during the entire month. As this is such a turning point for you in a key relationship, your home life will also come under the microscope for change. Be sure to avoid making rash decisions, especially at the end of the month.

LOVE LIFE

A changeable and busy start to the month may be intense and on occasion unmanageable, especially around the 5th and 8th. Rely on a good, strong set of personal values as these will help guide you towards making the right decisions as opposed to being impulsive. Couples may be drawn to be independent but must bear in mind that this phase will not last, so you must avoid making rash decisions.

WORK

Jupiter retrograde in your sixth house of work may add to a feeling that you are stuck or even going backwards. If you are lucky enough to be on holiday you will enjoy this dreamy phase, but if you are working it will be in your interest to be super patient, especially with long-term goals. Luckily, towards the end of the month you are likely to gain the incentive to explore new options. Be bold but not impulsive.

AQUARIUS · FEBRUARY

March

WEEK 1: 5–11 MARCH

A fresh direction will appeal in a business or personal relationship. You'll appreciate stepping into a new understanding of both yourself and others and a different timetable, as it will help you build your dreams with the benefit of realistic plans. There's romance around this weekend, so organise a date! You'll also enjoy being creative and music, film and dance, so be sure to organise something special.

WEEK 2: 12–18 MARCH

Keep an eye out for opportunities at work to prove yourself and show just how co-operative you can be. Some Aquarians' personal or family life will benefit from a little more focus, while for others extra attention at work and especially towards the 18th will be rewarding. You'll enjoy an impromptu get-together or will receive key news that could boost your circumstances.

WEEK 3: 19–25 MARCH

Thursday's Pisces new moon will be an excellent time to revitalise your personal life. Follow your instincts, and be optimistic but avoid being super idealistic. You may enjoy a reunion or news from the past and an unexpected boost in self-esteem. Some lucky Aquarians will enjoy a financial boost. Romance, the arts and music will thrive this weekend, so be sure to organise a treat.

WEEK 4: 26 MARCH–1 APRIL

A trip or get-together may bring out your sensitivities, so be sure to maintain an even approach. An unexpected or unusual development at home or due to a change of environment could have a therapeutic effect. If you have been overspending recently your debts could start adding up, so this will be a good week to factor in a mindful approach to your spending.

HEALTH

You will gradually notice an improvement in your energy levels if they have been slightly low in recent weeks and months. You'll relish increasingly investing in activities and ventures you enjoy as a result. Just keep an eye on stress levels, especially towards the end of March. Be sure to be mindful of how much energy you spend worrying and find ways to minimise this if it has been more than usual.

FINANCES

There will be important financial developments in March, especially between the 13th and 18th. If you feel that you have let your finances get out of hand this will be a good time to get the information you need to be able to sort things out, especially by reviewing existing agreements and arrangements and finding new ways forward. Some lucky Aquarians may be in for a financial boost this month.

HOME

You will be drawn to invest in your personal life and may be particularly drawn to invest in your home life and those you love on the weekend of the 21st. A reunion or return to an old haunt may produce a slight sense of nostalgia. A change in your environment may be unexpectedly pleasant towards the end of the month, so be sure to keep an open mind about visitors and visiting others.

LOVE LIFE

There is an upbeat feeling around your love life at the start of March, especially between the 5th and 9th, and this can certainly help you boost your love life whether you are a part of a couple or single. Bear in mind that you are looking for more adventure in your life over the coming weeks and months, and working together with those whose company you love will bring the added benefit of sharing your experiences.

WORK

Now that Jupiter has ended its retrograde phase you will gradually over the coming weeks and months experience more progress at work. Be sure in March to take the initiative and get in touch with important people you would like to spend more time with in the work arena, and to circulate your résumé and make phone calls if you are ready to move into a fresh environment as your efforts are likely to succeed.

WEEK 1: 2–8 APRIL

Thursday's full moon will spotlight a need, either of your own or of someone close at home or at work, to rearrange shared duties, finances or even your personal life. Be prepared to make commitments to a project or person or put your own happiness first at this time, but avoid arguments that will be counterproductive to establishing a new norm.

WEEK 2: 9–15 APRIL

Financial and personal developments may present like a runaway train as Mars enters Aries and steams through this upbeat sign until mid-May. This week's developments may be particularly busy but you will soon settle into the rhythm. It will be important to keep an eye on finances to avoid overspending. You may receive good news or enjoy a get-together this weekend or towards Monday.

WEEK 3: 16–22 APRIL

Events are likely to speed up this week and may even entail a surprise next week. Take unpredictable people and fresh options in your stride. Ensure you make the most of a new chapter in a contract, agreement or relationship, as this could affect your finances. Avoid accruing more debt than you can foreseeably manage. A strong link with your past may bring out your deeper feelings.

WEEK 4: 23–29 APRIL

You will appreciate the opportunity to meet people whose company you value. However, this weekend it will be in your interest to be careful with conversations that might touch a nerve with someone who is sensitive. You are likely to experience a financial, work or personal boost next week and developments will stimulate a productive and positive outlook in you.

HEALTH

April's developments are going to gather pace as the month goes by so it will be in your interest to be well prepared, especially after the new moon on the 17th. Consider developing a healthy schedule earlier in the month that keeps you on top of a busy time. You will find at the end of April that the comfort and security you gain from your home will improve your health, so be sure to create a healthy home.

FINANCES

If you have allowed your finances to take on a life of their own you are liable to need to sort out aspects of your finances that are no longer supporting you or your plans moving forward. Be prepared to look at ways to alter existing arrangements. Developments towards the 13th and 17th will shine a light on whether you are on top of your budget or whether your finances have a momentum of their own.

HOME

You may experience a surprise development towards the end of the month. Avoid trying to be too stuck on present circumstances and be sure to embrace a progressive approach to a new circumstance that is waiting in the wings regarding property, your domestic life or family. You will find as the months go by that developments that signify a great deal of change and may seem disruptive now will actually take you somewhere better.

LOVE LIFE

Early in April developments will be worth discussing carefully with your loved one, as you may otherwise risk working at cross purposes with each other. Luckily, you are communicating well this month so be prepared to take the initiative. Some of your communications may need to circle around finances and work duties so you are able to come to mutually acceptable arrangements. The end of April could bring romance your way, so be sure to organise a treat.

WORK

While you prefer to gain a degree of stability from your work you also need excitement and variety in your daily life. This month you may need to weigh your options to establish a middle road that allows you to achieve security through work and also excitement. To this end be sure to avoid a battle of wills, especially around the 4th and 5th and the 24th, that could diminish your chances of finding that middle ground.

AQUARIUS · APRIL

May

WEEK 1: 30 APRIL–6 MAY

Being philosophical, you sometimes need to remind yourself that you do have free will. This week, attention to details and research will help you. Key developments may mean you must look at a financial or personal situation from a fresh perspective. Negotiations, talks and new ventures point to the need for a different communications device or approach to your budget.

WEEK 2: 7–13 MAY

You will manage to gain a more settled outlook in your personal and financial lives this month, especially if you look for practical and realistic solutions to any issues that have arisen in either of these areas. You may experience a financial or ego boost. It is certainly an excellent week to discuss plans to gain both a sense of commitment and adventure within your personal life and work.

WEEK 3: 14–20 MAY

This weekend's new moon will bring news, get-togethers and social events that warm your heart. You may make changes at home. Keep your values uppermost in your mind for the best effect, because in this way decisions you make will sit better with you over time. An expense or investment is best approached from a level-headed point of view. Avoid impulse spending as you are likely to regret it.

WEEK 4: 21–27 MAY / WEEK 5: 28 MAY–3 JUNE

WEEK 4: you may be surprised by someone unpredictable, so keep communications clear for the best results. Avoid financial and emotional gambling. You'll enjoy a change of environment via travel or a visitor. **WEEK 5:** news at work or regarding your status signals the beginning of an exciting phase in which events could lead to adventure and more opportunities to indulge in your true interests.

HEALTH

In May you will appreciate the revitalising effect of short trips, either to visit friends and family or to enjoy a change of scenery, with the second and fourth weeks being particularly conducive to visits and brief trips. Just ensure you double-check itineraries and plans to avoid delays and frustration. The benefit on your health of taking breaks will be immeasurable. Be prepared in May to also schedule fun events to raise your spirits.

FINANCES

The full moon on 1/2 May will spotlight some of the financial arrangements you have made with other people. This would include those with, for example, housemates or the tax department. It is time to refresh some of your arrangements, for some Aquarians due to changes at work and for others to changes in your income. Be prepared to seek the help of an expert if necessary to ensure you avoid making mistakes.

HOME

You will appreciate the opportunity to embellish your home and/or environment in May. Venus in your domestic zone will also contribute to the likelihood that domestic interpersonal dynamics can proceed more harmoniously than usual, so be sure to invest in this lovely aspect of your life. Mid-month, however, you may be tempted to overspend or will need to address household spending if you have got into debt.

LOVE LIFE

There is a distinct sense of fate in May, so couples may ask whether they are meant to be together and singles may meet someone who seems strangely familiar yet who you have never met before. Prolonged periods of questioning could lead to confusion; aim instead to connect with an inner sense of direction. The key to determining the happiness of your relationship is to ask if you are both on the same spiritual path.

WORK

Pluto's retrograde phase will be making waves for you in your work life. This will manifest for some as boredom and for others as the necessity to overhaul your usual daily work routine. Be prepared to look at innovative ways to alter your work so that it suits you better over the coming months. The 11th to the 13th and the 31st will be particularly conducive to finding solutions to gain both more purpose and stability at work.

AQUARIUS · MAY

June

WEEK 1: 4–10 JUNE

A fresh daily schedule could arise due to changes at work or regarding your health. Some lucky Aquarians will enjoy a fun change of schedule such as a holiday or short break. The key to making successful decisions now lies in establishing common ground and aiming for a solid foundation. February-born Aquarians could see romance blossom despite vulnerabilities arising, either in yourself or someone close.

WEEK 2: 11–17 JUNE

You're ready to take a creative or work project to the next level and will be happy to reveal your projects once all aspects of your plans are in place. That said, an unexpected meeting or news could catapult them forward. You may be pleasantly surprised by family or domestic developments. However, if you experience a work or financial disappointment keep an open mind, as something better is on the horizon.

WEEK 3: 18–24 JUNE

A busy time at work or the chance to focus on your favourite activities will keep you on your toes. Circumstances may be intense but news will engage your interest, especially concerning your health, fitness and career. You may receive a financial boost or compliment from out of the blue that will boost your morale. Some Aquarians will enjoy an improvement at home.

WEEK 4: 25 JUNE–1 JULY

If you have been looking for a commitment from someone, either in your personal or professional life, this will be a good time to ask for it. Be prepared to venture into fresh territory. The full moon on the 29th/30th will spotlight your social and personal connections. If your social life has been particularly busy you will be drawn to slow it down or vice versa.

HEALTH

You will have a wonderful opportunity to boost your health and well-being in June, especially around the 9th. You may consider a new diet or fitness schedule that brings more of a sense of fun and enjoyment your way. Avoid subscribing to programs that are too strict and that you know in your heart you will not be able to maintain in the long term. Jupiter in Leo will help improve your energy levels from the 30th.

FINANCES

It will be important in June to organise your finances so they suit you, as you may need to adjust some of your budget or expectations. Avoid overspending and consider ways to repay debt if this has accrued considerably over time. Developments towards the 13th may spotlight a financial hole in the bucket, and the benefit of this will be that you will be able to fix it. Consider enlisting the help of a financial expert if necessary.

HOME

This will be an excellent month to make changes at home, with family or a property, as the new moon supermoon on the 15th will help you with your plans. If you are enjoying your domestic life at the moment you are likely to be busy and continue to enjoy this important aspect. Developments towards the 18th could also feel therapeutic due to a visit or change of ambience.

LOVE LIFE

You will enjoy being spontaneous, especially in mid-June. However, risk-taking is not something that will improve your love life so you must avoid gambling or making assumptions about other people's feelings, especially towards the 13th. An impromptu get-together could be unexpectedly pleasant, however, towards the new moon on the 15th. The full moon on the 29th/30th will spotlight your feelings about one particular relationship, and you may be drawn to make a fresh commitment.

WORK

If you have been looking for a lucky break at work this is likely during the first and second weeks of June, so be sure to circulate your résumé or schedule talks with your boss and/or business associates. However, you will need to adopt a realistic approach to finances at this time. A change in your usual working schedule is on the cards, so be prepared to negotiate so it suits you.

AQUARIUS · JUNE

July

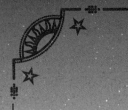

WEEK 1: 2–8 JULY

Surprise developments this week will benefit from a structured approach, especially if you feel you are outside your comfort zone. For many Aquarians, however, there will be excitement due to a visit, trip or spontaneous get-together. If finances have been an issue this will be a week in which you must finally review spending and reckon with your circumstances.

WEEK 2: 9–15 JULY

You will appreciate the opportunity to look into fresh options, especially in your working life. You'll need to think on your feet, as some developments may be unexpected or will ask that you draw on your inner resourcefulness and maintain high self-esteem. Be prepared to innovate within your working life but also maintain a knowledge of the nurturing and financial aspect of your work, which can't be overlooked.

WEEK 3: 16–22 JULY

Pluto in your sign makes a favourable link with Uranus, which could bring ideal developments. These are likely to be long term and will affect your daily routine, work and prospectively also health. Be prepared to discuss your options with those they concern. Avoid being caught in a spiral of intense emotions or a feeling of loss; it's far better to focus on the positives.

WEEK 4: 23–29 JULY

The Aquarian full moon on the 29th/30th and your sign's co-ruler Saturn turning retrograde point to a fairly intense week in which you may be prone to second-guessing yourself. See the positives of fairly rapid change in your personal or professional life even if it has been a long time coming, and be prepared to adequately research your circumstances.

HEALTH

July will be an excellent month to adopt a more upbeat fitness routine. If your current health routine has seen diminished energy levels, consider looking at a diet that is specifically geared to improve digestion. Be sure to consult expert advice with regard to this; it is certainly a good month to review your health practices. Developments towards the end of the month could bring surprise solutions to ongoing circumstances and/or the influence of positive people who raise your spirits.

FINANCES

The beginning of July brings the need for a serious review of your finances. If you have already accrued debt it will be necessary to restructure some of your arrangements in order to get on top of your finances. There is a non-negotiable aspect to some of your financial arrangements, and for this reason there is little wiggle room. However, in the long term it looks like positive or even surprise developments at work could improve circumstances.

HOME

Uranus and Mars in your fourth house of home will encourage you to make progress and transform this important part of your life in July. Developments are likely to be rapid, especially mid-month, and while these will largely be the result of previous decisions some Aquarians will enjoy unprecedented opportunities to improve your home life or family circumstances. Be sure to snap these up: pending due diligence, of course.

LOVE LIFE

Developments concerning a partner may bring out some of your vulnerabilities, so it will be important to properly manage your responses to other people's situations. The full moon on the 29th/30th will be in your sign and is likely to bring your emotions to the surface, especially if you were born in January, although all Aquarians are likely to experience an intense end of the month due to its transformative nature. Be sure to pace yourself.

WORK

A gregarious outlook at work will certainly be to your benefit. However, if you have overinvested in certain areas of your work you will find out this month and will need to adjust where you place your focus. You may need to review some aspects of your working life, and if you're lucky a holiday will enable you to do so in your own time and reorient your career direction.

AQUARIUS · JULY

August

WEEK 1: 30 JULY–5 AUGUST

You'll gain the potential this week to work towards constructive developments in your personal life, financially and at work, depending on when you were born. For some the drive towards building a more solid platform for yourself in your health and well-being will be hard to ignore, especially if you have found your energy levels are slightly lacking. A new daily work or health initiative or schedule will appeal.

WEEK 2: 6–12 AUGUST

Get set for an exciting, active new chapter at work, concerning your health or daily routine, especially if you were born in mid-February. If you were born beforehand be prepared to consider a fresh arrangement in a business or personal partnership that may even be beneficial financially, although you may need to undertake serious discussions first. Romance will thrive on the 10th: just be sure you're on the same page!

WEEK 3: 13–19 AUGUST

Some January-born Aquarians will receive key news from a business or personal partner. February-born Aquarians are likely to undergo a change in your usual daily schedule due to news at work or regarding your health. All the above will eventually create a sense of stability and at least direction, even if there is some upheaval in the process. This is still a romantic week, so be sure to organise dates.

WEEK 4: 20–26 AUGUST / WEEK 5: 27 AUGUST–2 SEPTEMBER

WEEK 4: keep an eye on good communication skills as you may gain the opportunity to create more stability and security in a work or personal relationship. **WEEK 5:** this is a good week to prioritise your personal life and find ways to settle differences with someone important in your life at work or at home to create a sense of healing.

HEALTH

Early August will be a good time for frank discussions about your health and ways to best maintain it. You may need to undergo some degree of research to establish the true state of your health. Be prepared to discuss it with experts and advisers for the best results, especially if you were born in February. August is a particularly good month to establish a fresh routine that benefits your health.

FINANCES

It is important to be able to collaborate financially with those you either share space with at home or regarding work duties. There is focus this month on exactly how you share and ideally who is owed what. For these reasons you are likely to experience considerable changes either within personal or business commitments or within key financial arrangements, especially towards the 21st and 28th. Be careful to formulate plans that are both practical and realistic moving forward.

HOME

Strong feelings are hard to ignore, but it is equally important to be careful about making major changes in your domestic life without adequate research or gaining impartial knowledge. Fact finding may be necessary as you have the option to improve your domestic, family or property circumstances this month, but on the other hand you have an equal chance of losing financial traction unless you are careful in the domestic realm, including your home and/or a property.

LOVE LIFE

This month's eclipse season spans your relationship sector, so you can expect considerable changes in this regard. For some this will pan out primarily as you make fresh financial arrangements, and for others this could mean the parting of ways if your relationship has already been on rocky ground. Singles may meet someone new but you must be prepared to be adventurous if you are willing to commit to someone.

WORK

The total solar eclipse on the 12th/13th will kick-start a fresh chapter for you at work if you were born after 12 February. That said, all Aquarians will be undertaking important conversations at work that could potentially transform your work scenario. It is possible in August to establish more of a sense of security and stability at work, so be sure to have discussions towards this outcome but also be prepared to innovate.

AQUARIUS · AUGUST

September

WEEK 1: 3–9 SEPTEMBER

You are generally a self-sufficient, independent character but, even so, there are times in your life when you need to collaborate with others. This week this will be very apparent, and you'll need to find ways to collaborate with a business or personal partner for the best results. When you do you will find by Sunday or Monday that you are able to bond over mutual territory.

WEEK 2: 10–16 SEPTEMBER

This week's Virgo new moon will kick-start the opportunity to improve relationships with someone important to you, either in your personal life or at work, so be sure to take the initiative. However, some interactions and financial transactions may be a little more confusing than usual, so be sure to be super careful with communications and finances to avoid making mistakes.

WEEK 3: 17–23 SEPTEMBER

Developments now will involve making a commitment to something or to someone new. Investigate your options very carefully and be prepared to discuss your arrangements with your business or personal partner. Some aspects of your decision-making may be challenging, but the discussion process will have a healing effect as long as you are both willing to see the other person's point of view.

WEEK 4: 24–30 SEPTEMBER

This weekend's full moon brings an opportunity to establish more peace and harmony in your life, but also to bring a little adventure and sparkle into your primary relationships and enjoy a romantic time. This is an excellent week for health and beauty appointments and also for breathing new life into your home, so be sure to take the initiative.

HEALTH

Mars in your health sector is providing you with additional energy and motivation, so be sure to tap into this whenever you can. If you feel, however, that your energy levels are drained, find concrete ways to boost these as your efforts will be successful. Be sure to use your intuition regarding your health, and if you have any worries to consult an expert. The end of September and early October will be especially conducive for health appointments.

FINANCES

Important joint financial decisions must be taken seriously at the start of September, as you otherwise risk making your financial situation more difficult than necessary. Be prepared to collaborate with people with whom you share financial responsibilities, especially towards the 18th and 27th, as you may experience a positive outcome. However, if either of you is unwilling to compromise then some developments will need to be reviewed at a later time if they cannot be resolved now.

HOME

If you'd like to change major aspects of your home life September is the month to do it, as your plans can be discussed at the very least if not acted upon. There may be variables at play connected with someone close, such as someone you share duties or finances with, so it will be important that communications are approached in a level-headed way. Avoid obstinacy, and if you see it in someone close know that there is a more progressive way forward.

LOVE LIFE

The new moon on the 11th begins a fresh cycle that could truly enhance your love life. However, if you find you or your partner tend to be perfectionists this trait may become more accentuated in September and may need to be addressed, especially if perfectionism is removing some of the spontaneity you would otherwise enjoy in the relationship. Communications will require extra focus, especially around the weekend of the 12th, to avoid misunderstandings.

WORK

Mars will help you be productive throughout September. However, you may also discover the need to be a little more intuitive about some of the arrangements at work as this will provide you with insight into your best way forward. Be prepared to discuss your options with those they concern, especially where financial matters are at stake.

AQUARIUS • SEPTEMBER

October

WEEK 1: 1–7 OCTOBER

You could make headway financially and in your personal life, so trust your ability to work well with fresh opportunities. You may need to make a tough call financially or sign a new contract. If you are unsure about your options, consider consulting an expert and avoid allowing negotiations to become difficult. You'll be drawn to embrace different ideas and beliefs and will enjoy art, music and creativity.

WEEK 2: 8–14 OCTOBER

You know what is and what isn't fun in life. This weekend your beliefs may be stretched to their limit and you'll need to look beyond your expectations, otherwise differences of opinion could get in the way of your enjoyment. You must avoid arguments, as they'll escalate. This weekend's new moon suggests the better you collaborate and co-operate with others the more you'll enjoy the upcoming weeks.

WEEK 3: 15–21 OCTOBER

You'll enjoy the company of upbeat and fun people towards the weekend, so be sure to organise an event if you don't already have one planned. You may even find it therapeutic. This is likely to be a busy week but also one in which you can establish a sense of security and balance. Be sure to avoid overspending and making assumptions about how other people feel.

WEEK 4: 22–28 OCTOBER / WEEK 5: 29 OCTOBER–4 NOVEMBER

WEEK 4: focus on what brings you happiness in life. Consider whether sharing chores and responsibilities in a new way could free up time for you. Be ready to negotiate. Aim to establish more financial stability where possible. **WEEK 5:** someone may need your help or vice versa. Be prepared to offer support and ask for it if necessary, as collaborations could excel as long as you avoid arguments.

HEALTH

Mars in your health zone early in October will encourage you to focus on this important aspect of your life, but as the month progresses you may find that relationships and your love life take more focus and you allow your health routine to slip. Be sure to maintain your schedule throughout the month, as you'll gain positive options towards the end of October to improve the fun and spontaneity in your daily life that will buoy your health and well-being.

FINANCES

This will be a good month to review shared finances such as taxes and household expenses. A business arrangement may require a fresh approach as circumstances change. Avoid taking for granted that everyone is on the same page and work towards establishing common ground so you reach agreements as opposed to conflict. If you can work towards collaborations you could make a breakthrough towards the 9th, 16th and 28th. Avoid speculating and following influential people, especially towards the 21st.

HOME

Venus retrograde in October points to your desire to share important aspects of your life in a fresh way and at least reconsider some of your existing arrangements, both financially and at home. Ask yourself whether you could improve the way chores are shared and whether equal investment in key aspects of your home life is warranted. There are positive aspects for making changes at home, especially towards the 7th.

LOVE LIFE

You will be clear early in the month about who really means the most to you, even if you need to undergo a degree of vulnerability to realise this. As you do you will gain strength and developments may be therapeutic. Singles may meet someone who has a healing influence so ensure you organise dates, especially early in October and towards the 24th. A difference of opinion towards the 9th and 30th is best managed carefully to avoid disruption.

WORK

You are in line to enjoy an improvement in your working conditions or daily schedule, so be sure to take the initiative and work towards an ideal outcome. You may see significant progress mid-month and at the end of the month. In the process you may need to negotiate. Some talks may be intense so be prepared to use your considerable negotiation skills, especially on the 9th, 10th, 20th and 30th.

AQUARIUS · OCTOBER

November

WEEK 1: 5–11 NOVEMBER

You'll be fuelled by passion this week so be sure to maintain perspective, especially with regard to a personal or professional relationship. You may reunite with someone and romance could certainly flourish, but you must maintain a sense of practicality. You may be easily distracted by adventure, travel and broadening your horizons. A trip and the pursuit of knowledge will be rewarding, so be sure to plan ahead!

WEEK 2: 12–18 NOVEMBER

Key news from a business or personal source signals change. Couples may decide to venture into new territory within the way you share aspects of your relationship. If you are single you are likely to meet someone who feels fated to be in your life. However, you must be discerning as always: they may seem ideal, but you need to find out! A partner or business situation may improve your finances.

WEEK 3: 19–25 NOVEMBER

You cannot control anyone else's behaviour but you can control your own, and this will become very evident now. Be prepared to be tactful with someone special. However, if some communications are too left of field you may decide the time has come for separate paths. This week's full moon supermoon will spotlight unexpected developments that are best handled with a view to long-term peace of mind. You may enjoy a change of environment.

WEEK 4: 26 NOVEMBER–2 DECEMBER

This is an excellent weekend for collaborations and romance. You may even discover that someone in particular has a therapeutic or healing influence over you. However, some communications will merit more focus than others, and you must avoid taking other people's vulnerabilities personally. Avoid making their problems your own. You will gain more of a sense of security towards Monday.

HEALTH

If you can put your mind to fun ways to improve your health, such as through team sport or any other activity you enjoy, this will help improve your health. Be sure to make fun a factor, as otherwise you are liable to put health on the back burner. You'll be drawn to adventure towards the end of the month and travel will appeal. You will be in a position to enjoy a romantic or exciting change of scenery.

FINANCES

You may need to discuss shared finances and obligations early and again later in the month. To avoid either party misunderstanding the actual arrangements of your financial circumstance it's important to spell out clear facts. If overspending has been an issue for you, this will be a good time to curb it so you can plan forward for exciting projects. If possible avoid taking on someone else's debt or loaning or borrowing money, especially towards the 29th.

HOME

You'll gain a real opportunity to make concrete changes for the better in your home life, even if someone you share space or are in a relationship with has a few surprises up their sleeve. Aim to create a therapeutic and nurturing space for yourself. You may be drawn to enter fresh territory towards the end of the month; for example, by returning to an old haunt or taking a break.

LOVE LIFE

There is a sense of destiny in your love life now. A serendipitous meeting around the 12th to the 14th for singles will help romance thrive. There is no doubt this is a soul connection, but you must consider whether this is an uplifting one or a potentially difficult one. Couples will enjoy a romantic time, especially around the 9th, 10th and 28th. However, if you discover you have slightly different plans you'll need to discuss these over common ground.

WORK

Developments at work may feel as though they have been a long time coming, especially if you were born after mid-February. However, the changes will be swift once they arise. Be careful with communications, especially towards the end of the month. You may receive unexpected news around the full moon on the 24th/25th, and at this time it's best to look at your long-term options with a view to improving your usual working day. Be prepared to negotiate.

AQUARIUS • NOVEMBER

December

WEEK 1: 3–9 DECEMBER

You may be surprised by some conversations this week but the more you discuss people's observations the better it will be, as this may avoid arguments. A change of environment will involve some upheaval but will bring adventure your way. You may feel ready to turn a corner in your work or career, and opportunity may knock. Be inspired, but avoid change just for the sake of it.

WEEK 2: 10–16 DECEMBER

A get-together with a close friend, group or organisation will create a positive ambience, and you are likely to enjoy it. A decision or trip may require debate, however, so be prepared to discuss your plans with those they involve. Some Aquarians will enjoy a work or financial boost. The upcoming weekend is perfect for romance, so be sure to organise a date if you haven't already.

WEEK 3: 17–23 DECEMBER

You'll appreciate the sense that your status, relationships and finances can improve. There is a great deal of motivation on your part to enjoy life this weekend, and you will experience an ego boost as a result. Some Aquarians may experience a financial boost, but you must avoid overspending as a result. There may be tension in an interaction towards the 21st, so be careful with details then.

WEEK 4: 24–31 DECEMBER

You'll appreciate the opportunity to truly engage in some of your favourite interests this week, and if cocooning is what you want then rest assured you'll turn a corner where your home or family becomes a true centre of focus and nurturance. You'll enjoy socialising too. Just be sure to avoid making rash decisions as these may cause unnecessary upheaval. New Year's Eve could be busy or eventful.

HEALTH

In the lead-up to the festive season you will gain the opportunity to put in place a contingency plan for when your social life gets busy. You may even wish to make a promise to yourself to avoid overindulgence. Luckily, Venus in Scorpio will encourage you to indulge in some of your favourite activities such as sport and self-development, which will enable you to maintain a more balanced approach to seasonal festivities this year.

FINANCES

You are likely to reap the rewards of past hard work well done with the possibility you gain a financial boost between the 11th and 14th and again towards the 23rd. If you share everyday finances with someone such as a family member or partner it's in your interest to be careful with interactions towards the 21st to avoid unnecessary arguments. You may be prone to misplacing valuables towards the 23rd, so be careful with finances then too.

HOME

The full moon supermoon on Christmas Eve will spotlight family, creativity and, for some, your home life. This will provide you with clarity about the importance of these aspects of your life that sometimes take second priority because you can get so busy. For this reason it's in your interest during the entire month of December to focus a little more than usual on your home, family or a property investment to ensure developments are smooth sailing.

LOVE LIFE

A change of environment or trip will be exciting but could bring into play different dynamics in your relationship, so good communication skills will be at a premium this month to ensure a smooth flow of events. The weekends of the 12th and 19th are perfect for romance, both for singles and couples. Someone special may feel particularly passionate or romantic at this time, so be sure to facilitate a lovely time.

WORK

You may be drawn to a more adventurous phase in your career and work and opportunity may knock, so be sure to investigate it but avoid rushing into something without adequate forethought, especially towards the new moon on the 9th. It's likely in the week before Christmas that you'll enjoy a positive change at work that may even involve the chance to prove yourself or shine. Be sure to take the initiative.

AQUARIUS • DECEMBER

January

WEEK 1: 1–7 JANUARY

You'll appreciate the sense that you're turning a corner in 2026, especially in your personal life or creativity. For some this will be reflected in changes in your family, while others may begin a fresh phase with a project or organisation. You'll enjoy taking your time to socialise and network, and if you're back at work this week after a break you may receive good news there.

WEEK 2: 8–14 JANUARY

The aspects between Uranus, Saturn and Neptune point to matters that may have an unexpected quality about them, so be prepared this week to be adaptable. Your attention is likely to go to other people, especially via groups and organisations, socialising and networking. Family and those you love will also draw your focus. Just keep an eye on finances as overspending will be a pitfall.

WEEK 3: 15–21 JANUARY

This is a lovely week for socialising and networking. You may begin a fresh chapter with a group, friend or organisation. You will also gain clarity about where you stand, and if the news isn't what you hoped for you will at the very least gain direction as a result and can step ahead with more certainty. Avoid taking the random comments of other people personally.

WEEK 4: 22–28 JANUARY

You'll enjoy taking time for yourself and your favourite activities. A social or networking event could be pleasant, but if you feel conflict is brewing you'll know who or what to avoid. There is a strong link with your past. A meeting or news from a group or friend could bring intense emotions, but as a result you'll gain insight into circumstances.

HEALTH

The start of January will be ideal for getting back to nature and enjoying soaking up the earthy vibes. Mid-January will be an excellent time to explore groups and organisations you feel could help to improve your physical, mental, emotional and spiritual health, so be sure to keep an eye out for courses or groups that appeal to you as this will be a good time to boost your self-esteem, appearance and self-confidence.

FINANCES

Keep an eye on your finances in the first two weeks of the month, as you may receive a bill you'd forgotten about or will tend to overspend. Above all, avoid gambling to overcome a financial shortfall and look for concrete ways to improve finances, such as via work or your career. Mid-January could see an unexpected development financially and for many this will be an improvement, so be sure to be positive about opportunities that arise.

HOME

You may need to make a tough call between your work, status and home life this month. If you're on holiday you must avoid overspending but you'll appreciate returning to your home. Domestic expenses may mount up, so be sure to budget carefully. This aside, there is something inspiring about your home life, a property or family in January. Be prepared to seek nourishment from your home space or offer it to others who may need a little extra care.

LOVE LIFE

You may be pleasantly surprised by some of the people you meet and the connections you forge in January, so if you're single be sure to embrace a sociable phase and keep an open mind about events, as an individualistic character may catch your eye. Couples will enjoy pepping up your love life by being open to fresh experiences and trips to new places. The end of the month will be particularly sociable, ideal for singles to mingle!

WORK

January is a good month to make solid progress at work and improve your status as a result. Be prepared to embrace fresh ideas and new companies, groups and organisations, but you must avoid uncalculated risks as these could truly trip you up, especially in the second week of the month. Mid-January you may experience an unexpected development in connection with a group or organisation that could bring a surprise improvement in your status at work or finances.

February

WEEK 1: 29 JANUARY—4 FEBRUARY

This is a good week to enjoy the company of friends, groups and organisations of like-minded people as you could turn a corner both in your social life and at work. You'll enjoy meetings and networking and may be super busy. A key get-together on Thursday could bring significant work or health news your way, and for some a change of routine.

WEEK 2: 5—11 FEBRUARY

Developments could cause restlessness and the sense that change is coming. Avoid feeling distracted and edgy; find purpose in your activities and you could excel. A personal, domestic or work matter may seem to take you a few steps back or will remind you of the past. A progressive approach to a healthy schedule will keep strong emotions in perspective and enable progress.

WEEK 3: 12—18 FEBRUARY

There is a strong link with your past this week. For some this will be a reunion with someone you love, and for others a return to an old haunt will appeal. The solar eclipse on the 17th will kick-start a fresh chapter at work or in your daily schedule. It's a good week to find new and revitalising ways to bring more health and well-being into your life.

WEEK 4: 19—25 FEBRUARY / WEEK 5: 26 FEBRUARY—4 MARCH

WEEK 4: if the solar eclipse already brought a new daily, health or work schedule your way you'll find ways to gain a foothold now. Be positive, as developments are part of a long-term process. **WEEK 5:** the total lunar eclipse on 3 March will solidify schedule changes for March-born Pisces and changes in a key partnership for February Pisces.

HEALTH

Early in the month you are likely to be drawn to investigate different ways to maintain your health. As a generally spiritual and philosophical person you may particularly be drawn to complementary or spiritual activities such as self-development, psychic development, meditation, yoga or even such psychological in-depth inquiries as hypnotherapy. The lunar eclipse on 3 March will help you gain a sense of stability in your new health regimes.

FINANCES

There is a possibility that you must attend to past financial errors in February and that these derail your financial progress. Bear in mind that this would only be temporary. However, the realisation that your income, investments or expenditure can be erratic will enable you to put in place safeguards that ensure you do not experience the situation again. Try to get key agreements in place before Mercury turns retrograde on the 26th.

HOME

It's a good month to feather your nest and make your home a truly nurturing aspect of your life, especially as this is likely to be a fairly intense month. A link with your past could add romance to your home life. Some Pisces may be drawn to return to an old haunt or will welcome family for visits. You'll gain a deeper understanding of the value of your home or domestic life as the month progresses.

LOVE LIFE

The solar eclipse on the 17th and the lunar eclipse on 3 March point to an intense month, so be sure to take this into account should you find that you or your partner are more stressed than usual. Try to keep pressure off your relationship. However, as you will be stepping into new territory in at least one area of your life such as work you'll need to discuss more topics than usual, so keep communication channels open.

WORK

A stop-start atmosphere at work or simply a change of schedule may be slightly disruptive, especially at the start and end of February. However, if you have been looking for fresh work opportunities this will be a good time to find them. The eclipse season will open new doors for you, so be prepared to take the initiative and look for exactly what you want even if a little upheaval must take place to attain your goals.

March

WEEK 1: 5–11 MARCH

You may notice the tide turning in your personal life, and while some developments may feel a little overwhelming you will enjoy the process so much more if you are able to see the merits of some of the new territory you are entering. You will enjoy a reunion this week or return to an old haunt. A fresh financial cycle is beginning for you.

WEEK 2: 12–18 MARCH

This is likely to be an eventful week. For February-born Pisces there could be movement in your personal life. Singles may meet someone inspiring, and couples will be drawn to invest more in your relationship and domestic and family lives. For March Pisces much focus is likely to be on your work or health life, with discussions and/or meetings with someone important who can help move your work or health forward.

WEEK 3: 19–25 MARCH

Thursday's Pisces new moon signals the chance to boost your appearance, profile and well-being and also romance. You'll find out whether you've been unrealistic about someone or a venture. If so you'll get the chance to focus on building more security. This is a good week to invest in your love life and home. March Pisces especially may receive news from someone from your past.

WEEK 4: 26 MARCH–1 APRIL

This week's events may bring your vulnerabilities to the surface although a surprise could ultimately boost your health or self-esteem, so be sure to maintain a positive outlook even if you initially feel a little sensitive. Avoid gambling on particular outcomes; do your research instead, as this will help you maintain an even keel. You'll enjoy a treat this weekend or early next week. Just avoid overspending.

HEALTH

An inspiring or influential character can help you if you have any niggling health or well-being issues. If you have been looking for the correct practitioner who you feel can help you this is likely to come about mid-month, so be sure to be proactive about seeking the support or information you're looking for. You will also notice how important your home life or family are in connection with your well-being.

FINANCES

You may be drawn to create more flexibility financially but must be careful not to throw caution to the wind in the process. As new opportunities present themselves you may be torn between an idealistic approach to your investments and income on the one hand and a more cautious attitude on the other. If you can find safe middle ground you will be happier with the arrangements you make.

HOME

If you are returning to a family home or enjoying a reunion with family in March you will appreciate the feeling of nurturance that having connections with family can bring you. Some Pisces will be drawn to review aspects of your home life that you could improve, and this is certainly a good month to consider any adjustments at home ranging from simply sprucing up some décor to considering a move.

LOVE LIFE

The start of the month will impress upon you how much change is actually going on in your personal mindset, which will invariably have repercussions on your relationships. You will be drawn to be more outgoing and active in the months to come. Just be sure to keep on the side of those in your life who provide security and stability. The new moon will be in your sign on the 19th and will bring inspiring insight into your love life.

WORK

Some Pisces will appreciate a fresh work opportunity, which could lead to an exciting commitment you must make that may prospectively boost your finances as well. Developments must be carefully weighed with your domestic life and how you can establish work-life balance. March Pisces may receive good news later in the month to do with work that may also have a knock-on effect in your home life or family.

PISCES · MARCH

April

WEEK 1: 2–8 APRIL

Thursday's full moon puts the spotlight on someone you must collaborate with, which will signify the end of a particular arrangement and the beginning of a new one. Be sure to display your excellent communication skills, especially where your personal life is concerned, as you could make great inroads in your personal life to create more stability and security.

WEEK 2: 9–15 APRIL

You may breathe a sigh of relief as pressures and the busyness of recent weeks subsides. However, for some Pisces the busyness will only increase this week so it is important to stay on top of developments, especially at home and in your personal life. Keep an eye on your finances. Some lucky Pisces will receive a financial or ego boost, while others will need to curb spending.

WEEK 3: 16–22 APRIL

Friday's new moon may point out one of your strengths, but if it points out a vulnerability it will enable you to strengthen your position in the long term. You'll appreciate a sense of progress, especially regarding people you love and the groups and organisations you associate with. You could turn a corner financially but must also be practical, especially regarding any contracts or arrangements you make.

WEEK 4: 23–29 APRIL

Be prepared to be on your toes as communications and news and, for some, travel are likely to bring a fairly upbeat week. However, for some this may be a slightly disruptive time, so be sure to always look at the big picture as opposed to looking only at the frustrations of current circumstances. You may receive unexpected financial or personal news that is best handled tactfully.

HEALTH

While many of the feelings of pressure or having to keep up with deadlines will begin to settle in April, for some Pisces the speed of events will increase. You will gain a good idea of which way the pace is turning early in the month and will be able to gauge the levels of energy you need as a result. Be sure to invest in yourself and your health so you can stay one step ahead.

FINANCES

You have the opportunity in the long term to improve your finances; however, there are no shortcuts. If you are tempted to gamble or invest in schemes that you have not adequately researched you risk making mistakes, especially early in April and towards the 24th, so be sure if you are making considerable financial arrangements that you are super clear about the terms and conditions. You may be surprised by developments at the end of the month. Avoid gambling.

HOME

The full moon on 2 April will spotlight certain arrangements and agreements you already have in place at home, and may also spotlight differences of opinion. Be sure to find ways to gain the middle ground and avoid allowing your differences to dominate. In the process you may need to discuss some arrangements with a friend, group or organisation. Communications may be particularly fraught over the weekend of the 25th and 26th, so be sure to be diplomatic then.

LOVE LIFE

You are communicating particularly well at the start of the month, which will be a useful quality as someone close will need to discuss important matters that have been on their mind or seek your reassurance. Mid-month is likely to be a busy and sociable time that will be ideal for singles to meet new people. Couples may need to keep partners in the loop as this will be a fast-moving time.

WORK

Mercury and Mars in Pisces at the start of April create a strong profile for you at work, so be sure to take the initiative with your projects and be confident that you can present and speak well to colleagues, employers and clients. However, towards the 4th, 5th and 24th you must avoid appearing dogmatic, even if someone else is displaying this characteristic, as otherwise you will enter a Mexican standoff that will be counterproductive.

May

WEEK 1: 30 APRIL—6 MAY

This week's full moon is likely to bring a degree of intensity to your relationships, both at work and in your personal life, so be sure to maintain perspective should you notice discussions becoming more heated than usual. Above all, avoid taking other people's inability to communicate well personally. This is a good week to focus on your well-being and give your finances a health check.

WEEK 2: 7—13 MAY

A project or get-together will deliver a feel-good factor this week, so if you've been planning something special be optimistic and push your plans forward. You'll enjoy meeting with friends and family and pushing creative projects through. A financial and personal commitment may be made to positive effect. Some Pisces will enjoy a beneficial development at home such as improved interpersonal dynamics.

WEEK 3: 14—20 MAY

This weekend's new moon supermoon suggests you're ready to revitalise a personal relationship or update your financial investments. The quality you're looking for is a degree of security and stability in both your personal life and finances. Paradoxically, there will also be a tendency towards making rash decisions at the moment, either your own or by someone close, so to maintain peace of mind ensure you avoid impulsiveness.

WEEK 4: 21—27 MAY / WEEK 5: 28 MAY—3 JUNE

WEEK 4: some developments will require you to dig deep and work out your priorities. A get-together or journey around the 22nd may be thought-provoking or out of the ordinary. **WEEK 5:** decisions could be long-standing, so ensure you weigh up options. The full moon on the 31st will be revitalising in a collaboration and you'll gain clarity about your options regarding agreements, including financial arrangements.

HEALTH

Both the start and end of May towards the full moon on the 31st will be an excellent time to ensure you're on track with your health and have not been taking it for granted. Consider organising talks with an expert if there is any aspect of your health that you have felt concerned about, either emotionally, mentally, spiritually or physically, as your efforts are likely to be productive.

FINANCES

The first week of May will be an excellent time to consider fresh ways to repay debt and service bills. It is also a good time to seek expert advice in this arena if necessary. Above all, avoid gambling with hard-earned money and find more stable and secure ways of managing finances moving forward. During the second week of the month you may be inclined to splurge on friends and family.

HOME

The first week of May could involve some misunderstandings or difficult conversations that require clarity, so ensure that discussions that escalate dangerously close to arguments have not done so due to a basic misconception. The second week of the month will be more conducive to visits and improved interpersonal dynamics. Just be sure to avoid overspending if you are engaging in DIY projects or remodelling.

LOVE LIFE

There will be an intense feeling to the start of the month, so ensure you enjoy the passion and excitement. However, should intense feelings escalate to a more negative aspect, look for ways to re-establish the peace and harmony you prefer. The new moon supermoon on the 16th will encourage you to look for a sense of stability in your love life but, paradoxically, you are also likely to feel restless so may need to find a happy middle ground.

WORK

Where do your true priorities lie regarding work: to your employer, clients, colleague or bank? May is an excellent month to decide this and work out whether you'd prefer your finances to be determined by your income or your income to be determined by your work. You may experience a surprise in connection with work towards the end of the month that will provide insight.

June

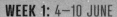

WEEK 1: 4–10 JUNE

This could be a particularly romantic and upbeat week for you. However, you will need to ensure that you employ tact and diplomacy as otherwise you may experience misunderstandings in complex or confusing interactions. Avoid sensitive topics if possible. A fresh agreement either in your personal life or financially may be required. You must avoid financial and emotional gambling.

WEEK 2: 11–17 JUNE

You may discover a vulnerability this week that will arise in different ways depending on your circumstances. For some there may be perceived emotional weakness, and for others financial vulnerability. The good news will, however, be that you'll be able to find a way forward as a result rather than the situation dragging on. You may even experience a lucky break towards the new moon on the 15th.

WEEK 3: 18–24 JUNE

You'll enjoy deepening strong relationships and forging new ones. Singles may meet someone compelling and attractive. Events may bring out people's creative sides or mystical interests, and you'll enjoy playing along. However, a family decision or talk may be intense. There will nevertheless be therapeutic aspects to developments, and some lucky Pisces may enjoy a financial or ego boost.

WEEK 4: 25 JUNE–1 JULY

You will appreciate the opportunity to look at your daily life and schedule and improve it this week. Just ensure you do not make any uninformed decisions based on a whim, as these are likely to backfire. You may be ready to make a commitment to someone or a group or cause. Some Pisces will turn a corner in your career or general direction.

HEALTH

Sometimes it is necessary to discover your weaknesses in order to become stronger. If you discover an emotional, spiritual, mental or physical weakness this month it will enable you to improve your circumstances and health. If you feel drawn to seek the help of an expert or adviser this is likely to beneficially support your aims. The new moon supermoon on the 15th will help you reach out.

FINANCES

You have equal chances of good and bad luck financially this month, and this will depend to a degree on your previous actions. For this reason some Pisces will need to reconfigure your budget as you discover a financial flaw. For others an unexpected financial boost that arises mid-month will boost your self-esteem. Some mid-March–born Pisces may reach a key turning point in your career towards the end of the month that could improve your finances.

HOME

Your home and family will take a considerable chunk of your focus early in June, and this is certainly a good time to devote your attention to these important aspects of your life. If you have been taking someone for granted recently or if you feel that you have been taken for granted, this situation will be carefully addressed. Avoid taking others people's opinions personally and look for common ground and the best way forward.

LOVE LIFE

The start of the month will be particularly conducive to romance, so be sure to organise some events. However, you must ensure that you are on the same page as your partner or lover as otherwise mistakes can be made. If you have been considering growing your family it's possible you'll make headway in this area. However, if you are disappointed you will find the help of an expert invaluable.

WORK

This will be a good month to forge deeper ties with colleagues and organisations, so it's a good time for networking. If you have been looking for a new career or simply to get on better terms with colleagues, this is a good time to make tracks. Just be careful that some conversations don't become too intense: be prepared to be tactful and diplomatic. The full moon on the 29th/30th could reveal a fresh path or arrangement.

July

WEEK 1: 2–8 JULY

There is a slightly chaotic feel to the week for you, largely because you prefer to live life on an even keel. Developments now will be a test of how far your Zen approach to life stretches. Many circumstances are going to take you backwards and forwards in negotiations and expectations. Some matters will be non-negotiable and others manageable, so be prepared to adapt.

WEEK 2: 9–15 JULY

The new moon supermoon on the 14th will bring a fresh chapter romantically, so be sure to consider your true romantic hopes and take action to allow fresh dynamics to birth. If you have been considering adding to your family this is a good time to take the initiative. Avoid looking only at what isn't working in your life and look at what is. Unexpected developments will merit a positive perspective.

WEEK 3: 16–22 JULY

Conversations, negotiations and developments this week are likely to be fairly intense, so steel yourself already early in the week for important discussions that could potentially take you into new territory. Some Pisces will enjoy a wonderful and potentially life-transforming trip, and others the opportunity to boost your finances and ego. Wherever your attention is now, bear in mind the changes you make are likely to be long term.

WEEK 4: 23–29 JULY

The lead-up to this weekend is an enjoyable time for romance, the arts and reconnecting with favourite people. As the full moon on the 29th/30th approaches, however, not everyone is going to see eye to eye, and it will be in your interest to maintain an even keel in relationships. Nevertheless, you'll gain the opportunity to truly enjoy some wonderful get-togethers.

HEALTH

July is an excellent month to discuss your health and well-being, both with experts and friends and colleagues, as you are likely to find out about health modalities and practitioners who may specialise in your growing areas of interest. Keep an eye on what you eat, as gut health could be a focus for you now. The end of the month may illuminate fresh modalities that could benefit you.

FINANCES

Discussions and financial arrangements could take you into fresh territory already early in July. If you experience loss as opposed to gain this July, be prepared to research your circumstances as you may discover unexpected avenues you could take that until now had really not been an option. A group, friend or organisation could be particularly helpful to you at this time. The full moon on the 29th/30th will spotlight important financial decisions and potentially also an improvement.

HOME

This is a good month to make arrangements concerning your home, a property or family that will provide you with more stability. However, if you have made or are considering making arrangements that could restrict your spending power it is important that you first review your options. Developments are likely to be fairly intense in your personal or family life towards the full moon on the 29th/30th, so be prepared to make reasonable and practical decisions then.

LOVE LIFE

July is a potentially romantic month. This will depend on the actions you take, but if you are outgoing and adventurous – whether you're single or a couple – this is a month to enjoy. If singles initially feel a little vulnerable stepping into fresh territory, consider joining like-minded groups where socialising becomes the focus as opposed to feeling you are in a dating pool. Emotions will be heightened towards the full moon on the 29th/30th, so avoid arguments then.

WORK

Ask yourself this month where your true interests lie. Where certain options lead you down a particular path, ask yourself how flexible you truly are in your career path. You may surprise yourself with some of the conclusions you draw, and also realise that when you step into fresh territory new opportunities can arise. You may be pleasantly surprised around the full moon on the 29th/30th as you take the opportunity to turn a transformative corner at work.

August

WEEK 1: 30 JULY–5 AUGUST

The full moon still has a powerful effect this week from the perspective that some relationships are likely to feel intense, so be sure to maintain an even keel. Luckily, you are ready to embrace a new understanding that could heighten your relationships and personal life. Be prepared to work methodically towards creating strength in your personal life and financially, as you could gain security and stability now.

WEEK 2: 6–12 AUGUST

This week's solar eclipse will help you turn a corner that brings more dynamism and independence to your daily life. In the process you may need to undergo serious conversations that revolve around your long-term ambitions. Be sure to initiate talks, as you could truly boost your circumstances and romance could thrive, especially towards the 10th. However, be sure to avoid misunderstandings.

WEEK 3: 13–19 AUGUST

You will enjoy a change of routine towards the weekend, which will benefit not only your self-esteem but also potentially your bank balance. Be prepared to discuss your options if you are unsure of your circumstances. An open-minded and curious approach to developments at home or regarding property will be beneficial to avoid making mistakes. Romance can still thrive this week, so be sure to take the initiative.

WEEK 4: 20–26 AUGUST / WEEK 5: 27 AUGUST–2 SEPTEMBER

WEEK 4: this will be a good week to consider making a commitment to a business or personal arrangement. However, you must avoid making impulsive decisions.
WEEK 5: the partial lunar eclipse is in your sign and will bring considerable change, especially at work and regarding your health and daily routine. There are therapeutic aspects to the week, so be sure to take the initiative.

HEALTH

You may be tempted once Venus enters Libra on the 6th/7th to indulge a little more in the creature comforts and allow your health routine to lapse. However, if you maintain self-discipline with a tried and tested fitness routine and combine this with attention to detail in your appearance you are less likely to allow bad habits to resurface. The days before the lunar eclipse on the 28th will be excellent for turning a corner in your health routine.

FINANCES

If your finances have been an area of concern, the first two weeks of the month are ideal for building a stronger financial profile. If you have tended to risk some of your income purely on speculation you will gain the necessary self-discipline to overcome this tendency. You may inadvertently discover that money is not always needed in order to have fun! It is definitely a good month to build financial security, as your efforts will be rewarded.

HOME

Mars in your home sector will bring activities at home or with family, especially in the second half of August. You may be drawn to visit someone's home or to receive visitors, which will add a new dynamic to your home life. Be intuitive about where you would like to go if you travel. You may be drawn to make a personal commitment to someone towards the 21st, and this could have an impact on your home life.

LOVE LIFE

The first two weeks of the month will be ideal for consciously working towards stability in your love life. This needn't be as boring as it sounds: you can find that spontaneous activities actually bring you closer together. The 10th, mid-month and towards the 17th are excellent times for romance, so be sure to organise dates then as this is potentially one of the most romantic times of the year. However, you must avoid making assumptions, as these could backfire.

WORK

Developments mid-month and towards the last 10 days of the month will provide invaluable information regarding your work and career prospects. Be positive this month as you could make considerable progress at work and in your chosen field of interest. You may need to discuss your options with an employer or business colleagues to ensure you are on the right track, so be sure to take the initiative and organise talks.

PISCES • AUGUST

September

WEEK 1: 3–9 SEPTEMBER

Be prepared to go that extra mile for someone you admire either at work or in your personal life. It may seem challenging, but it is likely to be worthwhile. You will appreciate spending quality time with someone special later on this weekend or early next week. If you're looking for work or a lucky break at work you may experience a breakthrough, so take the initiative.

WEEK 2: 10–16 SEPTEMBER

The new moon on the 11th signals a fresh chapter in a business or personal partnership: that is, unless you were born after mid-March, in which case this new moon signals a fresh chapter at work or in your health routine. Be prepared to take the initiative in your love life, as your efforts are likely to be successful as long as communications are clear and you avoid misunderstandings.

WEEK 3: 17–23 SEPTEMBER

This weeks' events will show where you could be healthier or work smarter. For March-born Pisces, where health is the mainstay of balance and harmony it's important to be in tiptop condition. For February-born Pisces the key to success this week resides in good communication skills, as developments will require you to be flexible and adaptable.

WEEK 4: 24–30 SEPTEMBER

This weekend's full moon will shine a light on a business or personal relationship and there may be ideal aspects to some of your interactions, including romance. However, you may discover a vulnerability in yourself, so if you need support be sure to reach out to a loyal friend or family member as it will be available. Avoid knee-jerk reactions or making snap decisions, as these may set you back.

HEALTH

Jupiter in your health sector contributes to positive energy levels: that is, as long as you do not overwork or overstress. Jupiter in Leo can provide more energy but it can also predispose you to using more, so be careful to look after yourself even if you're aware that you have more energy than usual. This is especially the case as a housemate or someone else who is close to you may need more of your attention than usual.

FINANCES

You will discover your financial vulnerabilities and these may be tied to a friend or organisation. Be careful with transactions towards the 10th, 12th, 19th and 27th, as mistakes can be made. If you must make arrangements with someone close such as a housemate or partner ensure you consider the long-term implications of shared finances before making commitments. If, however, you are happy with the circumstances, solid arrangements made now could be beneficial.

HOME

You will enjoy a sense of belonging and contentment at home as long as you feel comfortable within certain relationships, so ensure you gain peace of mind by investing in good communications and relationships as this is where you can truly gain a sense of well-being. You may find a partner or someone you live with needs to discuss their feelings, and the more you are able to work with them within reason then the better the outcome will be.

LOVE LIFE

You'll gain the opportunity to turn a page in your love life. If you have been looking for more commitment in an existing partnership this is something you are likely to gain. If you are single and have been looking for a loyal companion this is a positive time to find someone, so be sure to make dates and socialise. However, you must avoid conflict, especially between the 10th and 15th and on the 18th and 27th, as it is likely to escalate.

WORK

Early in September, despite the necessity for hard work and application you could experience positive developments at work. It will be a case of being industrious and finding the time and way to prioritise your favourite work-related activities within your working day. Towards the 18th, 22nd and 28th you may need to discuss important matters diplomatically that could put you on a fresh path at work. Be bold, as you could make a great deal of progress at work.

October

WEEK 1: 1–7 OCTOBER

You will enjoy socialising this weekend; however, you may be surprised by some developments. Someone's feelings may be heightened and intense circumstances arise. When well managed this could indicate an enjoyable circumstance but there is a dramatic aspect to developments now that could easily lead to conflict, so avoid arguments. A group or friend may be in touch, and you'll enjoy romance, creativity and the arts this week.

WEEK 2: 8–14 OCTOBER

While you prefer harmony in life, this week you risk focusing too hard on the negative aspects of a circumstance. Be discerning about your loyalties by carefully weighing up your options. Avoid peace at all costs regardless of who is involved, as this could land you in hot water; you may need to make a tough call instead. You'll enjoy a change of routine or trip.

WEEK 3: 15–21 OCTOBER

You will appreciate the chance to show off a little at work, and there are some therapeutic aspects to the week for this reason. However, if you feel under pressure to perform then rely on your good communication skills and ability to rise to the occasion. Mid-week next week, approach difficult communications in a balanced way and avoid feeling vulnerable by reminding yourself how strong and dedicated you are.

WEEK 4: 22–28 OCTOBER / WEEK 5: 29 OCTOBER–4 NOVEMBER

WEEK 4: the sun in Scorpio brings a passionate week. You'll enjoy feeling more vibrant in your personal life and at work. Try to get key meetings and ideas on the table before the 24th to avoid having to backtrack over the coming weeks. **WEEK 5:** keep communications on an even keel to avoid needless arguments, and as you do you'll enjoy an upbeat get-together or positive development towards 4 November.

HEALTH

There are aspects of your health and well-being that are non-negotiable; for example, the need for exercise and food. Your good health relies on practicalities, and as a result this month you'll discover how straightforwardly self-care can positively impact your health. You'll also enjoy the opportunity to bring more fun and spontaneity into your daily life and will notice the positive impact of this on your mental, emotional and spiritual health.

FINANCES

A financial circumstance you share with someone such as a bank, partner or organisation will require careful handling on your part early in the month, and also towards the 9th, to ensure transactions have been transparent. Avoid arguments over minor financial matters as these could escalate quickly, but you must be prepared to be diligent with a contract or arrangement that requires a commitment from both sides.

HOME

Try to get important domestic matters on the table for discussion before the 24th when Mercury turns retrograde, as you are more likely to be able to gain reasonable agreement before that date. However, if you have contentious topics to discuss be careful around the 20th and 30th to avoid a battle of egos. Mid-October will be a good time to be practical about creating more stability and security within a family context, as your efforts are likely to succeed.

LOVE LIFE

It's a romantic start to October, which you'll enjoy, but if some people in your environment can be drama queens then circumstances could become intense. You'll appreciate the opportunity to deepen your understanding of someone, but if you sense you are repeating past mistakes be sure to alter dynamics. Be careful with communications from the 26th to the 30th. The full moon on the 26th may usher in a phase when you look for more security in your relationships.

WORK

Mars in your work sector will continue to motivate you, and you may even experience a breakthrough towards the 7th, 15th and in early November. However, you will need to negotiate or discuss very carefully shared aspects of your projects with those they concern. If you need to negotiate terms and conditions such as finances you can make headway, but you may need to work hard towards an adequate outcome and you must avoid being easily influenced by others.

PISCES · OCTOBER

November

WEEK 1: 5–11 NOVEMBER

You will appreciate the opportunity to gain deeper insight into a colleague or partner. The new moon on Monday will kick-start a fresh cycle in which certain arrangements – for example, financial agreements – could be renegotiated. Be prepared to look at the best-case scenario and negotiate from there. A meeting or news early next week will provide perspective at work or regarding your health.

WEEK 2: 12–18 NOVEMBER

Meetings and get-togethers will move your circumstances forward quickly now, so be prepared to be on your toes. Significant news from a work colleague or personal partner could take you into fresh territory. Be careful with communications, especially towards Friday, to avoid misunderstandings. You may enjoy a change in your usual work or health schedule so be sure to factor in fun activities, especially this weekend.

WEEK 3: 19–25 NOVEMBER

You will enjoy a change of pace; just double-check some logistics such as travel schedules towards Friday to avoid delays. You'll enjoy a reunion with someone close to your heart. This week's full moon supermoon brings fresh dynamics in a key relationship. Be prepared to be patient with someone and look outside the box at ways to enjoy the relationship. Developments around a trip or finances may be unexpected.

WEEK 4: 26 NOVEMBER–2 DECEMBER

You may receive good news from a personal or work source that provides a true boost. However, this weekend it's important you avoid taking the ideas of other people personally. You may feel vulnerable or sensitive, so arrange to unwind when you can. Someone special may prove particularly supportive; however, if the opposite occurs be sure to find practical ways to support your aims and goals and enjoyment in life.

HEALTH

This will be a good month to consult experts if there has been anything on your mind health-wise, as you are likely to find a relevant expert who can help you. Be sure to reach out, especially between the 10th and 20th and on the 29th. A change in your health or daily work schedule towards the 12th will encourage you to be more upbeat about some of your health-related activities. Consider fun and upbeat activities that buoy your mood.

FINANCES

Developments at work or a change in your usual working hours or routine will have an impact on your finances, so be sure to keep this in mind if you are considering fresh working parameters. You may attain ideal outcomes with some of your arrangements at work or with someone special but you also have a predisposition to see your finances through rose-coloured glasses in November, so be sure to obtain expert guidance if it's needed.

HOME

You will enjoy a change of pace in November, and for some Pisces this will involve a trip or fresh way to share your important joint duties with someone close such as a housemate or your partner. Be prepared to be practical and realistic about any new arrangements you put in place at home or with a property as you may be a little more idealistic than usual, especially towards the end of the month.

LOVE LIFE

You'll appreciate seeing your love life gain more fun and spontaneity from mid-month on, especially if you feel that it has been stuck. You'll enjoy reconnecting with someone. Some Pisces may even reconnect with an ex towards the 23rd; however, you'll need to evaluate the merits or lack of them of this. Be sensitive to someone's feelings towards the 28th, but if they are insensitive to yours it may be a true hurdle in the relationship.

WORK

You'll gain a great deal of insight into exactly where you stand work-wise this month. A meeting or news towards the 12th and then again on the 28th will be particularly insightful. You may begin a fresh arrangement regarding shared responsibilities and duties. The lead-up, especially towards the new moon on the 9th and also on the 10th, will be an excellent time to discuss your options with those they concern as you may reach mutually agreeable outcomes.

December

WEEK 1: 3–9 DECEMBER

An adventurous phase is about to begin when you'll feel more optimistic about your projects, interests and relationships. A new legal, sporting or written project could excel. A secret may be revealed. This is a good week for self-inquiry and introspection but also for a change of scenery and pace. Be inspired, but avoid unnecessary delays and upheaval by planning ahead.

WEEK 2: 10–16 DECEMBER

Constructive plans made now will produce excellent results. You may already be in a position to appreciate past plans that have come to fruition. A change of pace or of place via travel or one of your favourite activities will be enjoyable, so be sure to organise a treat if you haven't already. This is a good weekend to organise your finances in readiness for seasonal festivities.

WEEK 3: 17–23 DECEMBER

A change of pace will raise morale and energy levels and will be therapeutic on many levels. Whether you have already planned travel or you will be welcoming the opportunity to take a break, you will appreciate developments. Just be a little careful to avoid impulsiveness early next week and also to keep an eye on forgetfulness, as you may be prone to being absent-minded towards Wednesday.

WEEK 4: 24–31 DECEMBER

Developments will demonstrate how important it is to have the love and support of those close to you and also to lead a happy life. You'll gain the opportunity to work towards these goals from a nurturing point of view even if circumstances are slightly disruptive due to work concerns or situations outside your control. You'll feel you're ready to embrace the new year.

HEALTH

You'll appreciate being more outgoing in December, and travel or more investment in your favourite projects will prove uplifting. A change of pace or of place towards the 12th, 18th and 23rd will be enjoyable and could improve your well-being. You'll appreciate being more physically active towards the end of the month, which in turn will boost your energy levels and positive mindset. If you feel that stress gets the better of you, exercise will certainly help defuse angst.

FINANCES

Be prepared to view your finances from a fresh perspective early in the month already, because you may experience a surprise towards the 8th and 9th that will merit careful appraisal. A change in your usual routine or working circumstance is liable to affect your finances. For many there will be positive developments financially; however, if you find that overheads and projects you've already committed to drain your resources then look for ways to mitigate these circumstances.

HOME

The full moon on Christmas Eve will spotlight how important your home life is. For some Pisces this will be because you finally gain the opportunity to relax, while for others a sense of missing out on something crucial in your life may resonate. If this is the case for you, you'll gain the opportunity and insight to make changes in your life so that by this time next year you are in a much stronger position.

LOVE LIFE

Venus in your partnership, love and marriage zones will amp up the passion in your life but may also contribute to a partner seeming more contrite. For this reason you will benefit from being more patient with your partner or love interest if necessary. You will nevertheless enjoy a more passionate time in December. Romance and a change of pace will enable love to thrive, especially over the weekend of the 12th.

WORK

Collaboration is the key to success at work, and you may already experience the benefits of teamwork and co-operation towards the 11th and will enjoy fulfilling activities connected with work. If you're working in the week leading up to Christmas you're likely to appreciate a change of pace that is both mind expanding and potentially adventurous. However, you will need to keep an eye on a battle of egos, as this could escalate.

ALSO BY PATSY BENNETT

SUN SIGN SECRETS
Celestial guidance with the sun, moon and stars
ISBN: 9781925946352

This comprehensive, ground-breaking astrology book is for everyone who wants to make the most of their true potential and be in the flow with solar and lunar phases. It includes analyses of each zodiac sign from Aries to Pisces and pinpoints how you can dynamically make the most of your life in real time alongside celestial events. Work with the gifts and strengths of your sun sign in relation to every lunar phase, zodiacal month, new moon, full moon and eclipse.
Look up your sun sign to read all about your talents and potential pitfalls, and discover how to express your inner star power during the various phases of the sun and moon throughout the days, months and years to come.

Available at all good bookstores.